Western Europe in Maps

Western Europe in Maps

Topographical Map Studies

Revised Edition of Europe in Maps Book 1 and 2

R. Knowles
Senior Lecturer
Polytechnic of North London

P.W.E. Stowe
Headmaster
Cedars Upper School, Leighton Buzzard

Longman

Contents

Maps

LONGMAN GROUP LIMITED
Longman House
Burnt Mill, Harlow, Essex. U.K.

© Longman Group Ltd 1982

First published 1982

ISBN 0 582 35260 6

Printed in Hong Kong by Sheck Wah Tong Printing Press Ltd.

Photographs

Figures

Acknowledgements

Thanks are due to many individuals and organisations who have helped in the preparation of this book by the provision of statistical data and other information about the study areas. Thanks are due in particular to the following: Statistisk Sentralbyrå, Oslo; Anton Jakhelin of the Norsk Meteorologisk Institutt, Oslo; Olav Liestøl of the Norsk Polarinstitutt, Oslo; Geological Museum, Oslo; Per Mietle of Fiskeridirektøren, Bergen; Sven-Eric Brunnsjö, Director of Public Relations for L.K.A.B., Stockholm; Eva Ericsson of Karlstads Stads Turistnämnd Turistbyrån; Lennart Forsberg and Klaus Janz of Skogsstyrelsen, Jönköping; Jan-Olof Seveborg of Planeringsavdelningen, Karlstad; Kungli Domänstyrelsen, Stockholm; Ulla Wikander of AB Svensk Bostäder, Vällingby; Stockholms Stadbyggnadskontor; Karl Rasmussen of Vestergaard Farm, Sönder Vissing; Centraal Bureau voor de Statistiek, s'-Gravenhage; Royal Netherlands Embassy, London; Dutch Ministry of Agriculture, Utrecht; G. Jackson; Information Service of the European Community; A. Dufrasne of the Institut National de Statistique Belgique; L. Van Malderen of the Ministère Des Affairs Economiques (Administration des Mines); Neiderrheinische Industrie und Handelskammer, Duisburg-Wesel; Dr Brustmann of Industrie und Handelskammer, Koblenz; R. Broschart of the Economic Section of the Embassy of the Federal German Republic, London; A. D. Wheatley of Volkswagen Motors Ltd.; Niedersächsisches Landesverwaltungsamt Statistik; Industrie und Handelskammer, Braunschweig; Industrie und Handelskammer, Hildesheim; Oberkreisdirektor, Landkreis Peine; Oberkreisdirektor, Landkreis Hildesheim-Marienburg; M. Jackson; P. J. T. Morrill; Institut National de la Statistique et des Etudes Economiques, Paris; French Embassy, London; Direction Général des Etudes et des Affaires Générales, Paris; Directions Départementales de l'Agriculture, Calvados and Marne; Chambres d'Agricultures, Eure-et-Loir and Aisne; Comité Interprofessionnel du Vin de Champagne; Direction Départementale de l'Agriculture, Var; Sacilor, Hayange; Chambre de Commerce et d'Industrie de la Moselle, Metz; R. Prat of the Chambre de Commerce et d'Industrie, Marseille: Institut de Recherches Economiques et Sociales, Marseille; U. Zwingli and Z. Lomecky of the Statistical Office, Zürich; Eidgenössisches Statistisches Amt, Berne; Oerlikon Engineering Co., Zürich; Office Economique Cantonal Neuchâtelois, La Chaux de Fonds; B. Jobin; Dr B. Ledermann, Chambre Suisse de l'Horlorgerie, La Chaux de Fonds; Dr G. Elliston of the Department of Geography, University of Hull.

Photographs have been obtained from a variety of sources which have been acknowledged individually throughout the book. Maps and diagrams have been especially drawn for the book by K. Wass, chief draughtsman in the Department of Geography, University College, London, and by A. W. Gatrell & Co. Ltd. Where these have been based on earlier published maps and diagrams the original source has been acknowledged in each instance. Fig. 22 is based on a map by the Industrie und Verkehrskarten Institut, Ivris-Verlag, Düsseldorf.

The choice of a sample district to illustrate some of the themes of Danish dairy farming was prompted by John Fraser Hart's study of Vestergaard published in 1964 in *Focus on Geographic Activity. A Collection of Original Studies* edited by R. S. Thoman and D. J. Patton. Study 7 is based in part on Hart's paper with more recent information derived from visits to Sönder Vissing and correspondence with the present owner of the farm. Similarly Study 10 of the old industrial landscape around Liège is based in part on a paper by T. H. Elkins on *Liège and the Problems of Southern Belgium* which was originally published in *Geography* in 1956.

Finally, thanks are due to the following Examination Boards for permission to reproduce questions from past examination papers: Oxford and Cambridge Schools Examination Board; University of Cambridge Local Examinations Syndicate; Welsh Joint Education Committee; Joint Matriculation Board; University of London Schools Examination Council.

Foreword

This book has been written with the aim of providing a series of studies of small and distinctive areas in Western Europe. The studies are based upon extracts from national topographical maps and aerial photographs. The commentaries are concerned with the information provided by the maps and photographs, but in many cases the limitations of these two sources are soon apparent and supplementary material has been introduced, especially on land use and industrial geography.

It is hoped that the book will be of value in two ways. Firstly, it should enable a student to become familiar with the cartographic styles of foreign maps and thus play a useful role in mapwork studies. Secondly, the use of such samples will be valuable in connection with regional work on Western Europe. It has been found that detailed studies of small, specific areas can usefully precede, or alternatively substantiate, the generalisations that are common in many standard regional geographies. The book is therefore complementary to regional texts rather than alternative to them.

Inevitably the choice of study areas is a subjective one. The aim has been to cover as wide a range as possible of aspects of physical, agricultural, industrial and settlement geography. However, the non-availability of both up-to-date map sheets and good photographs has precluded studies of many interesting areas. This is especially true of France, where much of the west and central part of the country is mapped only on outdated series.

The book has been prepared particularly with the needs of 'A' level and first year university students in mind, and assumes a basic knowledge of physical and human geography. Although many of the questions are based entirely on an understanding of the map extracts, others have been included which will require reference to regional texts and an appreciation of the geography of other parts of Western Europe. There is certainly much scope for further cartographical exercises, which may be devised to fit individual requirements. In many cases it would be valuable for students to have access to the full map sheets from which the extracts have been taken.

Finally, it should be emphasised that each district studied possesses its own individuality, a product of its landscape, its people and its history. Although parallels may be drawn with other areas, it would be unwise to think of these studies as 'type' areas representative of large tracts of Western Europe. The differences are frequently of more significance than the similarities. The studies should rather be thought of as illustrating the interaction of various geographical factors in the evolution of a distinctive landscape; only in this sense are they applicable to other parts of Western Europe from which the extracts have been taken.

In preparing this new edition of *Europe in Maps*, studies have been retained from the original two volumes which were first published in 1969 and 1971 respectively. The choice of study areas for inclusion in this book was partly determined by comments from reviewers and users of the earlier volumes, together with recent changes in examination syllabi. The aim has been to include in the present collection those studies which proved most useful to users of the earlier books. The opportunity has also been taken to up-date the statistical information included in the various studies and to refer to recent economic trends and developments where appropriate.

R. KNOWLES   P. W. E. STOWE

The Regional Setting of the Study Areas

The series of twenty-two studies presented in this book is an attempt to provide a cross-section of Western Europe from various standpoints. Their location is shown in fig. 1 which also represents the major structural components of Western Europe.

From the standpoint of physical geography the studies show contrasts in landforms which in part at least reflect both the structure and the erosional history of the area. Thus, the Caledonian mountains of Norway (1, 2) contrast markedly with the plateau blocks of Hercynian Europe represented in the uplands bordering the Rhine Gorge (11). The classic simple folding of the Jura Mountains shown on the Chaux de Fonds extract (21) contrasts with the scenery of the Gorner and Engadine districts (19, 22) which also belong to the last of the major orogenies which affected Europe. Scarpland topography is well expressed in the studies of the Paris Basin (15) and could be profitable compared with English examples on many O.S. sheets. Modern geomorphology is much concerned with the study of processes and their effects. Topographical maps are of value in this work and the student will find several extracts concerned particularly with glacial landforms, notably those of Finse (1), Aurland (2), Svolvær (3), Gorner (22) and the Engadine (19). The less spectacular glacial and fluvioglacial depositional landscapes are to be seen in Jutland (7) and Wolfsburg (12). Fluvial landforms may also be studied on various extracts.

Various themes in human geography have been explored in the different studies although the topographical map has severe limitations in these fields. Thus items of evidence on the map have been investigated with the aid of additional information particularly of a statistical nature to provide some explanation for the features observed. A wide range of agricultural types and patterns is to be found in Western Europe. The more difficult environments of Aurlandsfjord (2), the Engadine (19) and La Chaux de Fonds (21) impose considerable constraints and led to semi-subsistence forms of agriculture helped out by manufacturing industry, fishing, forestry or, especially today, by tourism. By contrast the fertile loess soils of the Börde country (13) and of much of the Paris Basin (15) support a prosperity undreamt of a few decades ago.

Specialism in agriculture is of course common in Western Europe. Studies of Le Pays de Champagne (15), the polders of Holland (8, 9), the warm lands of Provence (16) show the development of such specialities, capitalising upon one particular aspect of the environment while overcoming other problems of soil fertility, water supply or water control. Industrial geography can also be studied with success through the use of topographical maps, although additional statistical data are of vital importance in obtaining a balanced view. Extractive industries are represented in the studies of the timber industry of Karlstad (5) and the iron ore mining of Kiruna (4). The latter is especially interesting in highlighting some of the difficulties of working in an Arctic environment. Contrasts between old and new manufacturing industries stand out clearly in a number of studies. The old industrial centres of the Sambre-Meuse valley (10), the Ruhr (14) and more recently the Lorraine iron and steel industry (17) face difficult adjustments in the face of declining natural resources and the change in patterns of demand as new technology supervenes the old. The newer industries of Western Europe are shown in the automobile plant of Wolfsburg (12) and the vast oil and petro-chemical developments of the Etang de Berre (18). However, many industries of ancient foundation still survive and the watch-making of La Chaux de Fonds (21) epitomises the success of many of these in overcoming what appears superficially as an unpromising setting for a modern competitive industry.

It is hoped that the map extracts will provide useful material for work on settlement geography both in rural and urban areas. Patterns of rural settlement present many problems and the purely physical explanation is usually most unsatisfactory. Variations in economy, differing historical backgrounds and many other factors must be given full consideration as the studies of the Börde (13) the Geestmerambacht polder (9) and the various *pays* of the Paris Basin (15) will suggest. Most of the extracts depict towns of a wide variety of form and function. It is certainly instructive to consider them in detail and to attempt to relate to them the various models of urban morphology to be found in relevant textbooks.

Further reading

BEAUJEU-GARNIER, J. *France*, Longman, 1975.

BURTENSHAW, D. *Economic Geography of West Germany*, Macmillan, 1974.

CLOUT, H. D. *The Regional Problem in Western Europe*, Cambridge U.P., 1976.

CLOUT, H. D. (Ed.). *Regional Development in Western Europe*, Wiley, 1975.

CLOUT, H. D. *The Geography of Post-War France: A Social and Economic Approach*, Pergamon, 1972.

DOLLFUS, J. *France: Its Geography and Growth*, John Murray, 1969.

EGLI, E. and MULLER, H. R. *Europe from the Air*, Harrap, 1959.

GOTTMANN, J. *A Geography of Europe*, 4th edn, Holt, Rinehart & Winston, 1969.

HARRISON CHURCH, R. J., HALL, P., LAWRENCE, G. R. P., MEAD, W. R., MUTTON, A. *An Advanced Geography of Northern and Western Europe*, 2nd edn, Hulton, 1973.

HOFFMANN, G. W. (Ed.). *A Geography of Europe: Problems and Prospects*, 4th edn, Ronald Press. 1977.

HOUSE, J. W. *France: An Applied Geography*, Methuen, 1978.

HOUSTON, J. M. *A Social Geography of Europe*, Duckworth, 1963.

JORDAN, T. G. *The European Culture Area: A Systematic Geography*, Harper & Row, 1973.

MONKHOUSE, F. J. *The Countries of North-Western Europe*, 3rd edn, Longman, 1974

MONKHOUSE, F. J. *A Regional Geography of Western Europe*, 4th edn, Longman, 1974

PINCHEMEL, P. *France: A Geographical Survey*, Bell, 1969.

POWRIE, P. J. and MANSFIELD, A. J. *North West Europe*, 6th edn, Harrap, 1971.
SCARGILL, D. I. *Economic Geography of France*, Macmillan, 1968.
SHACKLETON, M. R. *Europe*, 7th edn, Longmans 1965.
SINNHUBER, K. A. *Germany: Its Geography and Growth*, 2nd edn, John Murray, 1970.
SMITH, C. T. *An Historical Geography of Western Europe Before 1800*, 2nd edn, Longman, 1978.
THOMPSON, I. B. *Modern France: A Social and Economic Geography*, Butterworths, 1970.

Exercises

1. In what ways has glacial deposition affected the agriculture of Western Europe excluding Britain? (O. & C.)

2. Assess the effects of glaciation on the human geography of one of the following: Norway, Scotland, Sweden or Switzerland. (London)

3. 'Scarpland topography in Western Europe takes many varied forms'. Discuss.

4. With reference to a selection of the study areas, examine the extent to which landscapes in Western Europe are determined by structural factors.

5. Describe the distribution of loess deposits in Western Europe and examine their influence on human geography.

6. Discuss the relative importance of physical and human factors in the agricultural geography of Mediterranean France. (W.J.E.C.)

7. Examine the relationships between slope and land use.

8. How far does agriculture in Western Europe reflect soil conditions?

9. What is meant by marginal land? Examine the factors which influence the cultivation or usage of such land.

10. In what ways have the rural areas of Western Europe had to adapt themselves to changing economic circumstances in the present century?

11. Discuss the problems of planning in agriculture.

12. With reference to Western Europe, examine the conditions under which farming becomes highly specialised.

13. How far does the study of a land use map enable one to understand the farming of an area?

14. What factors determine (a) the density (b) the distribution of population in agricultural areas?

15. Write an essay on the variation in village form in Western Europe.

16. Examine the geographical basis of one major area of steel production within north-western Europe. (London)

17. By reference to specific examples, discuss the factors which favour the growth of heavy chemical industries. (O. & C.)

18. Discuss the assertion that successful industrialisation requires more than the presence of raw materials. (O. & C.)

19. Why are certain of the areas of 'old' industry in Western Europe still flourishing and important while others appear to face a future of difficulty and decline?

20. Examine the factors which are producing changes in the pattern of industrial location in Western Europe.

21. Describe the specific problems associated with mining either in areas of highly folded and faulted rocks or in high latitudes. (O. & C.)

22. 'The genesis and development of towns have very often been due to some obstacle where man has had to halt and change his means of transport'. Amplify and give examples. (O. & C.)

23. 'All town planning has a built-in element of obsolescence'. Discuss.

24. Illustrate the statement that the type of rural settlement reflects both land use and history. (O. & C.)

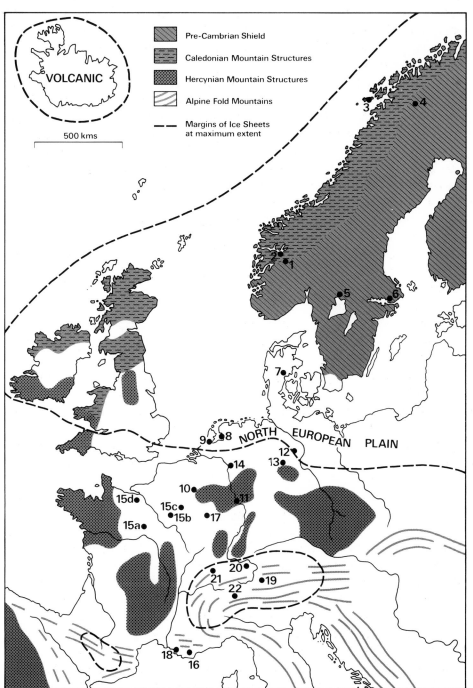

Figure 1. Structural map of Europe and location of study areas.

1   Finse
2   Aurland
3   Svolvær
4   Kiruna
5   Karlstad
6   Vällingby
7   Sönder Vissing
8   North East Polder
9   Geestmerambacht
10 Liège
11 Kaub
12 Wolfsburg
13 Gross Ilsede
14 Duisburg
15a Le Pays de Beauce
  b Le Pays de Brie
  c La Côte de Champagne
  d Le Pays d'Auge
16 Solliès-Pont
17 Hagondange
18 Marseilles
19 Engadine
20 Zürich
21 La Chaux de Fonds
22 Gorner Glacier

Pre-Cambrian Shield

Caledonian Mountain Structures

Hercynian Mountain Structures

Alpine Fold Mountains

Margins of Ice Sheets at maximum extent

500 kms

VOLCANIC

Key Symbols

Only those symbols necessary for interpretation of the map extracts have been listed. These are not comprehensive lists of symbols.

Norwegian 1 : 50 000 Map Series

Unsurfaced roads *Surfaced roads*

Motor way
State road { Road Number E=Europa-road }
County road
Commune road
Private road, toll
Road under construction
Cart-track
Marked path
Well-used track
Little-used track
Winter road
Car ferry
Small ferry

House, dwelling place
School: meeting place
Hotel, tourist hut
Hut, cabin
Saeter, tower, monument
Barn, boat-house, shed
Factory, power-station, large and small
Mine, quarry, sandpit
Trigonometrical point
Spot-height, controlled, without control
Surface level of lakes, controlled, without control
Airport, airstrip
Sea-plane harbour, berth for sea-plane, boat
Radio station, radio beacon
Lighthouse, light
Beacon
State boundary, boundary markers
County boundary
Commune boundary
Parish boundary
Boundary of public lands
Forest, forest boundary, Groups of trees
Marsh: peat-cutting
Coastline with inter-tidal area & submarine contours
Rock above or below water, depths

Railways

Double track, station
Single track, stopping-place
Narrow
Under construction or abandoned
Tunnel: built-over
Level-crossing
Road over a railway
Road under a railway
Electrified tramway
Cable railway: ski-lift
Telegraph-telephone line
Power line
Church, chapel
Cemetery
Farm

Norwegian 1 : 100 000 Map Series

Church
Farm
Smallholding, saeter
House, school, meeting house club-house, small business property, etc.
Hotel, tourist hut, boarding house
Fishing hut, shooting lodge
Factory, business property power station, mill, etc.
Trigonometrical point
Lighthouse, beacon
Buoy
Rock above water
Rock below water
Rural and urban district boundaries
Main road
Local road
Private road

Cart track
Farm track
Path
Marked path
Poorly marked path
Telephone, telegraph line
Beach with sand exposed at low tide and submarine contour
Coniferous woodland
Deciduous woodland
Marsh
County boundary
Commune boundary
Parish boundary
State property
Multiple track railway, station, stopping place
Single track railway, station, stopping place, guard's house

Norwegian 1 : 50 000 Map Series

50 — Main road, route number
Secondary road
Private road
Cart track
Winter road, track
Path, distinct
Marsh
Coniferous woods
Deciduous woods
Church, Parish church, chapel
Cemeteries
Factory, power station, etc., Mill
Brickworks, small mill; sawmill
Mine, mining claim, quarry
Wireless telegraph station
Airfield, parade ground
Trigonometrical points

Lighthouse, light; beacon; air navigation light
Fishers or hunters cabin, cattle camp, etc.
Farms: farm, mountain pasture
Cottage, school, hotel, meeting house, tourist shelter, inn, sports-hunters cabin, small farm, small power station, mill, etc.

Swedish 1 : 50 000 Map Series

Watercourse—At least 10m. wide
Watercourse—Less than 10m. wide
Underground watercourse
Timber flume or floatway
Canal with lock
Floating bridge
Swing bridge
Ferry
Small footbridge
Waterfall
Rapids
Ford
Direction of flow
Dam
Dam with footpath
Jetty
Submarine contours
Shallows
Depth in metres
Marked channel

Harbour
Lighthouse, lightship
Buoy or marker
Area of botanical interest
Area of geological interest
Prehistoric remains
Building of historical interest

Swedish 1 : 50 000 Map Series

R.r. 00 — State boundary with markers
County boundary
Commune boundary
Parish boundary
Village or settlement boundary
Boundary of shooting range
State road, dual carriageway
State road, at least 6 metres
State road—4.5 to 6 metres
E4 — 218 — Number of main road
Narrow road
Narrow road usually suitable for cars
Residential road
Track
Railway, not electrified
Railway electrified
Railway, double track
Suburban or factory railway
Station or stop with passing place and station buildings
Electricity pylon lines with transformer
Heavily built-up area
Built-up area (Residential)
Large individual buildings

Other large buildings
House or workshop
Hut or cabin
Hotel, motel, guest-house
Sports ground
Cemetery
Mine
Aerodrome with surfaced runway
Triangulation point
Spot height, Accurate
Spot height, Less accurate
Spot height, Least accurate
Contour & ice surface contours (V.I.-5 metres)
Quarry
Low ground sometimes water covered
Ditto with scattered trees
Ditto with woodland
Marsh
Ditto with scattered trees
Ditto with woodland
Garden, orchard
Dense forest
Large deciduous trees in forest
Scattered woodland

Swedish 1 : 10 000 Map Series

Public buildings
Apartment blocks or large buildings
Villas and smaller dwellings
Road or square
Projected road or square
Road closed to vehicular traffic
Park or other open space
Water
Railway
Tramway
Underground railway

Town boundary
Internal urban division
Junior school
Police-station
Fire-station
Post-office
Telegraph station
Underground railway station
Car park
Church
Sports ground
Football ground
Tennis courts
Ski-jump

Danish 1 : 20 000 Map Series

	Main road	..o...o...o..o.	Line of trees
	Country road with kilometre stone		Wire boundary fence
	Good secondary road		Fence
	Poor quality secondary road	△	Trigonometrical station with marker
	Track	✕	Windmill
	Private road	✿	Watermill
	Private track	▥	Glasshouses
	Path	•	Watertower
	Embankment	⬭	Chalk, clay or stone quarry
	Parish boundary	⊙	Monument
	Railway with level crossings	⬭	Sand or gravel pit
	Railway with road over	○	Tumulus
	Railway with road under	†	Cemetery
Ⓢ Ⓑ Ⓣ	Station, ticket-office, platform		Break of slope, drop
	Wall	○	Spring, well
..o..·..o..·..o..·.	Hedge	✕	Ruin

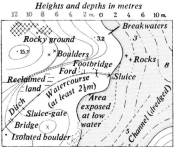

Heights and depths in metres
12 10 8 6 4 2 m 0 2 4 6 10 m.

Hollows shown with a **X**

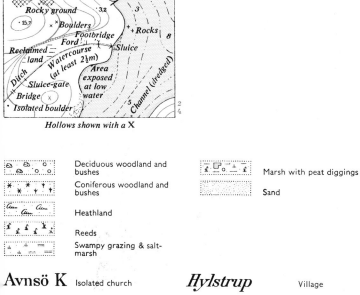

⬚	Deciduous woodland and bushes	⬚	Marsh with peat diggings
⬚	Coniferous woodland and bushes	⬚	Sand
⬚	Heathland		
⬚	Reeds		
⬚	Swampy grazing & salt-marsh		

Avnsö K Isolated church   *Hylstrup*   Village

Ramlöse Village with church bearing the parish name

Dutch 1 : 50 000 and 1 : 25 000 Map Series

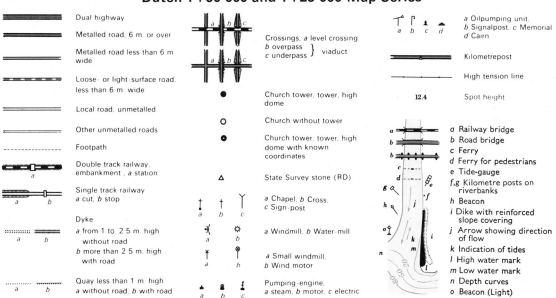

	Dual highway
	Metalled road, 6 m. or over
	Metalled road less than 6 m wide
	Loose- or light-surface road, less than 6 m. wide
	Local road, unmetalled
	Other unmetalled roads
	Footpath
	Double track railway, embankment, *a* station
	Single track railway *a* cut, *b* stop
	Dyke *a* from 1 to 2·5 m. high without road *b* more than 2·5 m. high with road
	Quay less than 1 m. high *a* without road, *b* with road

Crossings, *a* level crossing
b overpass } viaduct
c underpass

● Church tower, tower, high dome

○ Church without tower

⊙ Church tower, tower, high dome with known coordinates

△ State Survey stone (RD)

a Chapel, *b* Cross, *c* Sign-post

a Windmill, *b* Water-mill

a Small windmill, *b* Wind motor

Pumping-engine, *a* steam, *b* motor, *c* electric

a Oilpumping unit, *b* Signalpost, *c* Memorial *d* Cairn

Kilometrepost

High tension line

12.4 Spot height

a Railway bridge
b Road bridge
c Ferry
d Ferry for pedestrians
e Tide-gauge
f,g Kilometre posts on riverbanks
h Beacon
i Dike with reinforced slope covering
j Arrow showing direction of flow
k Indication of tides
l High water mark
m Low water mark
n Depth curves
o Beacon (Light)

1 : 50 000 Map Series

Built-up area with main road and other roads

ABBREVIATIONS

Bsc br	Bascule-bridge
Dr br	Swing-bridge
Gd r	Earth culvert
Km	Corn-mill
Oph br	Drawbridge
PK	Protestant church
pl	Pole
RK	Roman Cath. church
Sch sl	Lock
Sl	Sluice
Vbr	Footbridge
Wm	Watermill
Wt	Water tower

E10 International routes

a Canal
b Canal under construction

a Bridge, *b* Lock

a Culvert, *b* Earth culvert, *c* Footbridge, *d* Barrage, *e* Sluice

a Municipal hall, *b* Post, telegraph office

Contour lines

Municipal boundary

a Meadow with ditches, *b* Orchard, *c* Tree nursery, *d* Glasshouses, *e* Arable land, *f* Forest of high foliated trees or brushwood, *g* High or low pine forest, *h* Heath, *i* Sand

1 : 25 000 Map Series

Built-up area with main road and other roads

a Canal
b Canal under construction

a Bridge, *b* Lock

a Culvert, *b* Earth culvert, *c* Footbridge, *d* Barrage, *e* Sluice

a Municipal hall
b Post office
c Telegraph office

a Meadow with ditches, *b* Orchard, *c* Tree nursery, *d* Glasshouses, *e* Arable land, *f* Forest of high foliated trees or brushwood, *g* Brushwood, *h* High Pine forest, *i* Low Pine forest, *j* Heath.

West European Topographical Maps

The usefulness of topographical maps in geographical studies has long been appreciated by users of the map series published by the Ordnance Survey in this country. Foreign surveys can be equally rewarding, and a selection of maps from various West European countries can provide an insight not only into the geography of the countries concerned but also into the problems and limitations of the topographical map as an instrument of expression of geographical data.

The representation of relief

Perhaps the greatest problem that the cartographer has to face is that of the representation of relief. In earlier times this was achieved by a system of hachuring which, if well done, could produce an æsthetically pleasing result. Its greatest disadvantage lay in a lack of exactitude. It was impossible to ascertain with any accuracy the height and detailed form of mountain areas from such maps. In modern times, the contour line has become the universal answer to problems of showing detailed relief. However, its effectiveness depends upon two factors; firstly, the accuracy with which the line is drawn, and secondly, the vertical interval employed. The map series used in this book show a wide variation in this respect. The West German 1:50,000 series and the French 1:25,000 series show an interesting use of contours and form lines. On both types of map a vertical interval of 10 metres is used for the contours, but on gentle slopes where more space is available the information provided by the contours is frequently supplemented by form lines drawn at 5 metre and 2·5 metre intervals. Other series have a less flexible system. The Dutch maps use a vertical interval of 5 metres, and the French 1:50,000 series one of 10 metres. With the exception of the Norwegian and Swiss maps with their contour intervals of 30 and 20 metres respectively, all the other series represented in the book use an interval of 10 metres or less. Even so, the limitations of contours in the recognition of minor relief forms such as river terraces can be appreciated from a study of a number of the extracts. The representation of relief also involves the question of legibility as well as accuracy. One of the devices employed to increase this quality is that of hill shading. By this method the general layout of the relief can be seen before detailed investigation of contours is undertaken. Several of the map series represented in this book provide good examples of this technique, notably the French 1:50,000, the West German 1:50,000 (in some Länder) and the Swiss 1:50,000. Of these, the Swiss maps are among the finest produced in Europe. It is remarkable how landscapes with such complexity of relief become readily understandable through the use of finely toned shadows. The Swiss survey also illustrates another technique of the map maker, namely the representation of steep cliffs by rock drawing. The finely drawn detail on the Engadine and Gorner Glacier extracts are models of what can be achieved.

The portrayal of the human landscape

The representation of the human landscape involves a great deal of selection and compromise on the part of the cartographer. A topographical map cannot portray all features of the landscape as in the manner of an aerial photograph, and certain features are emphasised at the expense of others. Most maps use a basis of black for the representation of cultural detail although other colours are sometimes used to depict particular classes of buildings or other features. The representation of settlement groupings on medium-scale maps presents many problems and is also approached in a variety of ways. In village settlements buildings may be shown *en bloc* or as individual properties. In urban areas only the former technique is generally possible, apart from the portrayal of large properties in the urban fringe, with the result that details of site are frequently obscured by the 'cultural overlay'. In this respect much depends on the choice of colour and the intensity of shading or stipple employed. The range of symbols and other devices used to portray specific features of the urban landscape should be carefully considered. Roads should be shown in detail and classified according to width and condition, and different categories of railway should be indicated. Attention should also be given to the amount of information provided about non-visible elements such as boundaries and land ownership. The absence of *Gemeinde* boundaries on the West German maps, for example, reduces the value of statistical information published for these units, since this cannot be related to the map extracts with any degree of accuracy.

Representation of rural land use is another important aspect to be considered in attempting to interpret human geography from a topographical map. Many of the maps included in the book are inadequate in this respect, although most represent an advance on the limited amount of information provided by the maps of the Ordnance Survey. The British 1:50,000 maps show woodland and the buildings, roads and other works of man but there is no distinction between types of farmland apart from orchards and glasshouses. The distinction between arable land and permanent pasture thus becomes a matter of deduction and inference from location. By comparison, the West German 1:50,000 maps cover the same categories as the Ordnance Survey maps but have additional symbols for vineyards and hop gardens. The French 1:50,000 survey has a similar range of land use symbols. The most effective series in this respect are the Dutch 1:50,000 and 1:25,000 maps. Reference to the appropriate key sheets will show the wide range of land use symbols employed, possibly a natural reflection of the high value that the Dutch place upon their land.

It should be borne in mind that the key sheets on pages 10, 11, 126 and 127 include only those symbols required for the interpretation of the various map extracts. The keys on the full map sheets give additional symbols. These, in fact, show a wide variation in the amount of information that they provide. For example, the relatively small amount of information provided by the Norwegian 1:50,000 maps may be compared with the lengthy list of conventional signs used on the Swedish, Dutch, West German and Swiss maps at the same scale. These differences, of course, reflect not only the aspirations of the cartographers but also the varying complexity of the landscapes being portrayed. Some of the map keys are noticeably lacking in information about many symbols which appear on the map sheets. This is true of the French maps, which are also made more difficult to read on account of the frequent use of abbreviations on the maps, the meanings of which are not given in the keys.

The use of a grid system for map references is familiar to users of the Ordnance Survey maps. A similar practice is common throughout Europe, and the same kilometre square size is used for the grid. Usually a full grid system is provided, but in some cases, notably the French and most West German maps, reference numbers are provided in the margins but no grid lines drawn on the maps. In the cases of the Norwegian 1:100,000, and the Belgian 1:50,000 series no system of either grid squares or numbering is employed.

In using the various West European map series one is struck by the considerable variation in standards and styles of lettering employed on the map sheets. Poor legibility reduces the value of many maps. This is true of the Norwegian 1:50,000 series, on which heavy type frequently obscures significant detail. These considerations of legibility have in part determined the choice of study areas, for in many parts of Europe landscapes of great interest are still only covered by maps which have limited value to the geographer. The use of colour may similarly affect the legibility and usefulness of a map series. The Swiss sheets are restrained and economical in this respect, but nevertheless manage to portray a complex topography with success. Other maps employ more colours, notably those of the Netherlands and Belgium. The maps of the latter country suffer from an over-use of solid black shading for built up areas. This obscures much significant detail of relief etc., and is an unsatisfactory answer to the difficult problem of representing urban areas.

Exercises

1. To what extent would you subscribe to the dictum that what is unmappable is not geography? (S.U.J.B.)
2. How far are the considerations of legibility and the provision of detailed information compatible in the production of topographical maps? On which of the map extracts included in the book do you consider the problem to have been most effectively solved?
3. What information do you consider might be added to the following maps to increase their usefulness to the geographer: (a) Aurland; (b) Geestmerambacht; (c) Duisburg; (d) Marseilles?
4. Assess the problems of representing relief cartographically. (W.J.E.C.)
5. Take a single grid square on an Ordnance Survey 1:25,000 map, and draw maps to show the same area in the style of any four European map series.
6. Which of the map series included in the book do you consider to be of most value as an aid to the study of (a) landforms; (b) agricultural geography; (c) industrial geography? Justify your choice.
7. To what extent is the choice of land use symbols appearing on the various national map series a reflection of the geography of these countries?
8. Compare the cartographic techniques used on the Liège map extract with those employed in portraying a British city of comparable size on the 1:50,000 maps of the Ordnance Survey.
9. Compare and contrast the cartographic techniques employed on the Dutch 1 : 25,000, the French 1 : 25,000 and the Ordnance Survey 1 : 25,000 map series. Organise your answer under the following headings: representation of relief, land use, settlement, communications, and aesthetic considerations.
10. Make a critical assessment of the different ways of portraying land use on the Dutch and West German 1 : 50,000 map series.
11. To what extent do aerial photographs provide additional data which is not shown on the maps?
12. Comment on the relative merits and shortcomings of oblique and vertical air photographs for purposes of geographical interpretation.
13. With reference to a wide selection of map extracts, examine the extent to which many features of map design have become standardised.
14. Comment on the use of colour in cartographic design.
15. 'A topographical map cannot portray all features of the landscape as in the manner of an aerial photograph, and certain features are emphasised at the expense of others'. Comment on this statement with reference to the maps and photographs used in Studies 7, 13, 21.

Further reading

DEFFONTAINES, P. and DELAMARRE, M. J. *Atlas Aérien, France*. Vols. I–V, Librairie Gallimard, 1955–64.
DICKINSON, G. C. *Maps and Air Photographs*, 2nd edn, E. J. Arnold, 1979.
DURY, G. H. *Map Interpretation*, Pitman, 1960.
GARNETT, A. *The Geographical Interpretation of Topographical Maps*, Harrap, 1953
LOCK, C. B. M. *Modern Maps and Atlases*, 2nd edn, Clive Bingley, 1972.
RAISZ, E. *Principles of Cartography*, McGraw-Hill, 1962
ST. JOSEPH, J. K. S., (Ed.), *The Uses of Air Photography*, 2nd edn, Black, 1977.
SYLVESTER, D. *Map and Landscape*, Philip, 1952.
Textbook of Topographical Surveying, H.M.S.O., 1965. Especially chapters 16 and 19, 'Map Reproduction and Design' and 'British and Foreign Maps'.
WALKER. F. *Geography from the Air*, Methuen, 1953.

Study 1
FINSE
HORDALAND
NORWAY

Part of the
Norwegian High Fjell

Extract from Sheet D 33
Vest. Hardangerjökulen.
Norwegian 1 :100,000
(Gradteig) Series.

Published 1932. Field
Revision 1955.
Vertical Interval of
Contours 30 metres.
Longitude readings are
west of the Oslo meridian
(10°-43′22.5″ east of
Greenwich).

Map 1

Photograph 1. The *Bergensbanen* at Finse. Photograph taken in February. Notice the snow sheds and snow screens which shelter the railway below Finsentind.

Mittet Foto A/S, Oslo

Photograph 2. Finse from across Finsevatn. Notice the amount of lingering snow in August when the photograph was taken.

R. Knowles

The area covered by map 1, which is an extract from one of the Norwegian 1:100,000 sheets, is part of the Norwegian high *fjell* in the vicinity of Finse, a small mountain settlement on the Oslo–Bergen railway, some 110 km east of Bergen. The area portrayed on the map extract includes part of the main watershed of the Scandinavian Peninsula with the headwaters of streams flowing both west to the Atlantic fjord coast and south-east to Oslo Fjord. Among the latter the valley of the Hallingdalselv provides an important line of communication between Vestlandet and Östlandet, and the railway ascends its upper valley and a tributary valley, Ustedal, to reach the watershed just to the west of Finse.

Relief and Drainage

Apart from the extreme south-west, the area covered by the extract is everywhere above 1,100 metres and is a district of wild, dramatic scenery. The term 'dissected plateau' can be appropriately applied to the area which shows a predominance of gently sloping surfaces at levels ranging from c. 1,200 metres to c. 1,500 metres. Above this high plateau with its ice-eroded hollows and lake basins to which the Norwegians give the term *vidda* a number of peaks and areas of higher ground may be noted. To the south of Finse lies the ice cap of Hardangerjökulen with a summit height of 1,876 metres, while to the north-east is the western end of the Hallingskarvet ridge which rises steeply (1 in 1·3 in places) above the plateau to a height of 1,830 metres. The lake-studded valley of the Ustedalselv which runs from north-west to south-east across the area is generally broad and open, but becomes narrower and more deeply incised below Finse. (The river is unnamed on the map extract and reference should be made to a good atlas map or the full map sheet from which the extract is taken.)

The *vidda* surface of the interior *fjell* is an ancient peneplain uplifted in Tertiary times and since modified by fluvial and glacial erosion. Where mountains rise above the general plateau level these are either monadnock features owing their existence to greater resistance to erosion, or are, alternatively, remains of higher and older erosion surfaces. As M. Shackleton points out, 'the present cycle of erosion is still so youthful that there remain considerable areas of upraised peneplain scarcely attacked by the deepening of the river beds which has taken place in their lower and middle courses. Accordingly the high *fjelds* still retain the shallow valleys and meandering streams which date back to the days before the Tertiary uplift.'

Hardangerjökulen

The most immediately striking feature on map 1 is the ice cap of Hardanger-jökulen. This covers an area of 78·2 km² out of a total ice cover of 3,988 km² in Norway, and is the fifth largest ice cap in the country. (Olav Liestøl. *Breer i Norge,* Breen, Den Norsk Turistforening Årbok, 1961). The surface of the ice cap assumes a dome-like form with a maximum height of 1,876 metres. The margins have relatively steep gradients compared with the gently sloping upper surfaces. A series of glaciers extends from the main ice mass, the longest being Rembesdalsskaaki which extends for about 3 kilometres from the western margin of the ice cap. Others include Blaaisen, Forsteinsfonni, Leirbotnsskaaki and Isdölskaaki. (*Fonni* and *Skaaki* are old Norse words meaning glacier.) The surface of the ice is broken at a number of points by nunatak protrusions of the underlying rock surface, as at Nord Kongtind and Sud Kongtind. This fact, together with the spacing of the contours around the ice margin, suggests that the ice cover is of no great thickness. The scale of the map extract is, of course, inadequate to show the detailed surface features of the ice.

The present Norwegian ice caps are not, as is sometimes thought, remnants of the former Quaternary Ice Age cover. During the post-glacial period there has been a number of climatic fluctuations with consequent variations in the extent of the ice cover. The glaciers and ice caps reached a post-glacial maximum in the mid-eighteenth century, and records exist of many farms in Vestlandet and Nordland being overwhelmed by ice at that time. During the past two centuries the Norwegian glaciers and ice caps have generally been characterised by diminution. In recent decades this shrinkage has been relatively rapid. Between 1928 and 1960, for example, the summit height of Hardangerjökulen decreased by 17 metres, and this was accompanied by a decrease in area. However, since 1960 the ice has shown a slight increase, as indicated by mass balance studies made on the surface of the ice cap.

Hardangerjökulen: Annual Water Balance Measurements

1963	−14 grammes per cm²	1966	− 64 grammes per cm²
1964	+44 grammes per cm²	1967	+118 grammes per cm²
1965	+51 grammes per cm²	1968	+ 53 grammes per cm²

Source: O. Liestøl. Norsk Polarinstitutt, Oslo.

Map 1 shows the extent of the permanent ice cover in the vicinity of Finse in 1955 as determined by photogrammetric methods. Since then there has been an appreciable reduction in the area covered by ice, particularly in the vicinity of the Sankt Paal peak to the north of Finse where little permanent ice now remains.

In 1961 it was possible to write that 'The *fjell* is becoming free of ice at such a rate that the spread of vegetation cannot keep pace with it. Thus, one finds the zone of bare white rock around the ice caps which is so character-istic of the high *fjell* today.' (Olav Liestøl.) The map extract provides little information about the nature of the ground surface over most of the area. In fact the ground beyond the limits of the ice cover consists of boulders and rock rubble of glacial origin as well as bare ice-scraped surfaces. These areas beyond the ice are traversed by an irregular pattern of melt water streams. Apart from patches of marsh in ice-eroded hollows and along the valley floors only stunted vegetation exists on this bare uncompromising surface. Almost the whole of the area portrayed lies above the tree line. Only in the extreme south-west, on the south side of the deep valley below Rembesdalsvann, is there any map symbol denoting vegetation. Here on the steep valley walls and lower slopes a cover of deciduous woodland is shown to exist, although the cliff-like wall on the north side of the valley is devoid of vegetation.

Settlement and communications

Less than 50 buildings are to be found on the 455 km² covered by the map extract, of which only 28 appear from the map to be permanently occupied, the remainder being saeters and high-level mountain huts. The density of permanently occupied buildings over the area is thus as low as 0·06 per km². The only nucleation of any note is the small lakeside settlement of Finse (population 139) which is a tourist centre for mountain walking in summer and skiing in winter, as well as being the headquarters for winter snow clearance and repair work along this highest section of the Oslo–Bergen railway (photographs 1 and 2). Occupation statistics for Finse show that in 1970, 40 out of a working population of 52 were employed on the railway. The importance of tourism in the area is suggested by the provision of huts at various points on the mountain tracks shown on the map. A number of saeters, clusters of huts on areas of mountain grazing, is shown both along Ustedal below Finse and in the south-western part of the map area. These are probably connected to farms at lower levels and beyond the limits of the map extract.

Apart from the Oslo–Bergen railway, or *Bergensbanen* as it is known, communications in the area are almost non-existent. A narrow track is shown to follow the railway but there is no road in the area suitable for vehicular traffic. Until recently the railway, which was opened in December 1909, provided the only permanent all-year land connection between eastern and western Norway. The 480 kilometre long line reaches a maximum height of 1,301 metres near Taagavann to the north-west of Finse. This is almost as high as the Brenner and Mont Cenis Passes, which lie 15° further south in Europe. For almost 100 kilometres the railway runs above the tree line, and 30 kilometres of snow sheds as well as snow screens are necessary to protect the track from drifting snow in winter (see photographs 1 and 2). Seventeen tunnels may be noted on the section of railway shown on the map extract, and clearly the construction of the line over the mountain barrier between the two largest cities in Norway represented a great engineering achievement. In 1964 electrification of the line was completed, so that the journey between Oslo and Bergen now takes about eight hours.

While it would be an exaggeration to regard the limited area portrayed on map 1 as fully representative of the whole of interior Norway, it nevertheless provides a typical example of the bleak high *fjell* which constitutes almost 75% of the total area of the country.

	Bergen	Voss	Myrdal	Finse	Haugastøl	Geilo	Ål	Nesbyen	Lunner	Oslo
Height (metres)	43	56	870	1,220	995	841	464	164	375	22
Precipitation (mm)	1,933	1,369	1,265	1,090	744	678	587	433	731	680
Average number days snow cover p.a.	39	83	211	255	215	194	171	135	157	101

Source: *Nedbøren i Norge 1895–1943*. Vol. I. Middelverdier og Maksima. Oslo, 1949.

Either describe and comment on the relationships between the above sets of statistics *or* determine mathematically or graphically whether altitude or total precipitation is the greatest influence on the number of days snow cover per year.

2. Draw a cross section to show the form of the ice cap and the marginal relief and drainage features. Draw the section from the summit of Hardangerjökulen west down the centre of Rembesdalsskaaki and then across the lake and along the outlet stream to the margin of the map sheet. Label the main physical features shown and write a short description of the section.

3. Using the spot heights given on the map (including the surface level of the lakes) construct a cumulative altimetric frequency curve to show the relief of the area. *(a)* Comment on the result. *(b)* What are the limitations of this method of portraying relief? (See B. Sparks. *Geomorphology,* Longman, 1960, Chapter 9.)

4. 'An amelioration (of climate) has shown itself during the last century or two. The effects have tended to be cumulative. They have not commonly been perceptible within the human lifetime; but there are many records—natural and mathematical—which provide clues.' (W. R. Mead.) What are the ways in which climatic fluctuations have been determined?

5. Write an essay on 'The geography of winter in Scandinavia'.

Glossary of terms and abbreviations appearing on the map

The following terms and abbreviations appear at a number of points on the map extract. An appreciation of their meaning aids interpretation.

Bre	Glacier	*Seter (Sr.)*	Saeter
Foss (Fs.)	Waterfall	*Stölen*	Saeter
Haug (Hg. plural *Hgne.)*	Hill or peak	*Stöva*	Mountain hut
Hytta	Mountain hut	*Tind (T.)*	Pointed peak
		Vatn (Vn.)	Lake

Exercises

1. Profile along the Bergensbanen

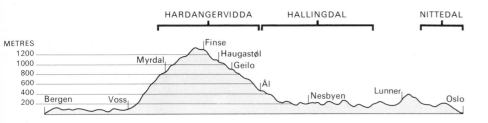

Further reading

AHLMANN, H. W. 'Glaciological Research on the North Atlantic Coasts', *R.G.S. Research Series*, No. 1, The Royal Geographical Society, 1948.

AHLMANN, H. W. 'The Present Climatic Fluctuation', *Geographical Journal* **112**, 1948.

AHLMANN, H. W. *Glacier Fluctuations and Climatic Variations*, American Geographical Society, New York, 1953.

BATESON, S. R. 'Preliminary Observations on Vegetation Succession and Environmental Influences in Front of a Glacier, *Horizon*, **19**, 1970.

EMBLETON, C. and KING, C. A. M. *Glacial and Periglacial Geomorphology*, Arnold, 1968. Norsk Polarinstitutt, Oslo, Arbok, 1964, 1965 and 1966.

FAEGRI, K. *On The Variation of Western Norwegian Glaciers during the Last 200 Years*, Oslo, 1948.

FAEGRI, K. *The Plant World at Finse*, Norway, Bergen, 1967.

LÅG, J. 'Preliminary Results of Investigations on Quaternary Geological and Soil Problems near Hardangerjökulen Glacier, Norway', *Meddelelser fra det Norske Skogforsøksvesen 85*, B XXIII, 1967.

LIESTØL, O. 'Glacier Dammed Lakes in Norway', *Norsk Geografisk Tidsskrift*, No. 3–6, 1955. (Refers to the ice-dammed lake on the north side of Rembesdalsskaaki.)

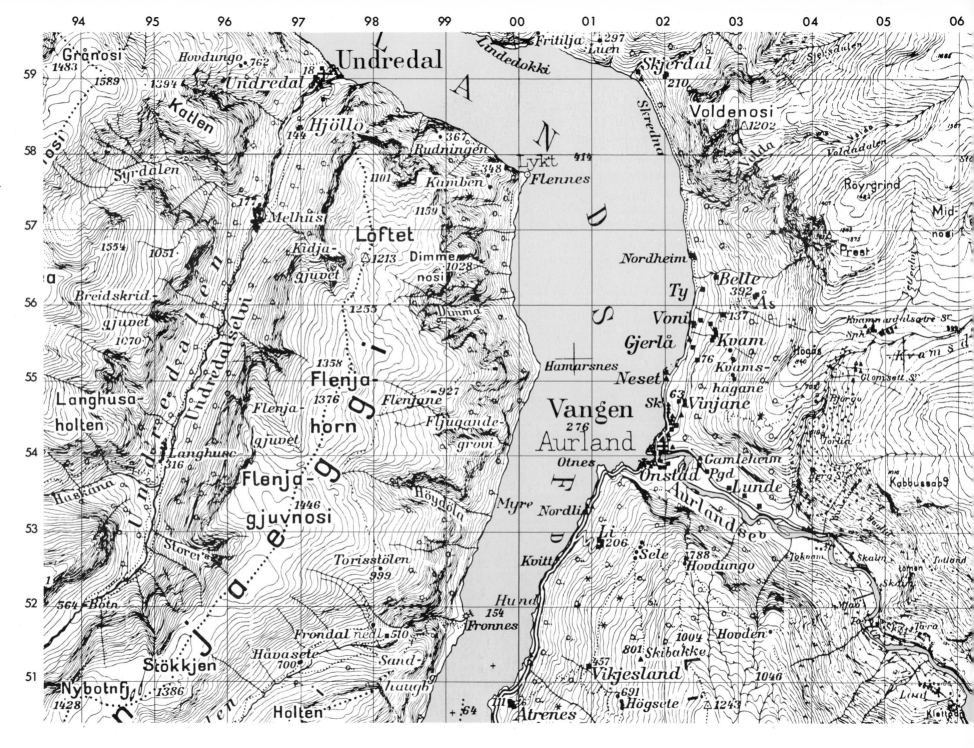

**Study 2
AURLAND
SOGN and
FJORDANE
NORWAY**

A Fjord Coast

Extract from Sheet 1416 IV.
Aurland.
Norwegian 1:50,000
Series

Published 1952.
Vertical interval of
contours 30 metres.

The map extract printed by
permission of the Geographical
Survey of Norway.

Map 2

Photograph 3. Aurlandsfjord.
View of the fjord slopes to the
north of the Aurland River.
The village of Aurland is seen
at the mouth of the river.

Mittet Photo A/S, Oslo.

19

The two principal series of Norwegian topographical maps are those at scales of 1:50,000 and 1:100,000. The Svolvær extract (Study 3) is an example of the older *gradteig* sheets which are based on late 19th-century surveys with subsequent revisions. The Aurlandsfjord study uses an extract from one of the 1:50,000 'tourist' sheets which were introduced in 1943.

Fjord coasts

Fjords may be described as long, narrow, steep-sided inlets of the sea penetrating in a rectilinear pattern of branching arms far into upland coastal regions. True fjords are found along the edges of mountainous areas which have been subject to glaciation, and it is thus held that they have resulted from former glaciers deeply eroding preglacial river valleys which in turn were probably guided by tectonic weaknesses. Many fjords are characterised by extremely great depths and yet are relatively shallow near their mouths. For example, Sogne Fjord, of which Aurlandsfjord is a branch, reaches depths of 1,200 metres, considerably deeper than the floor of the North Sea into which it opens, and yet is only about 150 metres deep at its mouth.

The formation of fjords has long been a subject of controversy. For example, they have been attributed to faulting on account of their rectilinear plan in many areas, but this fails to explain their restricted distribution to glaciated regions. Thus, while fjords are now generally accepted as being partially submerged glaciated valleys, their great depth and the presence of a threshold of apparently solid rock has led to much discussion as to their detailed mode of formation. Such a form implies a vast amount of glacial overdeepening of the inner parts of the fjord. It is necessary to assume that the inner parts of the pre-glacial valleys were greatly eroded as the glaciers flowed steeply down from the nearby ice-caps but were much less deeply cut where the ice entered the sea. It has been suggested by A. Cailleux that variations in the depth of frozen ground before the advance of the ice might be a significant factor in this respect, the ground being less deeply frozen and shattered near the sea than inland and thus less easily eroded by the glaciers. (A. Cailleux. 'Polissage et Surcreusement Glaciaires dans l'Hypothèse de Boyé'. *Revue de Géomorphologie Dynamique, 3,* 1952.)

Aurlandsfjord

Aurlandsfjord is a southern arm of Sogne Fjord and lies about 160 km from the open sea (fig. 2). Even at this distance from the main fjord entrance a sounding of 414 metres is indicated. The walls of the fjord are extremely steep, especially on the western side where gradients in excess of 1 in 2 are encountered. This side of the fjord is broken by two hanging valleys. Undre-

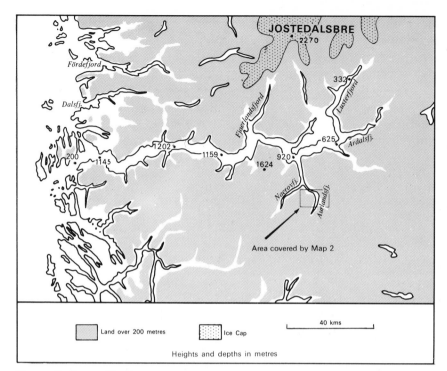

Figure 2. Sogne Fjord.

dal and Frondal, although in the case of the latter the typical glaciated form is modified by a deeply incised post-glacial stream valley. The floor level of Undredal corresponds closely with the level of submergence of the fjord valley, but the stream occupying Frondal plunges steeply down into the fjord and has built out the small deltaic platform on which the saw mill at Fronnes is sited (993519). On the opposite shore the mouth of another hanging valley, Skjerdal, may also be noted. The eastern side of the fjord is generally less steep, apart from the slopes below Voldenosi (030584), and is also breached by the valley of the Aurlandselv. Elsewhere small streams in incipient valleys plunge precipitously down from the mountain crags.

Settlement, occupations and communications

The settlement of the area shows a close correlation with topography both in amount and distribution. Nucleation occurs at Aurland/Onstad (0254), Undredal (9759) and to a much lesser degree on the more gentle slopes at Kvam (0255). These villages have populations of 606, 191 and 67 respectively. Elsewhere scattered farms and houses take advantage of the limited number of safe and suitable sites for building offered by the terrain, for rock and snow avalanches and landslips are a constant threat to property. The highest parts of the area are, of course, devoid of settlement.

The means of livelihood in fjord areas such as Aurlandsfjord is based essentially on farming, tourism, forestry and fishing, but clear distinctions cannot be drawn. Fishing, which is far less important than along the open coast, and forestry, which attains its maximum importance in south-east Norway, are merely supplements to what is essentially a farming economy, and tourism in West Norway is markedly seasonal.

Aurland. Principal occupations of the working population. 1970

Building and construction	353	31·2%	Retailing	62	5·5%
Agriculture	260	23·0%	Administration	34	3·0%
Service trades and professions	255	22·5%	Others	88	7·8%
Industry	80	7·0%	Total working population	1132	

(Note: The commune of Aurland extends beyond the limits of the map extract. Total commune population 2372)
Source: Folke -og Boligtelling. 1 November 1970. Statistike Kommunehefte. No. 1421.
Aurland. Statistisk Sentralbyrå. Oslo. 1974.

Farms in the area are generally small, owner-occupied and divided into what is known as the *innmark* and *utmark*. The former consists of small enclosed fields supporting crops of oats, barley and hay, while the latter, the outfield, takes the form of sæter grazing in these fjord districts. The typical sæter pastures with their collection of small huts such as Kvammardalsætre (049557) and Glomsett Sæter (046552) generally lie just above the treeline so that timber is available, but on the least accessible of the fjord slopes they are found at much lower altitudes as at Fritilja (003595), Luen (011594), Rudningen (989583) and Kamben (996577). The sæters lie at varying distances from the farmsteads to which they are linked by rough trackways. Notice the interesting clusters of sæter buildings at Melhus (965571) and Langhusc (952540) in Undredal. The pattern of transhumance or *seterdrift* varies widely from area to area both in timing and duration. In some cases a single sæter may be used, while in other instances a farmer may make use of several sæters during the summer. The high level pastures above Aurlandsfjord are used chiefly for the grazing of goats for about 3 months each year.

The map extract, published in 1952, shows a poorly developed system of local communications. Aurland's only links with the outside world at that time were by ferry steamer or the secondary road running south from the village to the head of the fjord where the famous Flåm Railway climbs in a series of spirals to join the Oslo/Bergen Railway at Myrdal. However, in recent years the isolation of the district has been broken down by the opening of two new roads. In 1966 a summer road was opened between Aurland and Lærdal to the north, followed in 1975 by a new road along Aurlandsdal to Hol on the Oslo/Bergen route. Construction of the latter which has over 16 km of tunnels no doubt accounted for many of the workers engaged in building and construction in 1970. The western side of the fjord is virtually devoid of roads and the village of Undredal relies entirely upon boats for its links with outside areas, a situation which is by no means uncommon among the fjord communities of West Norway.

Fjord districts such as Aurlandsfjord constitute some of the most distinctive landscapes in western Europe. The relief of these areas provides probably the most spectacular example of glacial erosion, and the human occupancy of the fjords shows a close adjustment to the conditions imposed by a unique and often difficult environment.

Abbreviations

In addition to the key symbols given on page 10 the following abbreviations occur on the map:

Bg—Berg Hill; mountain	*Pgd—Prestegård* Vicarage
Ev—Elv River	*Sk—Skole* School
Fj—Fjell Mountain	*Sph—Sportshytte* Sports Cabin
Nedl—Nedlagt Abandoned	*Sr—Seter* Saeter

Exercises

1. Draw a sketch section from the spur Katlen (955585) to the slopes of Kabbussaberg (052542). Estimate the depth of the fjord at the point where it is crossed by the section line and extend the valley sides to give an approximate submarine profile. Mark the treeline on your section and label the landforms shown.

2. 'Where the larger side valleys meet the main fjord valley there are generally a cluster of houses and a pier which act as a focal point. . . . Settlement on the fjord sides takes three main forms; it may climb an embayment of gentler slope, it may follow a raised beach, or it may occur as isolated units on shelves high up on the fjord sides or on the floors of side valleys which "hang" to the main valley.' A. C. O'Dell, *The Scandinavian World.*

How far do you consider this description to be applicable to the settlement of Aurlandsfjord?

3. 'Settlement shows a close correlation with topography both in amount and distribution.' With the aid of a map showing the distribution of both permanent settlement and sæters, amplify this statement.

4. Construct two frequency curves to show the relationship between altitude and the distribution of *(a)* sæters and *(b)* permanent settlement. Comment on your result.

Further reading

GREFFIER, M. J. *Le Pays d'Aurland dans la Région du Sognefjord.* Bull. de l'Ass. des Géog. Français, 1952.
GREGORY, J. W. *The Origin and Nature of Fjords,* Murray, 1913.
MEAD, W. R. *An Economic Geography of the Scandinavian States and Finland,* London U.P., 2nd Edition, 1968, chapter 7.
MEAD, W. R. 'Sogn and Fjordane in the fjord economy of western Norway', *Economic Geography* **23,** 1947.
O'DELL, A. C. *The Scandinavian World,* Longmans, 1957, chapter 10.
STRØM, K. M. 'The geomorphology of Norway', *Geographical Journal* **112,** 1948.

Study 3
SVOLVAER
NORDLAND
NORWAY

A Lofoten Fishing Town

Extract from Sheet K10.
Svolvær.
Norwegian 1:100,000
Series.

First published 1902.
Revised in the field 1956.
Roads up-to-date 1958.
Vertical interval of contours
30 metres.
Note. Longitude readings
give the number of degrees
east of the Oslo meridian.
(Oslo meridian = 10°-43'-
22.5" east of Greenwich.)

*The map extract printed by
permission of the Geographical
Survey of Norway.*

Map 3

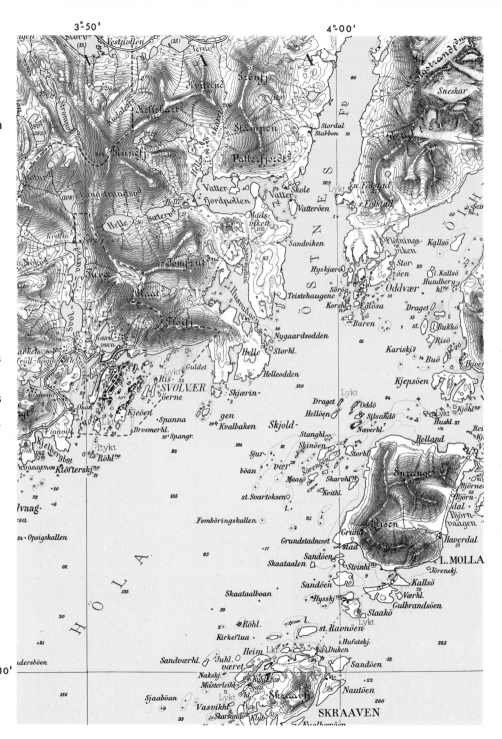

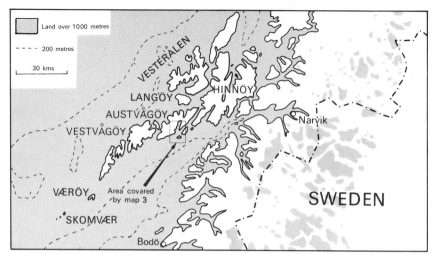

Figure 3. The Lofoten Islands.

The Lofoten Islands are among some 150,000 islands which border the coast of Norway. The group stretches south-west for about 160 kilometres from Hinnöy to the rocky outpost of Skomvær, and, like the Vesterålen group to the north, lies on a submarine ridge which separates Vestfjord from the North Atlantic. The map extract shows the southern part of Austvågöy together with smaller islands in the vicinity of the small town of Svolvær. The area portrayed lies almost 200 kilometres within the Arctic Circle.

Relief features of the Svolvær district

The land in the area covered by the map extract rises with extraordinary steepness to a maximum height of 1,062 metres. The southern slopes of the island of Lille Molla, for example, exceed 45° and comparably steep slopes can be found at many other points in the area. The plutonic rocks of the district have been deeply dissected by glacial erosion to produce a landscape of sharp, rugged peaks and narrow ridges or arêtes. These pyramid peaks are denoted by the term *Tind* (abb. *Td.*) which occurs frequently on the map extract. The mountains are deeply cut by corries and the extract provides several examples of these features with their small lakes and steep bounding walls. It will be noted that whereas corries are found only at high elevations in the mountain areas further south in Europe, in this arctic region they occur close to, or even at, sea-level as well as at higher levels. The figures on the various corrie lakes indicate the surface height of the lakes, so that it is

Photograph 4. Svolvær. Lofoten. Notice the nature of the strandflat upon which Svolvær is built and the steepness of the distant peaks.

Widerøe's Flyveselskap og Polarfly A/S. Oslo.

reasonable to suppose that the floor of Helle-sæter Vand (16 metres and 2 metres) lies below sea-level. It is generally believed that during the latter stages of the Quaternary glaciation the Lofoten Islands supported a local ice-cap detached from the main mass of inland ice on the Scandinavian Peninsula to the east. It is interesting to note that the map shows permanent ice and snow on the flanks of Langstrandtindene to the east of Östnes Fjord. Elsewhere the mountains are less high and fail to reach the level of permanent snow, although in such high latitudes there is, of course, a long duration of snow cover.

A striking feature of both the map and photograph is the fringe of low, flat ground just above sea-level. This rock platform which is found along much of the coast of West Norway is known as the strandflat. In addition to the fringe of low ground at the foot of the mountains the strandflat is also represented by the multitude of small, low islands which rise only just above sea-level and the rocks which lie just below sea-level. Norwegians refer to the 'dry' and 'wet' strandflat to denote those parts of the platform which lie just above or just below sea-level. The various rock formations of the strandflat are of vital significance to the maritime communities of Norway's west coast and figure prominently in the local vocabulary. The following terms signify particular features of the strandflat and many occur as part of the local names on the map extract.

Bo	Shoal near the surface	Holme (abb. Hl.)	Small island
Brake	Rock with heavy breakers	Klakke	Shoal or fishing ground
Bråt	Shoal with breakers	Öy or Ö	Island or islet
Drag	Long rock	Skjær (abb. Skj.)	Small rock, skerry, or shelf
Fall	Shoal with breakers	Slu	Long skerry below water
Fles	Flat skerry; low-lying island	Stabbe	High rock; stack
Flu	Skerry showing at low tide	Tare	Seaweed seen at low tide.

(It should be noted that where these terms are found on the map sheet they occur in the definitive form ending in 'et', 'a', or 'en'.)

The date and mode of formation of the strandflat is still a topic of controversy. One of the most detailed studies of the feature is that of Fridtjof Nansen, who considered that it was produced by marine denudation aided by sub-aerial frost action. (F. Nansen, *The Strandflat and Isostasy,* Oslo, 1922.) Nansen also believed that the strandflat consisted of three platforms with inner edges at *c.* 8 metres, 15–18 metres and 30–40 metres above the present sea level. The vertical interval of the map is, of course, inadequate for any determination of these subdivisions. A more recent explanation is that of the German geomorphologist Wolf Tietze, who envisages planation by shelf-ice on a tidal coastline. Erosion is thought to have resulted from the former movement of the ice due to tidal fluctuations. (W. Tietze, 'Ein Beitrag zum geomorphologischen Problem der Strandflate', *Petermanns Geographische Mitteilungen,* **106**, 1962.) Notice on the map sheet the way in which a broken line indicates water that is dangerous for shipping. This 'danger line' encloses much of the submerged portion of the strandflat. From the limited number of depths marked on the map it would seem that a deep channel, Höla (156 metres deep at one point), lies about 3 kilometres offshore from Svolvær. This is probably a submerged continuation of Östnes Fjord which extends across the strandflat.

Climate and vegetation

Since the Lofoten Islands lie within the Arctic Circle (Svolvær 68°15′ N.) the climate is, as would be expected, very severe in winter. However, the North Atlantic Drift has a pronounced ameliorating effect on winter temperatures along the whole of the west coast of the country, so that the littoral zone of North Norway has in fact the highest temperature anomaly, not only in Europe, but in the world. That is to say, if one finds the average temperature for a particular line of latitude it is then possible to examine deviations from the mean for particular places along that parallel. This deviation is known as the 'thermal anomaly', and near the Lofotens there is a record positive anomaly of 25·5°C. in January.

The mean January temperature for Svolvær is −0·7°C, which is less cold than the mean January temperature of Oslo (−4·2°C) almost 1000 kilometres to the south. Winter temperatures in Norway in fact decrease more rapidly inland than northwards. The arctic position of the Lofotens is more apparent in summer when the mean July temperature of Svolvær is only 11·9°C. Total annual precipitation is 592 mm with an all-seasonal distribution and much of it in the form of snow. Mention should also be made of the frequent gales which are a feature of the weather of the Lofoten district and which often occur during the winter fishing season. The arctic position of the islands means that they experience the 'midnight sun' effect in summer and a period of continuous and oppressive darkness in winter.

These climatic conditions are reflected in the natural vegetation of the area covered by the map. The combination of short growing season and poor, thin soils results in an absence of tree cover over much of the area. As can be appreciated from photograph 4, these outer coastal districts are generally bare and windswept, although scattered patches of deciduous trees (probably birch) are marked on the lower, more gentle slopes and rise to heights of *c.* 150 metres. (This may be compared with the tree-line at *c.* 800 metres in the Aurland district. See Study 2.) The valley floors and much of the strandflat appear to be badly drained, as is indicated by the frequent occurrence of the symbol denoting marsh. The lingering snow cover and the slight gradients of the strandflat are probably significant factors in this respect.

Settlement and occupations

The most striking feature of the settlement pattern is the marked concentration of population along the coast. Almost all the settlement lies on the strandflat. Much of the building is scattered, and the only nucleated settlement is Svolvær on the south coast of Austvågöy. In 1970 Svolvær had a modest population total of 3,905, but this figure shows marked seasonal fluctuations according to the movements of the fleets of small fishing vessels. At the height of the Lofoten fishing season as many as 10,000 fishermen move into the region from all parts of the north and west coasts of Norway so that 'some villages have up to ten times the off-season population' (Tore Sund). In the Lofoten Islands as a whole about three times as many people have fishing for their chief occupation as farming, although a combination of fishing and farming is a common means of livelihood. In the county of Nordland 26% of the working population has more than one occupation. Only very rarely is fishing subordinate to farming.

The map extract gives little information about farming. Farmsteads are shown at various points along the strandflat as, for example, along the shores of Östnes Fjord and on the eastern shore of Lille Molla. Two sæters, Bergs Sæter and Helle Sæter, are shown on the shores of Svolværvand and Vatterfjordpollen respectively. Agricultural emphasis in such an area, with its lack of soil, steep rocky slopes and severe climate must clearly be on livestock and the growing of fodder crops.

The sea, with its rich fisheries in this area, offers greater possibilities for making a livelihood than the land. The indented coast with its numerous bays and inlets provides many sheltered harbours for small vessels, but on the other hand an indication of the difficulties of navigation is suggested by the numerous marker lights (Lykt, abb. Lkt = a light), and the multitude of small islands, rocks and shoals. Strong tidal currents run through the narrow channels, and frequent storms add to the hazards of navigation. The Lofoten shores are visited by shoals of arctic-water fish such as cod, saithe, haddock and ling. The cod fishing is particularly important during the period January to April, and the Lofoten Banks rank as one of the most important fishing grounds in Europe. Unfortunately the area lies distant from markets and the bulk of the catch must therefore be dried (stockfisk) or salted (klipfisk). Of the total catch of Lofoten cod almost 80% is dried and salted for South American and Mediterranean markets, and only 20% sold fresh or frozen. A close examination of photograph 4 shows the wooden scaffolds on which the fish are hung to dry. They are to be found, for example, on the small islet beyond Svolvær church. Although the map provides no specific information, it may be assumed that many of the larger buildings along the quays of Svolvær are used for the processing, freezing, packeting and marketing of fish, the production of fish-meal, fish-oil and fertilisers, or the repair of boats and fishing equipment.

In conclusion it may be said that the Lofoten Islands constitute a very difficult and hostile environment. The population in the map area is of low density and unevenly distributed. Few roads are shown, and, as in many districts in North Norway, the chief means of communication in the area is by the sea. Svolvær itself has daily calls from the express coastal steamers (Hurtigruten) travelling both north to Tromsö, Hammerfest and Kirkenes and south to Bodö, Trondheim and Bergen. The economic resources of these northern islands are extremely limited and life in high latitudes can never be easy. Agriculture provides only poor returns, and fishing, the chief occupation, constitutes a hazardous and uncertain livelihood.

Glossary of geographical terms

The following terms and their abbreviations occur frequently on the map extract.

| Dal | Valley | Fd., | Fjord | Fjord | Vd., Vand, Vatn | Lake | Vaag | Inlet or bay |
| Fj., | Fjell | Mountain | Poll | | Creek | Vik | | Bay | Vær | Fishing village |

Exercises

1. Calculate the number of days of continuous darkness in winter at (a) Svolvær (68°15′ N), (b) Tromsö (69°40′ N) and (c) Hammerfest (70°33′ N). Suggest how this period of continuous darkness affects the life of North Norway.
2. Identify the observation point, direction of view (full circle bearing) and angle of view of photograph 4. Find the names of features A, B, C and D marked on the photograph.
3. From a careful examination of both the map extract and the photograph write a description of Svolvær. The description, which should be illustrated with an annotated sketch map, should include reference to the site, the density and arrangement of buildings and the type of buildings in the town.
4. 'North Norway would be practically uninhabited without its rich marine resources' (Axel Sømme). Discuss.

Further reading

ALGÅRD, G. 'A farm in northern Norway', Geographical Magazine, 27, no 4, 1954.
HANSEN, J. C. 'Regional Disparities in Norway with Reference to Marginality', Trans. Inst. Br. Geographers, 57, 1972.
LANDMARK, K. et al, 'Northern Norway, Nature and Livelihood', Norsk Geografisk Tidsskrift, 17, 1960.
MEAD, W. R. An Economic Geography of the Scandinavian States and Finland, London U.P., 2nd Edition, 1968, chapter 8.
MILLWARD, R. Scandinavian Lands, Macmillan, 1964, chapter 11.
O'DELL, A. C. The Scandinavian World, Longman, 1957, chapters 10 and 17.
SØMME, A., ed. 'The Geography of Norden', Heinemann, 1961, chapter 11.
SUND, T. and SØMME, A. Norway in Maps, A. S. John Greigs Boktrykkert, Bergen, 1947.
VORREN, ϕ., ed. Norway North of 65, Allen and Unwin, 1961.

Study 4
KIRUNA
NORRBOTTEN
SWEDEN

An Arctic Mining Settlement.

Extract from Sheet 29 J.
Kiruna.
Swedish 1:100,000 Series.

Surveyed 1959-60.
Published 1961.
Lines of latitude
and longitude at
0°-10′ intervals.
Vertical interval of
contours 10 metres.

Reprinted from the topographic
map Geographical Survey Office
Sweden. Release nr 6767, SRA,
Vällingby 1, Sweden.

Map 4

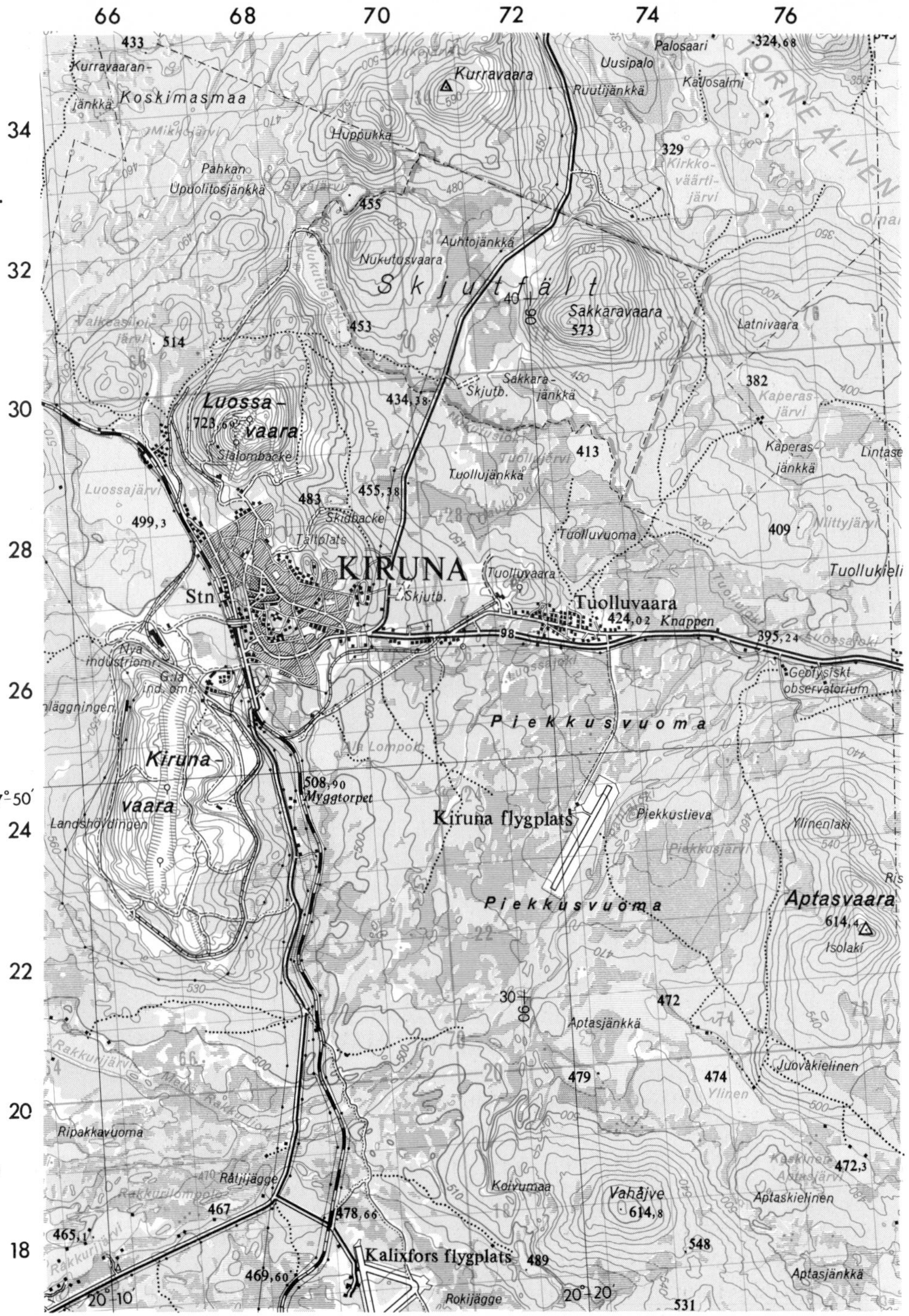

Sweden has map coverage at scales of 1:50,000, 1:100,000 and 1:250,000. The map extract provides an example of the new, coloured 1:100,000 sheets which are replacing the older, hachured editions at that scale. Within the limitations imposed by a scale of 1:100,000 these new maps give a quite detailed representation of the Swedish topography in a style which is both legible and æsthetically satisfying.

Kiruna is one of the largest centres of population in Arctic Europe and is situated at a higher altitude than any other town in Scandinavia. It lies among the forests of Norrbotten, Sweden's northernmost *län* or county, over 1,400 km north of Stockholm by rail and about 160 km north of the Arctic Circle, a latitude equivalent to northern Alaska or the Siberian tundra. The town stands on the railway between Luleå on the Bothnian coast and Narvik on the Norwegian coast, but is poorly served by roads. It can only be approached by route 98, a branch road which terminates in the town and carries traffic from North Norway via Karesuando and, more particularly, from the more southerly districts of Sweden via Gällivare. The minor roads shown on the map all terminate a short distance beyond the map area and merely link Kiruna with small surrounding settlements.

Relief and drainage

The Scandinavian Peninsula consists of a basement of extremely ancient pre-Cambrian rocks which had been folded and reduced to a peneplain even before Palaeozoic times. On top of this peneplain, known as the Baltic Shield, sediments were deposited during Cambrian and Silurian times and folded in late Silurian times into the Caledonian mountain system. The Caledonian mountains in their turn were reduced to a peneplain, and their present elevation is due to an epeirogenic uplift in late Tertiary times. The present relief of the Scandinavian peninsula is thus the result of a complex polycyclic erosional history. To the east of the main watershed a series of uplifted erosion surfaces dominate the landscape. Sten Rudberg uses the term 'Monadnock Plain' to describe the landscape of inner Norrbotten with its isolated hills rising above the plateaux surfaces.

The map extract shows a dissected plateau with a series of peaks rising up above the general level of the region. Notable among such peaks are Aptas-vaara (614 metres), Kirunavaara (*c.* 930 metres), Luossavaara (723 metres), Sakkaravaara (573 metres) and Kurravaara (*c.* 590 metres). Gently sloping surfaces are also evident, and at many points the direction of drainage appears to be indeterminate, as is indicated by the numerous marsh areas and temporary lakes. The pre-Cambrian rocks of the district consist of granites, porphyries, leptites and gneisses, but due to the complicated

Photograph 5. Kiruna and the Kirunavaara iron working. View from Luossavaara.

L.K.A.B. Fotografi, Stockholm, Börje Rönnberg.

erosional history there is little or no correlation between relief and geology.

The Quaternary glaciation produced considerable modifications to the relief and drainage of the area. North Sweden was not free of ice until *c*. 6500 B.C. (the Ancylus Lake period) and consequently the results of glaciation have been relatively little modified by post-glacial weathering and erosion. Much of the Baltic Shield is covered with a hummocky deposit of coarse morainic and fluvioglacial material which is deficient in lime and has a permafrost layer about 1 metre below the surface. Gley soils have developed and support a cover of poor forest which in the Kiruna district consists chiefly of stunted birches and scrub. Only along the Torneälv valley is there any indication of coniferous forest. Due to the impermeability of the soil and the extensive areas of slight gradient, many pockets of marsh and swamp may be noted (horizontal brown shading on the map).

Kiruna lies between two of the largest rivers in North Sweden, the Torneälv (*älv* = a river) and the Kalixälv (the latter lies just beyond the southern edge of the extract). The Torneälv, to the north-east of Kiruna, is more than 1 km wide in this area and really forms the southern end of the 130 km long Lake Torneträsk, which stretches from the Norwegian frontier. These rivers are two of a series of roughly parallel, consequent rivers which rise on the high *fjäll* and drop steeply in a south-east direction to the Gulf of Bothnia. They have all been rejuvenated as a result of post-glacial iso-static uplift which, in the case of North Sweden, is estimated to have been as much as 200 metres. In the vicinity of Luleå isostatic uplift is still continuing at a rate of 1 cm per year, although the actual rise of the land in relation to the sea is slightly less due to an eustatic rise of sea-level. The Swedish rivers are therefore characterised by irregular, ungraded longitudinal profiles with numerous falls and rapids.

The view from the summit of the hill on which Kiruna is built is described by Noel Watts as follows: 'From this point to the north nothing is to be seen but flat swampy land covered with small bushes and scrub. The view westwards is somewhat similar except that the horizon is dominated by a range of snow-covered mountains. It is when one looks south that the reason for the existence of such a large community in this barren and inhospitable land becomes apparent. Below the station lies a long lake and on its further shore another hill rises to a considerable height. It is split in half by a great gash many hundreds of feet deep and in this gash is the world-famous iron-ore mine. Every person in Kiruna depends directly or indirectly on this great man-made hole for his or her living.'

The iron working of Kiruna

The existence of ore deposits at Kiruna was known as early as the seventeenth century, but no attempt at exploitation was made until 1898, when the company of Luossavaara-Kiirunavaara Aktiebolag (generally known as L.K.A.B.) began the opening up of the Kiruna mines. The problems to be faced were immense. A labour force had to be attracted to this desolate region and a completely new settlement built to house the mining community. Facilities had to be established to allow the continuation of mining throughout the long arctic winter, and, most important of all, a railway had to be driven for more than 160 km over the mountains to the Norwegian coast where an export port could be established. Luleå was unsuitable as the main outlet for the ore, since it is normally closed by ice from November to May, but the Norwegian coast remains ice-free in winter as a result of the North Atlantic Drift. (See Study 3.)

In 1902 a railway was completed from Kiruna to Narvik on the Norwegian coast, descending through a series of great gorges and tunnels to the sea at Ofot Fjord. At the same time a line was constructed to connect with the older mining centre of Malmberget (Gällivare) which had already been linked in 1888 with Luleå. The map extract shows that the Ofot Railway, as it is known, is a single-track electrified line flanked with a power cable carrying more than 20,000 volts.

The iron deposit at Kiruna occurs as an enormous slab about 4 km long and 100 metres wide, running north-south through Kirunavaara and pitching eastwards at an angle of 40°–75°. Some sixty years of opencast mining have split the mountain with a huge terraced trench which extends down almost to the level of Lake Luossajärvi. Since 1962 all mining has been underground, and test drills have shown that the ore body extends down to at least 1,000 metres below the surface. The deposit continues northwards under the lake to Luossavaara where a similar, though much smaller, trench has been cut into the mountain. The symbol indicating a mine or quarry also appears on the map at Tuolluvaara to the east of Kiruna. This is a relatively small iron working which was acquired by L.K.A.B. in 1970. Production at Luossavaara and Tuolluvaara ceased in 1976 and 1980 respectively.

At a scale of 1:100,000 the map extract is unable to provide much information about the iron workings. However, it does show how the three mines have been connected to the main railway by a system of branch lines. In the case of Kirunavaara, zones of both old and new industry are marked. (*G.la ind.omr.* and *Nya industriomr.* respectively). The sketch map gives a more detailed picture of the workings. The central block (*Centralanläggingen*) which is just visible beyond Kirunavaara in the photograph consists of the main hoisting gear together with a concentrating and pelletizing plant constructed in 1965. The new lakeside industrial zone includes a thirteen-storey administrative block which can also be clearly seen in photograph 3.

The ore mineral of the Kiruna district is magnetite, although hematite occurs in small quantities. The iron content is very high (60–70%), but much of the ore is phosphoric, a fact which rendered it unusable until after the invention of the Thomas steel converter (Basic Bessemer) in 1879. This single technical innovation transformed the geography of northern Sweden.

At the present time there is an almost constant flow of crushed ore from Kiruna and Malmberget to the exporting ports of Narvik and Luleå. At peak periods as many as 32 trains, each carrying over 4,000 tonnes of ore, leave Kiruna for Narvik every 24 hours. This section of line in fact carries a greater tonnage per kilometre than any other railway in the world, and day and night the ore is constantly moving to the coast. Even during the most severe spells of winter weather the railway is kept open by snow ploughs, but snow-sheds and drift-fences are essential along the exposed sections of line. In 1977 the Kiruna mines produced 13·7 million tonnes of ore (Kirunavaara 13·0 million tonnes, and Tuolluvaara 0·7 tonnes). In addition, Malmberget produced 6·1 million tonnes giving a total of 19·8 million tonnes. Of this, 14·8 million tonnes were exported via Narvik, 3·5 via Luleå, and 1·5 carried by rail to southern Sweden. West Germany is the biggest importer of ore from Norrbotten, followed by Belgium and Great Britain. Relatively small amounts are sent to Poland, The Netherlands, France, Spain and the U.S.A.

Settlement of the Kiruna district

The actual urban district of Kiruna covers a vast area. It is in fact one of the largest in the world (14,340 sq kms), although the total population is only 31,000 of which about 24,000 people live in the actual settlement of Kiruna, which is referred to as Kiruna C. In 1977, 4,300 workers were employed in the Kirunavaara mine, and a further 300 in the Tuolluvaara working. Various incentives are offered to attract and maintain such a labour force in this remote arctic district. Wages are 25% higher than in central Sweden for the equivalent work, and the standards of housing and amenities are as high as in any other part of the country. The problem of isolation and the great distance from the main centres of population in Sweden is to some extent reduced by

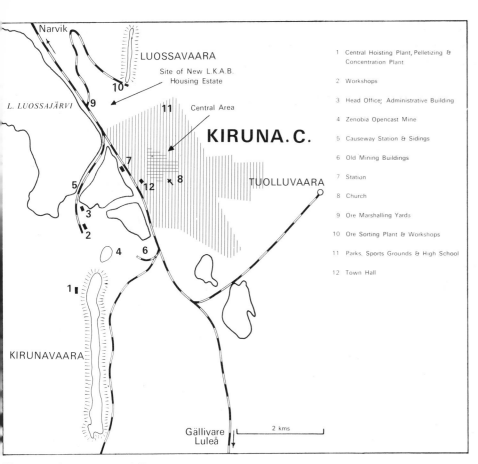

Figure 4. Sketch map of Kiruna.

Map legend:
1 Central Hoisting Plant, Pelletizing & Concentration Plant
2 Workshops
3 Head Office; Administrative Building
4 Zenobia Opencast Mine
5 Causeway Station & Sidings
6 Old Mining Buildings
7 Station
8 Church
9 Ore Marshalling Yards
10 Ore Sorting Plant & Workshops
11 Parks, Sports Grounds & High School
12 Town Hall

the air services operating from the two aerodromes shown on the map extract (Kiruna Flygplats 7223, and Kalixfors Flygplats 6817).

However, life is not easy in Kiruna, especially in winter when there is a six weeks period of continuous darkness and temperatures may be as low as −40°C. Snow lingers in the streets until June. A combination of lack of sunlight in winter and the intense cold forces many people from the south to return to a more congenial climate after several years in the north.

A key factor in the development of Kiruna has been the abundant supply of cheap hydroelectric power from the ungraded, rejuvenated rivers of the region. The map shows numerous power lines converging on the town. These carry the essential power for the iron workings, the town and the railways. The bulk of the electricity comes from the generating station at Porjus, almost 100 km to the south of Kiruna, but this source is supplemented by smaller, local power stations along the Torneälv and Kalixälv.

Apart from Kiruna, the only nucleated settlement shown on the map extract is Tuolluvaara (population 1,100), which lies just to the north of the main road about 5 km from the centre of Kiruna. Otherwise the settlement is both scanty and dispersed. Isolated buildings are shown along the road south from Kiruna and by the shores of many of the lakes. The latter are linked to the roads by mere tracks and the map gives no indication of their function. It seems unlikely that they can be farms at such a high latitude, and they are more probably mountain huts belonging to the people of Kiruna. It is interesting to note that at 648176 there is a symbol denoting a Lapp camp. Such camps consist of a collection of tents and turf-huts (*Kåta*) occupied by reindeer-herding Lapps. About 800 reindeer-owning Lapps with over 30,000 animals are found in the Kiruna district.

Although life is hard in Kiruna it is also clear that the iron deposits constitute one of the great assets of Sweden. The continuing importance that is attached to these metal resources of the north was indicated by the opening in 1964 of a new mine at Svappavaara, approximately midway between Kiruna and Gällivare. This mine, which has the third largest output in Sweden after Kiruna and Malmberget, is already attracting settlement in a manner reminiscent of Kiruna at the beginning of the century.

The following terms which are of Finnish origin occur frequently on the map extract.
Jänkä Marsh; swamp   *Joki* River; stream
Järvi Lake   *Vaara* Mountain

Exercises
1. Explain the difference between isostatic and eustatic changes of base level. Describe the effect of such changes on the coastal and inland features of the Scandinavian Peninsula.
2. Make a comparison of the economic development of Arctic Norway and Arctic Sweden.
3. Explain precisely the meaning of the following terms which occur in the chapter: *(a)* polycyclic erosion; *(b)* monadnock; *(c)* porphyry; *(d)* permafrost; *(e)* gley soil.
4. Illustrate the statement that people will live in the most inhospitable areas provided that the incentives are sufficiently great. (O. & C.)
5. Describe the evolution and present character of two contrasting regions of iron ore production. (W.J.E.C.)

Further reading
MEAD, W. R. *The Scandinavian Northlands*, Oxford U.P., 1974.
MEAD, W. R. *An Economic Geography of the Scandinavian States and Finland*, London U.P., 2nd Edition, 1968, chapter 12.
O'DELL, A. C. *The Scandinavian World*, Longmans, 1957, chapter 8.
SØMME, A., ed. *The Geography of Norden*. Heinemann, 1961, chapter 12.
STONE, K. 'Swedish Fringes of Settlement', *Annals of the Association of American Geographers*, **52**, 1962.
WATTS, N. 'Kiruna. Sweden's northernmost mining town', *Geographical Magazine*, **38**, 1955.

Study 5
KARLSTAD
VÄRMLAND
SWEDEN

A centre of the Swedish timber industry

Extract from Sheet 10 D.
Karlstad N.V.
Swedish 1:50,000 Series.

Published 1962.
Vertical Interval of
Contours 5 metres.

Reprint from the Topographic map, Geographical Survey Office, Sweden. Release nr 4668, Swedish National Map and Printing Organisation, SRA, Vällingby 1, Sweden.

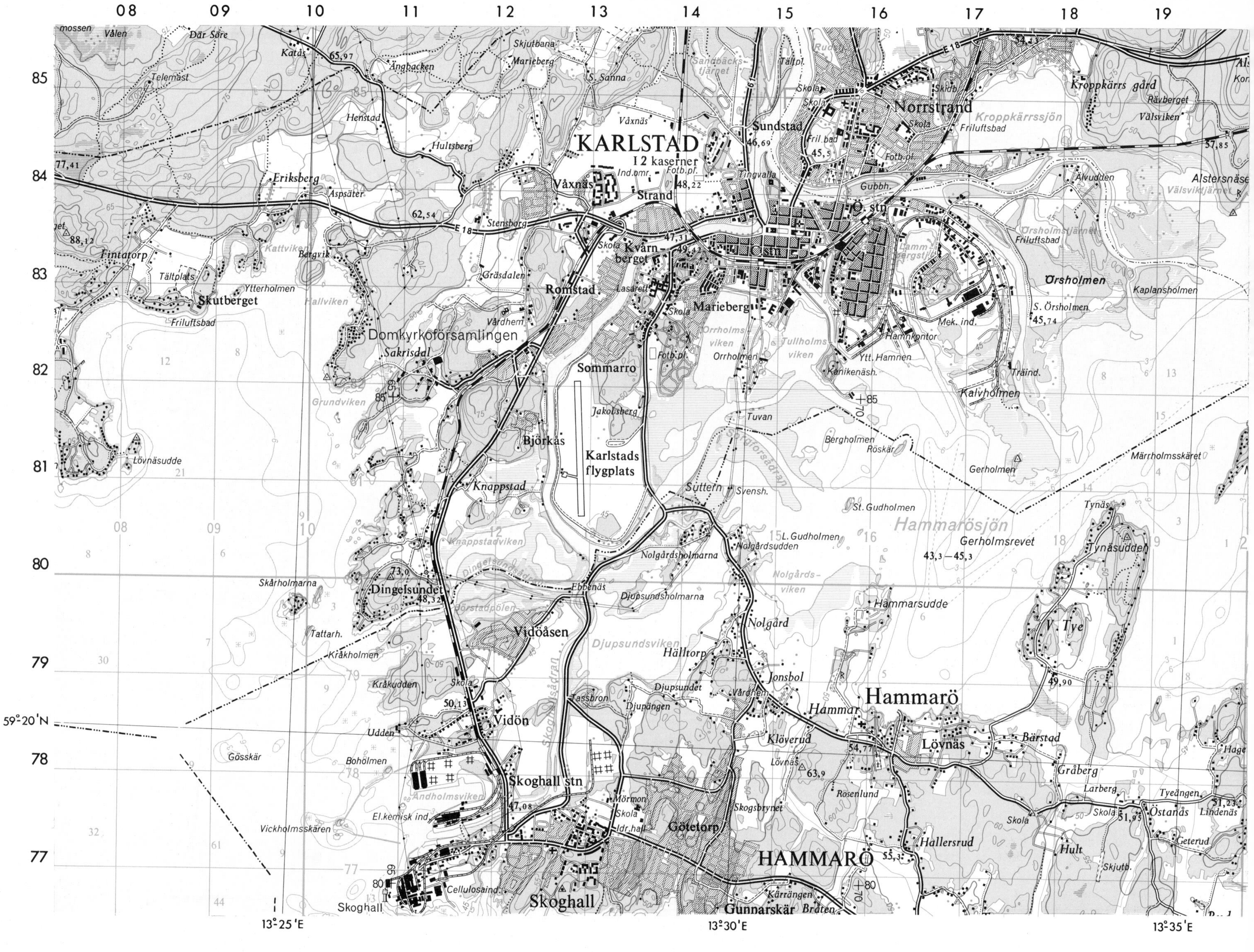

Map 5

KARLSTAD
I 2 kaserner
Ind.omr.
Våxnäs
Strand
Kvarn-berget
Romstad
Skola
Lasarett
Marieberg
Domkyrkoförsamlingen
Sakrisdal
Sommarro
Jakobsberg
Björkås
Karlstads flygplats
Knappstad
Sättern
Svensh.
Skutberget
Hallviken
Friluftsbad
Ytterholmen
Tältplats
Fintatorp
Kattvike
Bergvik
Eriksberg
Aspsäter
Stensborg
Gräsdalen
Vårdhem
Grundviken
Knappstadviken
Lövnäsudde
Skårholmarna
Dingelsundet
Tattarh.
Vidöåsen
Kråkholmen
Kråkudden
Skola
Vidön
Udden
Gösskär
Boholmen
Andholmsviken
Skoghall stn
Vickholmskären
El.kemisk ind.
Skoghall
Cellulosaind.
Gunnarskär
Bråten
Göteforp
HAMMARÖ
Djupsundsviken
Hälltorp
Djupsundet
Djupängen
Tassbron
Jonsbol
Vårdhem
Hammar
Hammarö
Lövnäs
Bärstad
Klöverud
Rosenlund
Skogsbrynet
Hallersrud
Hult
Geterud
Östanäs
Lindenäs
Tyeängen
Larberg
Gråberg
V. Tye
Tynäs
Tynäsudden
Hammarudde
Nolgård
Nolgårdsudden
Nolgårdsholmarna
Djupsundsholmarna
Ebbenäs
St. Gudholmen
L. Gudholmen
Gerholmsrevet
Gerholmen
Hammarösjön
Märrholmsskäret
Bergholmen
Röskär
Kalvholmen
Tuvan
Kanikenäsh.
Ytt. Hamnen
Hamnkontor
Mek. ind.
Träind.
Orrholmen
Orrholms-viken
Tullholms-viken
S. Örsholmen
Kaplansholmen
Örsholmen
Örsholmstjärnet
Friluftsbad
Gubbh.
Älvudden
Alstersnäs
Välsviktjärnet
Östra stn
Ö. stn
Tingvalla
Sundstad
Norrstrand
Skola
Kroppkärrs gård
Kroppkärrssjön
Välsviken
Rävberget
Sandbäcks-tjärnet
Tältpl.
Skjutbana
Marieberg
Ängbacken
S. Sanna
Växnäs
Katås
Där Säre
Valen
Telemäst
Telemäst
Hultsberg
Henstad
mossen
Domkyrkoförsamlingen

59°20'N
13°25'E
13°30'E
13°35'E

Photograph 6. The Skoghall Works from Lake Vänern. The saw mill, pulp mills and chemical plants were built between 1914 and 1918 to replace older factories in Central Värmland. The paper mill was added in 1930. Annual production includes 35,000 standards (160,000 cubic metres) of sawn timber, 130,000 tonnes of sulphate pulp, 80,000 tonnes of sulphite pulp, 80,000 tonnes of kraft paper and a wide range of chemical products.

Uddeholms Aktiebolag. Photo Esse Zetter-qvist

Forestry and timber industries of Värmland

The county of Värmland in south-west Sweden assumes a roughly triangular form. The base of the triangle is formed in part by Lake Vänern and the county both rises and tapers northwards towards the high ground along the Norwegian–Swedish border. The county is bisected by the River Klar which rises in Norway, enters Sweden in the extreme north of Värmland and flows south to discharge into Lake Vänern by a delta at Karlstad. Värmland ranks among the most important of the Swedish counties for forestry and related industries. Woodland and forest cover 72% of its area, of which more than 90% is productive. The table below shows that not only does Värmland possess a greater proportion of forest than Sweden as a whole but that the pattern of ownership also differs significantly. State forests are poorly represented, but ownership by industrial corporations is well above the national average. The forests of Värmland consist of 57% spruce *(Picea abies)* and about 32% pine *(Pinus silvestris)*. The remaining 11% is chiefly hardwood timber with birch *(Betula alba)* dominant. The spruce is of first rate quality and yields a sawn timber in great demand, but the pine is only of average quality by Central Swedish standards. Although figure 5 shows the forest cover to be greater in northern and central Värmland, natural replacement is faster in the south. Much of the timber from the upper county is floated down the main rivers to saw mills and pulp and paper factories along their lower valleys. The following figures give some indication of the enormous volume of timber floated down the Klar River alone.

Ownership of forest lands

Ownership of forest lands	Värmland[1]	Sweden[2] (National average)
Percentage area forested	72%	54%
Percentages of total forest lands		
State owned forests	2%	18%
Parish or communal ownership	4%	5%
Company forests	38%	25%
Private ownership	56%	52%

Sources: 1. *Värmlands Läns Näringsråd*. Karlstad 1967.
2. Skogsstyrelsen, Jönköping, 1977.

Timber floated down the Klar River 1971–1977

Thousands of cubic metres: unbarked timber

	Saw logs	Sulphite pulpwood	Sulphate pulpwood	Total volume	Estimated total number of logs
1971	125	323	236	684	8,845,000
1972	65	319	195	579	7,488,000
1973	74	356	252	682	8,820,000
1974	12	242	178	432	5,587,000
1975	49	190	104	343	4,436,000
1976	78	134	81	293	3,789,000
1977	53	163	116	332	4,293,000

Source: Skogsstyrelsen, Jönköping, Sweden, 1979.

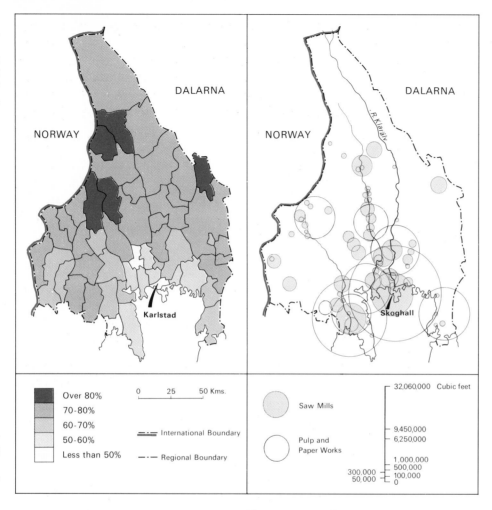

Figure 5. Värmland: distribution of productive forest. Plotted by Communes.
Sources: Commune areas from *Atlas över Sverige*; Forest Statistics provided by Skogsstyrelsen, Jönköping, Sweden

Figure 6. Värmland: distribution of timber processing industries.
Source: Skogsstyrelsen, Jönköping, Sweden

■ Over 80%	
70-80%	
60-70%	
50-60%	
Less than 50%	

0   25   50 Kms.

═══ International Boundary

─·─ Regional Boundary

Saw Mills

Pulp and Paper Works

32,060,000 Cubic feet

9,450,000
6,250,000

1,000,000
500,000
300,000   100,000
50,000   0

Figure 6 shows the predilection of companies to choose sites close to the main rivers or along the shore of Lake Vänern. By far the largest of these is the Billerud-Uddeholm Company's plant at Skoghall to the south of Karlstad.

The Skoghall works

'The outstanding feature of forest ownership in Sweden is the part played by the industrial corporation. Many of the company forests, particularly to the north of Lake Vänern, are inherited from an earlier industrial age of countless scattered forges and smelting mills. Firms that formerly produced iron have now entered the field of pulp and paper manufacture. The woodlands that were carefully tended as a source of charcoal now form the company forests of the new industries.' (R. Millward.) The process is well illustrated by the giant Billerud-Uddeholm Company. 'It owns land as extensive as the island of Gotland (nearly 3,000 square kilometres), it is interested in three principal ore fields (Persberg, Nordmark and Långban), it has concentrated smelting at four sites (Munkfors, Hagfors, Storfors and Nykroppa) and controls about 30 power plants. Its own railway links the main industrial points in this metallurgical complex with the pulp-, paper- and timber-mills at Skoghall on Lake Vänern.' (W. R. Mead.) The company also controls a great number of subsidiary firms engaged in a variety of production and employs over 14,500 workers. In 1967 Billerud-Uddeholm substantially added to its assets by taking over timber companies, power stations and forest lands belonging to the Borregaard Company. By this transaction it acquired ownership of virtually all the power stations along the Klar River.

The Skoghall plant, which is the centre of the company's forest and timber activities, may be subdivided into a number of distinct works. The saw mill is situated on the north side of Andholmsviken (113779). Timber supplies are either floated down the Klar, or towed from collection points along the shore of Lake Vänern, or brought from upper Värmland either by road or by the company's own Nordmark-Klarälven Railway. Five timber storage areas are shown to the east of the saw mill. The pulp and paper mills lie to the south *(Cellulosaind.)* and are connected by narrow-gauge railways to the saw mill (to receive saw waste) as well as to the company railway and further timber yards north of Skoghall (132781). Two main processes are used for the production of chemical pulp: the sulphate process whereby wood chips are reduced to pulp by cooking with sodium sulphate, and the sulphite process which uses calcium bisulphate. The Skoghall pulp mills produce chemical pulp for the production of viscose rayon and plastics as well as high quality paper pulp, some of which passes directly to the mill which specialises in heavy papers. By-products from the pulping process include ethyl alcohol, ether and other chemicals. The chemical plants (115775), like the saw mills, are situated on the island of Vidön and are separated from the pulp works by the Skoghallsådran arm of the Klar delta. The original purpose of these works was to supply bleaching agents to the pulp mills, but present production has extended far beyond these original needs and now includes chlorine, sodium hypochlorite, sodium hydroxide and ammonia. In association with the chlorine-alkali processes, other products based on chlorine, ethyl alcohol and acetylene have been developed. These include the production of degreasing agents, solvents for dry cleaning, acetic acid, ethyl acetate and other industrial chemicals.

The various plants at Skoghall are powered by hydro-electricity from the company's power stations along the Klar. The power lines may be seen on map 5. Vast amounts of water are required for the pulping process (700,000 litres per tonne of bleached sulphite pulp), and thus the waterside location is an advantage. Apart from the enormous timber requirements, other raw materials such as oil, sulphur, sodium sulphate and common salt are shipped direct to the company's wharves at Andholmsviken, from which the finished products are also sent via Lake Vänern and the Trollhätte Canal to Göteborg for transshipment to overseas markets. The Skoghall plant employs 2,200 workers, many of whom live in company houses in the urban district of Hammarö (population 11,500). However, the plant also draws large numbers of employees from Karlstad, some 10 kilometres distant.

Karlstad

Karlstad, the provincial capital of Värmland, had a population of 51,800 in 1978. The city core, which lies between the two main distributaries of the Klar delta, has a rectilinear pattern of streets. The original settlement, founded in 1584, lay around the present site of the cathedral (153836), an easily defended position accessible only by bridges across the swift-flowing Klar. The city has subsequently expanded south-westwards along the western branch of the Klar and has also spread northwards into the districts of Sundstad and Norrstrand. These are residential suburban areas.

Industrial developments have taken place chiefly in the south-east of the town near the harbour which is the largest on Lake Vänern. The inner harbour lies to the immediate east of the Central Station (C.stn. 148833) while the outer harbour (Yttre Hamnen) with its customs buildings and offices (Hamnkontor) lies near the mouth of the small channel that runs through the central town (160824). Another small quay and connecting railway is shown at Kalvholmen (169820). In 1978 Karlstad, excluding the Skoghall harbour, handled 817,000 tonnes of goods (chiefly exports of timber and timber-products). More than 100 industrial premises are located in the town, the largest being AB Karlstads Mekaniska Verkstad (170830) which produces machinery for the pulp, paper and wallboard industries as well as turbines and ships' propellers. Other fields of production include foodstuffs, textiles, clothing and furniture. An industrial area (Ind.omr.) is shown at Våxnäs (133842) and timber industries are shown at 075821 and 175823 (Träind.—timber industry). Altogether Karlstad has a working population of 29,437 of which 5,862 are employed in manufacturing industry.

In addition to its port and industrial activities the functions of Karlstad also reflect its status as provincial capital of Värmland and its position on the main road and rail routes between Stockholm and Oslo. The town is a regional centre of administration, education and other services and a tourist centre of some standing. However, its importance derives essentially from its position at the mouth of Värmland's chief timber-floating river, the forested nature of its hinterland and the Billerud-Uddeholm Company's choice of Skoghall as the site for its gigantic timber processing operations.

Karlstad: employment structure 1979

Percentage of total working population

Government and administration	36·2%	Transport, storage and communications	7·9%
Retail business, restaurants and hotels	18·6%	Banking and insurance	6·9%
Engineering, metallurgy and textiles	11·0%	Chemical industries	5·4%
Building and construction	10·5%	Pulp and paper production	3·5%
			100·0%

Source: Figures supplied by Jan-Olof Seveborg. Planeringsavdelningen, Karlstad, 1979.

Exercises

1. Discuss the importance of forest products in the economy of Sweden. (J.M.B.).
2. Describe the different types of ownership of the Scandinavian forest lands. Examine the ways in which variations of ownership affect the exploitation of forest resources.
3. 'Waste is a marked feature of the softwood industry.' (W. R. Mead.) Discuss.
4. 'The Norden wood processing industries show all the signs of developing into chemical industries.' (A. Sømme.) Discuss.
5. Analyse the difficulties under which Karlstad operates as a port with particular reference to (a) its harbour (b) its approach routes (c) its hinterland and (d) competition from other transport routes.
6. Make an accurate tracing of the Klar delta within northing 79 and easting 10 on map 5. Mark on your map the coastline, the 50 metre contour, intertidal areas and offshore channels. Comment on the form of the delta.

Further reading

GUTKIND, E. A. *Urban Development in the Alpine Lands and Scandinavia*, International History of City Development, Vol. II, Collier-Macmillan, 1965.

HARE, K. 'Boreal Forests of the Northern Hemisphere', *Geographical Studies*, I, London, 1954. *The Swedish National Atlas (Atlas Över Sverige)*. Svensk Sällskapet för Antropologi och Geografi, Stockholm, 1958 and 1959. (Pages 89–100 and 105–6 deal with forestry and related industries.)

HOLTHAM, B. W., CHAPMAN, E. S. B., ROSS, R. B. and HACKER, N. G. 'Forest Management and the Harvesting and Marketing of Wood in Scandinavia', *Forestry Commission Bulletin* 41, H.M.S.O., 1968.

LINDBERG, O. 'An Economic-Geographical Study of the Localization of the Swedish Paper Industry', *Geografiska Annaler*, **35**, 1953.

MEAD, W. R. *An Economic Geography of the Scandinavian States and Finland*, London, 2nd edn. 1968. (Chapter 8 includes maps of the Uddeholm Company's forest lands and industrial sites.)

SUNDBORG, A. 'Klarälven. A Study of Fluvial Process', *Geografiska Annaler*, **38**, 1956. (Especially Chapter 4, 'A Study of the Fluvial Morphology of Klarälven.')

Yearbook of Forest Statistics, F.A.O. Rome, annually.

A new town in greater Stockholm

Extract from Sheet 31.
Hässelby.
Greater Stockholm
1:10,000 Series.

Published 1967.
No Contours.

*Reprint from the Official
town plan of Stockholm,
Stockholm Urban Survey
Section/Esselte Map Service,
Sweden.*

Map 6

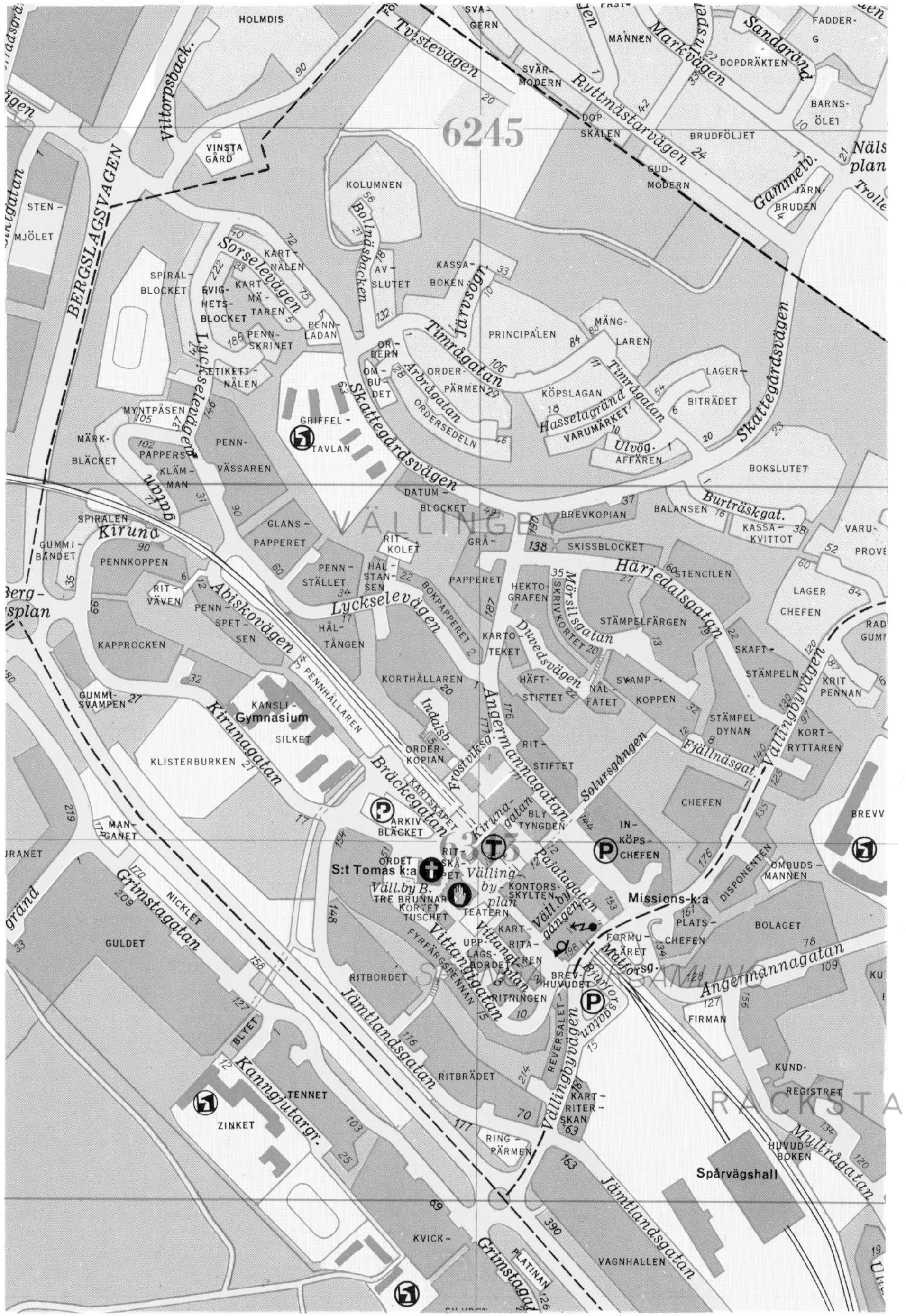

Stockholm, in common with other European capitals, has been characterised by extremely rapid population growth during the present century.
From a population of about 300,000 in 1900 Greater Stockholm has grown
with such speed that it has now joined the ranks of the world's 'millionaire'
cities. An immediate expression of this growth in numbers has been a
demand for living space and a resultant expansion of the city involving the
development of extensive new sites for housing. Without ambitious planning
such urban expansion can easily produce a random growth of ugly, inefficient
and socially sterile suburban districts, half town and half country and
lacking the advantages of either, the type of semi-urban sprawl that is to be
seen around most urban fringes in Europe today.

The growth of Greater Stockholm has been met in the postwar period by
the development of a series of new towns and neighbourhood centres
around the city, the sites of which are closely related to the pattern of the
electric suburban railways *(Tunnelbana)* which radiate from the city centre
(figure 7). Growth points have been selected chiefly along these pre-existing
lines of communication and impressive new developments have taken place
around the city.

Early new housing, as at Fredhäll and Hammarbyhöjden, although well
designed, was built without any social facilities, thus creating 'dormitory
towns'. 'Whereas "sun, light and air" were the overriding considerations in

Figure 7. 'New Town' developments in Greater Stockholm

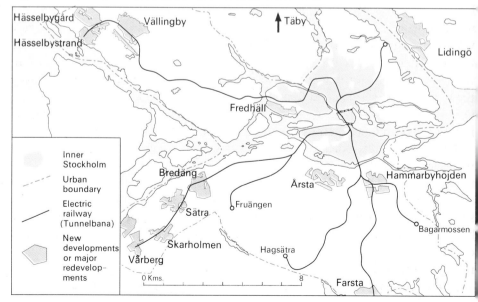

	Inner Stockholm
	Urban boundary
	Electric railway (Tunnelbana)
	New developments or major redevelopments

0 Kms. 8

he 'thirties, the sociological aspects of planning came to dominate in the forties. They were most notably expounded by Lewis Mumford, whose *Culture of Cities* had come out in a Swedish edition in 1942 . . . His chief importance for Sweden was as a spokesman for neighbourhood planning. The city and its districts were to be divided into well-defined residential areas, each of them sufficiently large to sustain its own small centre with room therein for a school, places of assembly, and stores' (K. Åstrom). The concept of new residential developments integrated with a full range of local urban functions is typified by the later development at Årsta, which was opened in 1954 and now has a population of some 25,000 inhabitants. This principle was followed in the new towns at Vällingby (centre opened in 1954). Hässelbystrand (1958), Farsta (1960), Skårholmen (1968) and Täby (1969). 'In this latest phase of development Stockholm's town planning and architecture have influenced building all over the world. The urban area of Greater Stockholm now stretches for 50 km from east to west and about 30 km from north to south. Former villages are now transformed into city satellites, their glistening factories of glass and concrete and slab-like blocks of flats and tiny rectangular villas set in the immemorial Swedish landscape of pines and silver-grey birchwoods.' (R. Millward.)

The planning of new centres in Greater Stockholm
In 1975 Greater Stockholm contained 1,370,000 inhabitants (one-seventh of the total population of Sweden). Of these, 300,000 lived in the inner city. It has been estimated that by 1990 Greater Stockholm will have 1,600,000 inhabitants of whom only 250,000 will live within the existing city boundary while the rest will be dispersed around the new suburban centres. Different types of new centres have been developed, their size and range of urban functions being determined by customer potential. Four types may be noted: the local centre (serving 4,000 to 7,000 inhabitants), the neighbourhood centre (15,000 to 25,000 inhabitants), the district centre (80,000 to 120,000 inhabitants) and the regional centre (500,000 inhabitants).

The local centres include only a few shops for everyday requirements, while the neighbourhood centres contain a greater range of shopping facilities and some civic buildings. A group of such units will in turn be served by a district centre in which specialist shops, department stores and shops of city character will be present, together with entertainments, civic buildings and offices. The regional centre in the case of Stockholm is the core of the inner city, especially the Lower Norrmalm district which was extensively redeveloped in the sixties.

One of the most important principles of town planning is the differentia-tion and spatial separation of the various urban functions, both with respect to the buildings of the townscape (zoning) and the movement of traffic (segregation of different categories of traffic). This differentiation is, of course, lacking where a town has grown spasmodically and matured over a long period of time. It is only when a completely new town is developed that a fully efficient differentiation of function is to be expected. This may be seen in Vällingby.

The Vällingby Centre
The town plan for Vällingby was authorised in 1951, and the centre opened three years later in the autumn of 1954, on land where three years earlier the last harvest was being reaped. The astonishing speed of construction by Svenska Bostäder Ltd was achieved by using pre-stressed concrete cast *in situ*, followed by prefabricated concrete elements. The plans for the centre, by Sven Markelius, Sven Backström, Lief Reinius and others, were based in part upon American models. The layout incorporates a large plaza directly accessible from the *tunnelbana* station, with pedestrian malls leading to the various sections of the Centre. Together the plaza and malls define a precinct

Photograph 7. Vällingby from the south-east. Notice the way in which the railway and roads run beneath the central area. The variety of housing units and their different arrangements may be appreci-ated from the photograph.

Swedish Tourist Traffic Association, Stock-holm. Photo E. Claesson

Photograph 8. Vällingby Centre. View south-eastwards from the station. Between 1962 and 1966 the central area was extended along its north-eastern flank by the addition of four new blocks of shops and a car parking building. This photograph was taken prior to these extensions and should be carefully compared with photograph 7 which was taken in 1968

Swedish International Press Bureau, Stockholm

barred to vehicles. The centre may be functionally divided into three parts: the shopping centre, the cultural centre and the social centre. The shopping centre comprises about 100 shops and restaurants, including two large department stores, housed in three main blocks. Beneath the shopping district are three tunnels, one carrying the underground railway and two for the supply and distribution of goods to and from the shops. The cultural centre comprises a church, chapel, library, study premises, youth centre, cinema, theatre and civic hall. These are housed in a series of buildings which lie chiefly on the south-western side of the central area (figure 8). The function of the central area as a social centre is represented by a series of buildings which house medical, dental and maternity welfare services, health insurance, pension and welfare offices and a student hostel.

The whole central area thus forms an impressive focus for the urban community and is spaciously located in a pedestrian precinct with both lateral and vertical segregation of pedestrians from vehicular traffic, which passes either round or under the central area. As can be seen from photographs 7 and 8, the central area is sufficiently small to be traversed easily on foot and also has ample parking space around its margins. In fact within a 125 metre radius of the centre there is parking space for 1,250 cars.

Vällingby Centre has proved to be a powerful commercial magnet in north-west Stockholm, partly at the expense of other nearby shopping centres, and had to be enlarged in the decade following its inauguration.

By 1966 both the original retail floor space and office accommodation had been almost doubled. The Centre at present employs a labour force of *c.* 2,000 persons.

Residential areas

Vällingby lies on the north-western branch of Stockholm's suburban railway system (figure 7). The city centre lies some 16 kilometres away and can be reached by rail in 20 minutes. The underground railway station on the north-western side of the centre is the focal point around which the housing developments have been constructed. All dwellings lie within easy walking distance of the station. Housing is of two types, apartment blocks and small, detached one-family houses. The distinction is made on map 6 by two coloured tints. The apartment housing consists of nine- to twelve-storey point or tower blocks and three- to four-storey linear or lamella developments such as Fyrfärspennan on the south side of the central area (see photograph 7). Vertical and horizontal forms thus complement each other in the urban landscape. All apartment blocks lie within a 500 metre radius of the station, while the small villas all lie within 900 metres, almost all in the northern part of the town. In general terms housing density thus tends to be highest at the centre and is reduced radially. Notice the way in which traffic in the housing districts is segregated by introversion whereby feeder roads on the perimeter branch off into cul-de-sacs which terminate in park-

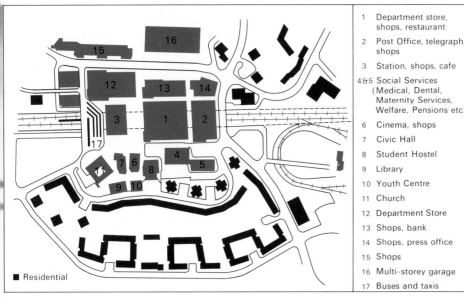

1	Department store, shops, restaurant
2	Post Office, telegraph, shops
3	Station, shops, cafe
4 & 5	Social Services (Medical, Dental, Maternity Services, Welfare, Pensions etc.)
6	Cinema, shops
7	Civic Hall
8	Student Hostel
9	Library
10	Youth Centre
11	Church
12	Department Store
13	Shops, bank
14	Shops, press office
15	Shops
16	Multi-storey garage
17	Buses and taxis

Figure 8. Vällingby Central Area
Source: A. Westerman, Swedish Planning of Town Centres, Stockholm, 1965.

ing areas or service access points. These in turn are connected with dwellings by a system of footpaths. Only one junior school is actually shown within Vällingby, but three others are indicated just beyond its boundary. In addition a secondary school *(gymnasium)* is shown to the north-west of the centre. A point which is evident from the map and which is typical of the Swedish new towns is the high proportion of open space that has been retained within the urban area.

Vällingby has a population of 25,000 within 900 metres of the centre, a size and concentration of population that is typical of Stockholm's larger neighbourhood units. However, its central area is built according to the requirements of a district centre and is used not only by the residents of Vällingby but also by the inhabitants of the bordering neighbourhood centres of Blackeberg, Råcksta, Ängby and Hässelby together with certain older housing areas. This gives the centre a customer potential of some 80,000 people. In addition some 15,000 people now work in the town's shops, offices and factories. The chief industrial premises lie south of the centre close to Jämtlandsgatan.

Vällingby is an example of what is sometimes termed in Sweden an ABC-town; that is to say, one which gives its inhabitants possibilities of work *(Arbete)*, housing facilities *(Bostäder)* and a well-developed centre *(Centrum)*. It is widely acknowledged as one of the best examples of modern Swedish town planning and may be regarded as a transitional stage between the earlier dormitory towns such as Fredhäll and Hammarbyhöjden and the even more ambitious multi-level development completed in the early 1970s at Skärholmen in south-west Stockholm.

Exercises

1. Examine the reasons for the rapid twentieth century growth of Stockholm.
2. With the aid of sketch maps describe the site and position of Stockholm.
3. Compare Vällingby with any other new town known to you.
4. Compare the economic and social problems involved in *(a)* urban renewal (rehabilitation), *(b)* urban reconstruction (redevelopment), and *(c)* new town building.
5. 'One of the most important principles of town planning is the differentiation and spatial separation of the various urban functions.' Discuss.
6. Examine the suggestion that most urban fringes in Europe today take the form of 'a random growth of ugly, inefficient and socially sterile suburban districts, half town and half country and lacking the advantages of either'.
7. Examine the problems involved in *(a)* assessing the size and range of urban functions to be included in new town centres, *(b)* developing pedestrian precincts in existing town centres and *(c)* landscaping new housing developments.

Further reading

AHLBERG, G. 'Population Trends and Urbanization in Sweden, 1911–1950', in *Lund Studies in Geography*, Series B, 1956.

'Migration in Sweden. A Symposium', ed. D. Hannerberg, T. Hägerstrand and B. Odeving, in *Lund Studies in Geography*, Series B, 13, 1957.

ARONSON, A. *Vällingby*, A. B. Svenska Bostader, Stockholm, 1966.

ÅSTROM, K. *City Planning in Sweden*, The Swedish Institute, Stockholm, 1967.

HALL, P. *The World Cities*, Weidenfeld & Nicholson, 2nd edn, 1977.

HAMRIN, E. and WIREN, E. *Town and Country Planning in Sweden Today*, The Swedish Institute, Stockholm, 1964.

HOLMGREN, P. *Integration of Public Transport with Urban Development in Stockholm*, The Stockholm Building Office, Stockholm, 1965.

MARKELIUS, S. 'Structure of Stockholm', *Town and Country Planning*, 24, 1956 and 25, 1957.

MERLIN, P. *New Towns, Regional Planning and Development*, Methuen, London, 1971.

PASS, D. *Vällingby and Farsta: From Idea to Reality*, M.I.T. Press, Cambridge, Mass., 1973.

POPENOE, D. *The Suburban Environment, Sweden and the USA*, University of Chicago Press, Chicago, 1977.

SCARLAT, A. *The Development of Shopping Centres in the Stockholm Area*, The Swedish Institute, Stockholm, 1963.

SIDENBLADH, G. 'Stockholm: A Planned City', *Scientific American*, Sept. 1965.

Stockholm, Tapiola and Cumbernauld, *American Institute of Architects Journal*, 48, 1967.

WESTERMAN, A. *Swedish Planning of Town Centres*, The Swedish Institute, Stockholm, 1965.

WILLIAM-OLSSON, W. 'Stockholm; Its Structure and Development', *Geographical Review*, 30, 1940.

WILLIAM-OLSSON, W. 'Stockholm; Structure and Development', *I.G.U. Congress*, Norden, 1960, Uppsala, 1961.

Study 7
SÖNDER VISSING
SKANDERBORG
DENMARK

A dairy farming district in East Jutland

Extracts from Sheets
M 2611 (Rye) and M2610
(Byrup).
Danish 1:20,000 Series.

Published 1872.
Revised 1951.
Partial Revision 1963.
Vertical Interval of
Contours 2 metres.

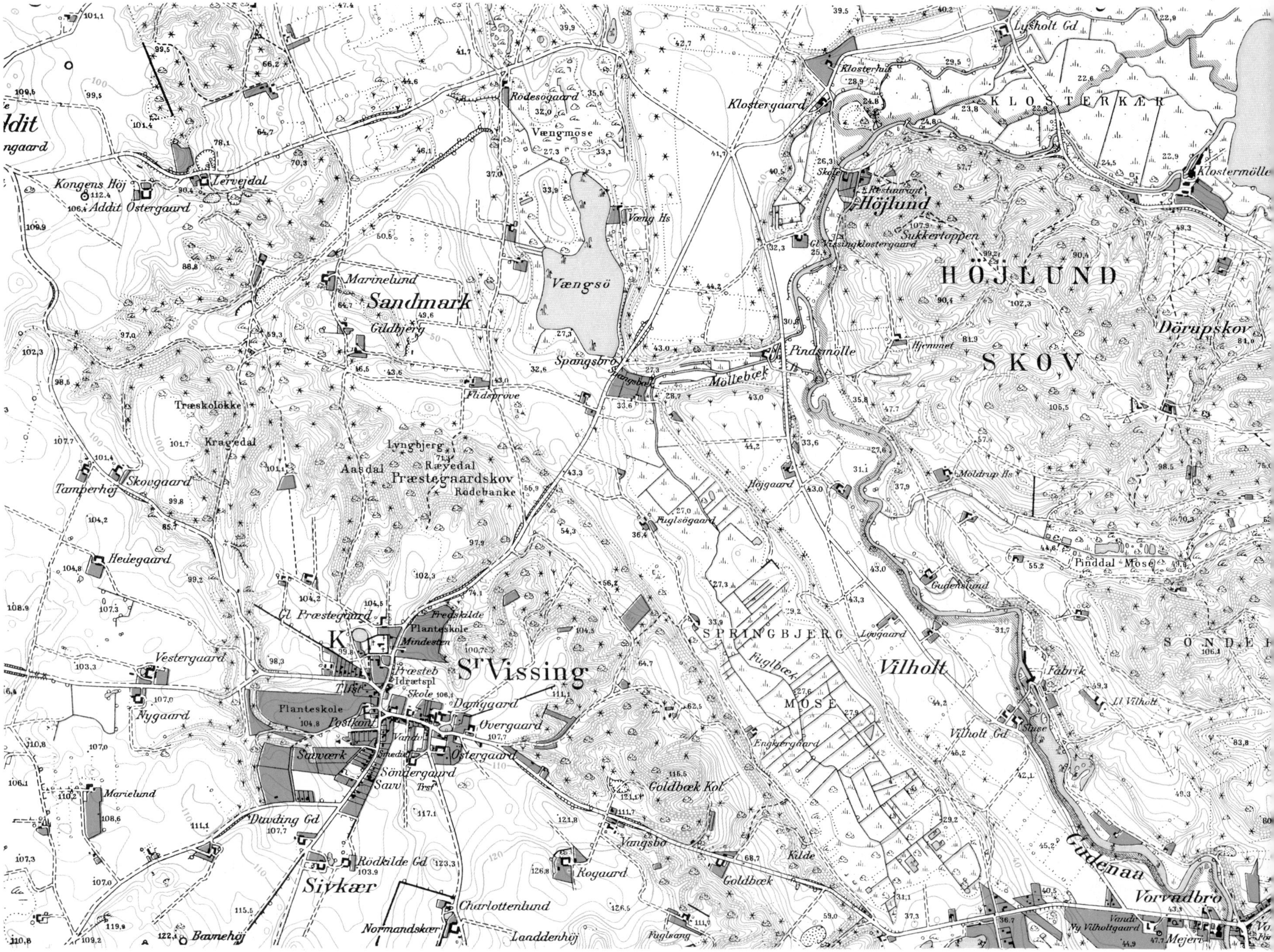

By permission (A.199/68) of
the Geodetic Institute of
Denmark.

Map 7

Photograph 9. Sönder Vissing. Note the intensively farmed upper surface of the moraine plateau and the heavily wooded slopes which separate it from the marshy grazing land on the floor of the melt-water valley to the east.

The village of Sönder Vissing shown on the map extract lies 22 km north-west of the small town of Horsens in East Jutland (Jylland). Like the islands of the Danish archipelago to the east, this eastern section of the Jutland Peninsula consists of drift deposits which relate to the Pomeranian phase of the last (Weichsel) glaciation of northern Europe. This is in contrast to south-west Jutland which consists of sandy fluvioglacial material from the Weichsel ice partly overlying deposits from the earlier Saale glaciation.

In detail the 'young' glacial deposits of East Jutland assume a great variety of forms. In places moraine clays form extensive plains and flats, while elsewhere moraine deposits of sand and clay form small hills and ridges which are frequently dissected by melt-water valleys formed along the former ice margin and tunnel valleys formed by subglacial streams. The latter have been partially drowned in many cases by postglacial marine transgressions to produce the distinctive *fjard* coast of East Jutland. Drumlins, eskers and kames all add further interest and variety to the Danish landscape.

Although the range of elevation in Jutland is only modest (the highest point in Denmark, Yding Skovhöj, 173 metres, lies just beyond the map area to the south-east), gradients can be locally quite steep, and the landscape is frequently hummocky and irregular. These small-scale variations of relief may be appreciated by reference to the area selected for examination.

Relief and drainage

The map area forms part of the region of Jutland which is sometimes referred to as the Danish Glacial Lake District. In very broad terms the area portrayed consists of two upland areas separated by a belt of lower ground. The western upland upon which Sönder Vissing is sited rises to a maximum height of 126·5 metres. Its surface is gently undulating for the most part, although a number of narrow, steep-sided dry valleys such as Kragdal and Aasdal penetrate the upland from the steep but dissected east-facing edge of the higher ground. Reference to a soil map of Denmark *(Jordbundskort over Danmark* by C. H. Bornebusch and K. Milthers: *Danmark's Geologiske Undersögelse* 1935) shows that this area consists predominantly of glacial clays with some glacial sands. It can be seen that the symbols for both clay pits and sand-and-gravel pits occur on the map in this western area. At Lervejdal, in the north, both symbols occur in close proximity. The whole of the western area is in fact part of a stadial moraine.

The eastern upland area, Höjland Skov, has a more rugged and fragmented appearance and rises slightly less high, to a maximum of 107·9 metres at Sukkertoppen. The area is much dissected by small dry valleys and again many small steep slopes are evident. The area is composed of sandy morainic material. Notice the sand or gravel pit cut into the river cliff north of Vorvadbro. Apart from the small west-flowing stream occupying Pinddal, the Höjlund Skov area, like the western upland area, is characterised by a general lack of surface drainage.

The belt of lower ground which separates the two upland areas is part of a melt-water valley which formed along a former ice front. Along its centre is a flat-topped ridge, some 15 metres higher than the bordering river, which separates the drainage of this lower ground into two channels. Along the western flank of this low ridge lies the small lake, Vængsö, and the stream

Figure 9. Denmark: Geomorphology. Based on *Landskabskort över Denmark* published by Geodætisk Institut, Copenhagen 1949

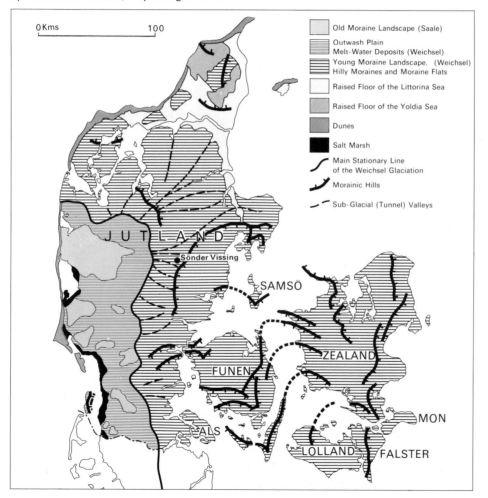

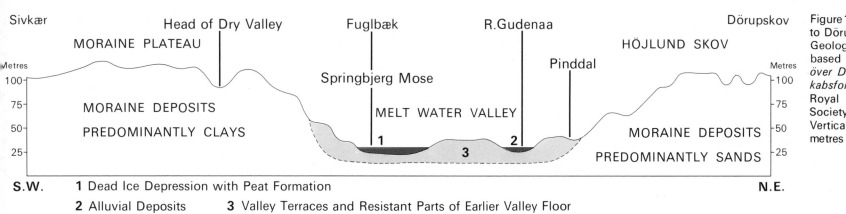

Figure 10. Section from Sivkær to Dörupskov. Geological information is based on fig. 20B in *Atlas över Denmark.* Vol.1. *Landskabsformerne.* A. Schou. Royal Danish Geographical Society. Copenhagen, 1949. Vertical Scale, 1 cm: 39.37 metres

S.W. **1** Dead Ice Depression with Peat Formation N.E.

2 Alluvial Deposits   **3** Valley Terraces and Resistant Parts of Earlier Valley Floor

Fuglbæk which drains the swampy area of Springbjerg Mose (*mose*—marsh). Drainage from this western side of the low ridge is carried by the Möllebæk through a narrow gap to join the Gudenaa which drains the eastern flank of the ridge before swinging east near Höjlund to enter Lake Mossö (unnamed on the map extract). The Gudenaa is the dominant drainage channel in this area, and reference to detailed maps will show that it follows a strangely irregular course which is in fact related to both old longitudinal melt-water valleys and transverse tunnel valleys. (See *Landskabskort over Danmark.* 1:250,000. *Geodætisk Institut.* Copenhagen, 1949.) The belt of low ground between the two upland areas consists of fluvioglacial outwash deposits with peat and alluvial deposits on the western and eastern sides of the central ridge respectively (see figure 10). The central valley ridge calls for explanation. It is, together with narrow terrace features that may be noted along the valley sides, a remnant of a former valley floor level. Since the original deposition of outwash material along the valley in late glacial times the Gudenaa has responded to changes of base level by eroding down into the fluvioglacial deposits of the old valley floor. The low ground of Springbjerg Mose is the result of a different process. This is a dead ice depression due to the subsidence of the outwash material which accompanied the melting of large masses of enclosed dead ice.

Settlement

Apart from the two villages of Sönder Vissing and Vorvadbro (only partially shown on the map extract) the settlement in this area is quite evenly distributed. Out of a total population of some 620 people in the area covered by the map extract, about 350 are found in Sönder Vissing and a further 100 in Vorvadbro, the remainder living in scattered farms and cottages. The distri-

bution of farms (*gaard* abb. *Gd.*—a farm) can be related in part to the conditions of relief and drainage. The intensity of farms is greatest on the rolling moraine country of the western upland. By contrast, few farms are found on the sandy, wooded upland of Höjlund Skov. The low, marshy sections of the melt water valley are virtually devoid of settlements, but several farms have taken advantage of the slightly elevated sites provided by the central ridge in the valley and the bordering terraces.

Sönder Vissing stands on gently undulating ground of the moraine plateau at a point where, in the past, water would be available locally. The map indicates a well *(kilde)* to the north of the village as well as a number of ponds *(kær)*. To the north and east lie the steep wooded slopes overlooking the melt-water valley, while to the west is the head of the steep-sided dry valley, Kragdal. The village has grown up at the intersection of two local roads and assumes an imperfect cruciform pattern. From the number of institutions shown on the map it seems fair to assume that the village is an important local centre for the surrounding rural population. As well as the church, school *(skole)*, post office *(postkontor)* and telephone station *(telefon station)*, the village is also shown to include a waterworks *(vandværk)*, two sawmills *(Savværk)* and a forge *(smedie)*. Photograph 9 also shows a large new school under construction to the west of the village.

Apart from the evidence at Sönder Vissing, and the sand and gravel workings mentioned earlier, the map gives little indication of non-agricultural activity. A factory *(fabrik)* lies on the bank of the Gudenaa at Vilholt. This in fact produces paper. Two mills *(mölle*—a mill) are also marked; Pindsmölle on the Möllebæk and Klostermölle on the Gudenaa where it discharges into Lake Mossö. However, there is no means of identifying the type of mill, or even of verifying whether they are still operational.

Land use

One of the most immediately striking points about photograph 9 is the heavily wooded nature of the steep edge of the western upland. Stands of conifers can be differentiated from deciduous species by their darker tonal values on the photograph. Although not covered by photograph 9, the map extract shows that Höjlund Skov has a similar cover of mixed woodland and bushes. The low-lying ground of Springbjerg Mose and Vængmose to the north of the reed-fringed Vængsö has an alternation of swampy grazing and heathland vegetation. Springbjerg Mose has numerous artificial drainage channels and peat digging appears to have taken place at a number of points. Similar swampy grazing can be seen at the western end of Lake Mossö. The remainder of the area is divided up into small fields with few enclosing hedges. The key for the Danish 1:10,000 map series shows a symbol for wire boundary fences but few of these are even shown, probably a reflection of the fact that most farmers use temporary electric wire fences which are constantly moved in position. Photograph 9 shows a number of areas around Sönder Vissing and Spangsbro divided up into narrow strips and devoted to nursery cultivation (*planteskole*—a nursery).

The area portrayed is part of the dairy farming region of East Jutland. Few cash crops are grown and most of the cultivation is concerned with the production of grass, fodder grains and root crops for the winter feeding of the large numbers of dairy cattle kept in the region. The farming pattern in the area may be illustrated by reference to one specific farm, namely Vestergaard, to the immediate west of Sönder Vissing.

Vestergaard

(The following section is based in part on an account of Vestergaard by John Fraser Hart in *Focus on Geographic Activity: a Collection of Original Studies*, edited by R. S. Thoman and D. J. Patton, and also on information provided by K. and G. Rasmussen of Vestergaard Farm.)

Vestergaard lies on the north side of the road running west from Sönder Vissing. The buildings lie around a small courtyard, and, apart from the farmhouse and recent additions to the farm buildings, they are of brick construction with thatched roofs. The farm covers an area of 37 hectares, of which 30 hectares were under cultivation in 1978 (sown grass, cereals and roots). The plot occupied by the farm buildings accounts for c. 1 hectare, and a further 4 hectares are taken up by the steep wooded side of the valley, Kragdal. In addition the farm owns a further 2 hectares of swampy grazing in the Klosterkær district at the western end of Lake Mossö. Vestergaard is a typical Danish farm in respect of both size and function. Its 37 hectares

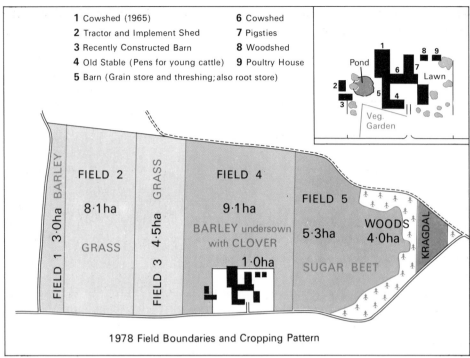

Figure 11. Farm plan of Vestergaard

are not greatly in excess of the average Danish farm size of 32·4 hectares, and, like most farms in East Jutland and on the Danish islands, Vestergaard is concerned with dairy production.

Vestergaard: Land use 1978

	hectares		hectares
Sown grass	12·6	Swampy grazing land at Klosterkær	2·0
Barley (9·1 hectares undersown with clover)	12·1	Farm buildings	1·0
Sugar beet	5·3		——
Woodland	4·0		37·0

The owner of the farm, Mr Gunnar Rasmussen, who took over the farm from his father in 1963, practises a five-year rotation of grass, grass, barley, sugar beet, and barley undersown with clover. 'He cuts hay from his rotation grass the first year, but grazes cattle on it the second year so that their droppings will fertilise the land for the grain crop which he sows in the third year . . . Rasmussen follows his fodder roots with a crop of barley and sows a mixture of grass and clover seed in the same field. The barley, which grows much more rapidly, serves as a 'nurse crop' to protect the young pasture plants and enable them to become firmly established by the time the grain is ready for harvest.' (J. F. Hart.) The following table shows the pattern of land use for the years 1976–78.

	Field 1	Field 2	Field 3	Field 4	Field 5
1976	Grass	Barley/Clover	Sugar beet	Barley	Grass
1977	Grass	Grass	Barley/Clover	Sugar beet	Barley
1978	Barley	Grass	Grass	Barley/Clover	

Field numbers correspond with figure 11.
Information supplied by K. Rasmussen, Vestergaard.

All cultivation at Vestergaard is directed towards the production of animal feed. The fields of grass and clover are grazed or cut for hay. The barley and sugar beet are used for cattle feed; the latter is a special type not grown for sugar production but used merely as a fodder crop. The green tops of the beet are also used to make silage for winter feeding. In 1978 Rasmussen had a herd of 48 mature Danish Red cattle and 30 young cattle for fattening. Some of the younger animals are raised as replacements for the older milking cattle, while others are sold at stock sales in Horsens after fattening. However, milk sales provide the greater part of the farm's income. Vestergaard and some 260 other farms in the district form a co-operative organisation with a modern dairy and creamery *(mejeri)* at Vorvadbro (see map 7). Milk from the farm is processed into butter and cheese, and until recently Rasmussen used to buy back skimmed milk from the dairy to feed a herd of 200 Landrace bacon pigs, but profit margins were small and this practice has been discontinued, so that no pigs are now raised at Vestergaard. In this respect the farm differs from the typical Danish pattern, for most farms combine milk and bacon production. However, the co-operative organisation does supply supplementary foodstuffs (oil cake) and chemical fertilisers. The soil here on the moraine plateau tends to be sandy and requires heavy applications of manure and artificial fertilisers.

Comparison of figure 11 with both the aerial photograph (taken in June 1965) and the map extract (partial revision 1963) will reveal a number of differences. The field pattern of the farm differs in several respects. The reason for this is that the farm has no internal hedge boundaries, and field divisions are made by moveable electric wire fences. A former track linking the farm buildings with the minor road that forms the western boundary has been ploughed up to facilitate the working of the western fields. What appears on the photograph to be a new track approaching the farm from the north-east is in fact the line of a new water main that was being laid to supply the large new cowsheds which were constructed to the north of the other buildings during 1965. By a long history of such adjustment and improvement Vestergaard, an old family farm, is now an extremely efficient production unit and typifies the high standards of agriculture in Denmark.

Glossary of terms and abbreviations used on the map
(These are in addition to those translated in the text.)

Bæk	Stream	*Hus (Hs.)*	House	*Lund*	Small wood
Bjerg	Hill	*Höj*	Hill	*Skov*	Wood
Gammel (Gl.)	Old	*Lille (Ll.)*	Little	*Sönder (Sr.)*	Southern

Exercises
1. Calculate *(a)* the vertical exaggeration of the section in figure 10; *(b)* the scale of the vertical aerial photograph, and *(c)* the scale of the farm plan (figure 11)
2. Define precisely the following terms which occur in the text.
(a) Tunnel Valley; *(b)* Stadial Moraine; *(c)* Fjard; *(d)* Dead Ice Depression; *(e)* Kame.
3. Write a description of the Gudenaa and its valley between Vorbadbro and Lake Mossö.
4. 'There are three distinct relief elements in the landscape of eastern Jutland; the tunnel valleys, the low plateau, and the terminal ridges.' (M. R. Shackleton.) Discuss.
5. The line marking the limit of the Weichsel glaciation is 'the most significant physical-geographical and economic-geographical borderline in Denmark'. (A. Schou.) Discuss.

Further reading
BUNTING, B. T. 'The Present Reorganization of Agriculture in Denmark', *Geography*, **53**, 1968.
Denmark. An Official Handbook, Press and Information Department, Ministry of Foreign Affairs, Copenhagen, 1970.
HANSEN, V. 'The Danish Village; Its Age and Form', *Denmark, Guidebook for the 19th I.G.U. Congress*, Stockholm, 1960.
HART, J. F. 'Vestergaard. A Farm in Denmark', in *Focus on Geographic Activity: A Collection of Original Studies*. ed. R. S. Thoman and D. J. Patton, McGraw-Hill, New York, 1964.
HUMLUM, J. and NYGÅRD, K. *Denmark Atlas*, Gyldendal, Copenhagen, 1961.
JENSEN, E. *Danish Agriculture. Its Economic Development 1870–1930*, Copenhagen, 1937.
KAMPP, Aa. H. 'Some Changes in the Structure of Danish Farming, particularly from 1940–1960', *Collected Papers, Denmark*, 20th I.G.U. Congress, London, 1964, published by the Geographical Institute, Copenhagen University.
KAMPP, Aa. H. 'Agricultural-Geography Studies on Denmark', *Kulturgeografiske Skrifter*, **6**, 1959.
SCHOU, A. *Atlas of Denmark*, Volume 1, The Landscapes, Royal Danish Geographical Society, Copenhagen, 1949.
SCHOU, A. and ANTONSEN, K. 'Denmark' in *The Geography of Norden*, ed. A. Sømme, Heinemann, 1961, Chapter 8.
SKUBBELTRANG, F. 'Agricultural Development and Rural Reform in Denmark', *F.A.O. Agricultural Studies*, **22**, Rome, 1953.

Map 8 shows part of the south-western section of the North East Polder in the Netherlands. The landscape is flat, having a maximum range of altitude of only 9·1 metres. Along the coast runs a dyke at 4·6 metres above sea level in the west, declining to 3·7 metres in the south-east. Behind the dyke the polder floor lies below sea level, the greatest depths being between 4·0 and 4·5 metres below sea level west and south-west of Tollebeek (7421). Two areas stand out as being very close to sea level, the town of Urk in the west and Schokland in the south-east. Drainage is obviously artificial and judging from the relative widths there appears to be a heirarchy of water-courses. The only one to connect with the Ijssel Meer is the Urkervaart which has a diesel pumping station at its mouth (Gemaal). Feeding into the Urkervaart is a number of secondary watercourses such as the Zuidermeertocht and the Nagelervaart, which in turn have even smaller tributaries dividing the land into sections of a regular size.

The reclamation plan

The history of this landscape is a recent one, originating in the project for the reclamation of the Zuider Zee. Though the idea had been under consideration even before the nineteenth century, it was only made official policy by an Act of the Dutch Parliament in 1918. There were many strong arguments in favour of the reclamation plan. Scarcity of food during the 1914–18 war fostered the consideration of schemes for greater agricultural production in Holland. The Zuider Zee scheme would add 10% to the arable land of the Netherlands. Furthermore, the productivity of lands lying around the Zuider Zee would be increased through greater safety from floods (such a flood had occurred in 1916) and by the easier regulation of drainage and water table levels in these lands. Not least among the advantages of the scheme would be the shortening of the Dutch coast: less maintenance of costly sea dykes would be required and the north-east provinces would be brought within easier reach of the rest of the country. In recent years consolidation schemes for agricultural improvement in areas suffering from fragmented holdings required the resettlement of many farmers; new land in the Zuider Zee would provide farms for many of these people.

The North East Polder was the second of the five polders to be constructed, having been preceded by the reclamation of the Weiringemeer Polder between 1930 and 1940. By the time the North East Polder was drained the enclosing dam across the Zuider Zee from Den Oever to Friesland had been completed. Thus the project was carried out in fresh water conditions which made the subsequent soil maturation processes much easier. In 1937 the enclosing dyke was built, part of which is shown north and south-east of

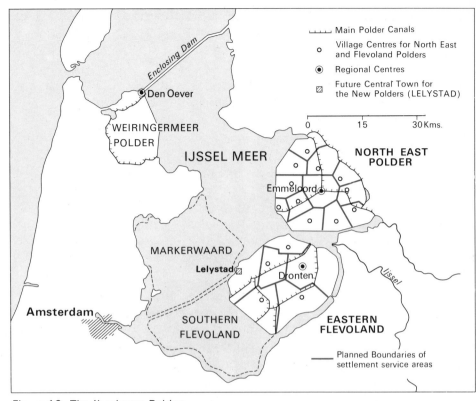

Figure 12. The Ijsselmeer Polders
Based on structure plan for the southern Ijsselmeer Polders, *Rijkswaterstaat Communication No. 6*, Board of Zuyder Zee Works.

Urk on the map extract. The sea bed was then pumped free of water, a stage which was reached by 1942. The main drainage canals were dredged before the polder was pumped dry. The materials from these (peat, sand and clay) were put to different uses. The clay was mixed with sandy soils in order to improve them; the sand was dumped at future road junctions or near future villages for building purposes; while the peat was scattered over a large area for working into the soil. In the North East Polder three main drainage canals were constructed from Emmeloord. Each of these has a pumping station at its mouth. The Vissering pumping station (696189) has three diesel-powered centrifugal pumps, each with a capacity of 120,000 gallons per minute. The three pumping stations together can remove water to a depth of over half an inch from the surface of the whole polder in 24 hours. At the side of each station is a lock which allows cargo ships of up to 300 tons access to the interior of the polder. Since the depth below sea level of the polder surface increases towards the west, the general water table level in the western section has to be maintained at a lower level (5·72 metres) than that in the east (4·42 metres below sea level). Main ditches feeding into the canals were dredged at distances of 1,600 metres apart and subsidiary ditches spaced along these at intervals of 300 metres. The detailed drainage pattern of land within these ditches has been the subject of considerable investigation. The distance apart varies according to soil conditions from 8 to 48 metres. Initially a system of field ditches was excavated by trench-cutting machines, but after a few years in which the very young soils were allowed to mature, the ditches were replaced by permanent tile drains at a depth of about 1 metre. On sandy soils the problem of summer drought is solved by using the ditch and drain system for sub-surface irrigation. Such areas are found north-east of Urk and north of Schokland. By using a series of check dams on the main drainage ditches it is possible to vary the level of the water table in each field according to soil type and the needs of individual crops.

Land use

Land use within the polder varies according to the soil type. Figure 13 is a simplified soil map of the south-western section of the North East Polder and may be compared with both figure 14 and the map extract which give details of land use. The relation between soil and land use is not simple, but is affected considerably by economic considerations. Only a small part of the land is unsuitable for agriculture: this is mainly composed of an infertile boulder clay or very coarse sands, and is given over to woodland (note the area of boulder clay near Urk). By far the largest area is used for arable farms (60% of all farms are purely arable) which have areas of grassland only as part of their rotations. Crop growing is certainly the most profitable form of land use but certain soils with less than 8% clay content are liable to wind erosion on these flat surfaces. Thus on sandy soils purely arable farming is rare and livestock assume some importance. In fact only 16% of all farms in the polder can be classified as livestock farms with over half of their area under permanent grass. There are few areas devoted to intensive fruit and vegetable cultivation. Though most of the sandy loam and clay soils are suitable for this purpose, the threat of over-production has led the planning authorities to restrict this type of agriculture to certain small areas in the east. The productivity of farms in the North East Polder is very impressive. The following statistics compare yields for the major crops in the North East Polder with those of similar crops in Noord Brabant (largely polder land of a much earlier date) and in the Netherlands as a whole.

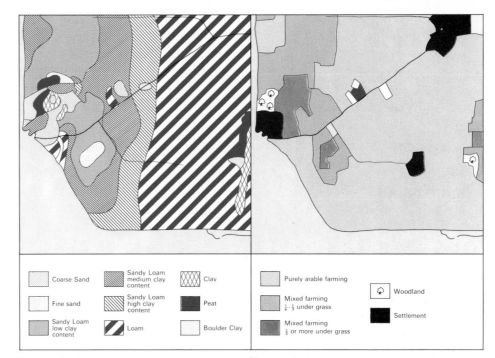

Figure 13. North East Polder: soils   Figure 14. North East Polder: land use

1978: yields per hectare in kilograms

	Netherlands	Noord Brabant	North East Polder	Crop areas in hectares in North East Polder
Wheat	6,567	6,289	7,248	4,982
Barley	4,997	4,644	5,602	721
Oats	5,576	4,748	6,400	889
Green peas	4,322	3,841	4,538	13
Flax	8,309	8,250	8,500	40
Potatoes	38,572	41,003	37,558	9,365
Sugar beet	48,418	45,987	58,000	8,915
Onions	43,827	41,151	48,000	3,154

Source: Centraal Bureau Voor de Statistiek, 's-Gravenhage.

The farms

The pattern of field boundaries is a simple one, dictated by the need for drainage and by the advantages of rectilinear fields for mechanised farming. Parcels of land are generally 800 metres long by 300 metres wide, bordered on one short side by a canal and on the other by a road. Down each long side runs a ditch carrying water from the tile drains and in turn feeding into the larger canal. Reference to the map extract shows that variations occur,

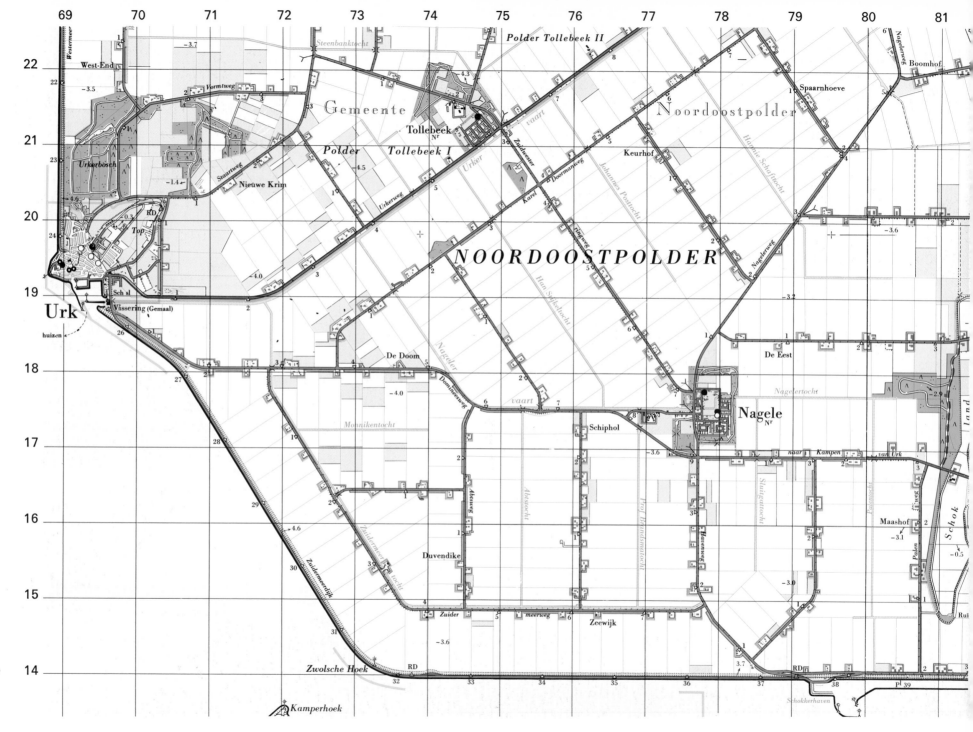

NORTH EAST POLDER NETHERLANDS

Extracts from Sheets 21 West (Zwolle) and 20 East (Enkhuizen). Dutch 1:50,000 Series.

Sheet 21 West Published 1962.
Sheet 20 East Published 1960.

Map 8

Photograph 10. North East Polder. Note the regular spacing of groups of farmsteads. An attempt was made to produce a series of small communities by locating farm buildings at the corners of their plots adjacent to each other.

Aerofilms Ltd

largely because of the circular shape of the polder and the centrifugal lines of main drainage from Emmeloord.

Farm sizes in the North East Polder are given in the following table:

Hectares	Number of farms	% of total number
12–17	194	14·2
18–23	148	10·9
24–29	567	41·6
30–35	133	9·7
36–41	135	9·9
42–47	35	2·6
48 and over	151	11·1
	1,363	100%

Source: Royal Netherlands Embassy, London.

The figures do not include the intensive market gardening and fruit growing holdings which occupy about 1,800 hectares and are generally smaller than 10 hectares. The size of the smallest arable or mixed farm is determined by the need to provide an adequate income for one family. In the North East Polder this was held to be 12 hectares, but it is noticeable that ideas on this have changed since 1930. In the earlier Weiringemeer Polder, a minimum size of 10 hectares was planned, while in the later Flevoland Polders the minimum size is 20 hectares. These changes have come about through the increased efficiency of labour largely resulting from the greater number of machines now used. Variation in the size of farms is a function of several factors, some of which are conflicting. Large farms are certainly cheaper initially because the cost of buildings and equipment per hectare is lower. However, the smaller farm is often held to be socially more desirable, giving a greater density of population and obviating the need for a large number of labourers. Suggestions that larger farms be created in the new polders meet with strong protests since the demand for farms is so great. Furthermore, the distances involved in working a very large farm may well lead to the cultivation of the furthest fields being less intensive (see M. Chisholm, *Rural Settlement and Land Use*). Soil and land use also exert an influence. Thus a farm with more than half of its land under grass needs to be 20–30 hectares in size to be economically viable. The smallest farms are not established on very heavy land, which would require too much tractive power for the resources of the small farmer. Finally, social considerations decreed that variations in farm size should exist in order to meet the variety of personal ability and financial means of the new farmers.

Generally farms of a similar size and type were grouped together; the smallest close to and the larger at some distance from the villages. Most of the smaller farms followed the traditional style of Dutch farm architecture with a living room, kitchen, three or four bedrooms and a storage shed grouped under one roof. On the larger farms the house and sheds are completely separated and the latter are generally a product of the new prefabrication techniques. The small farms (less than 20 hectares) are normally worked by the family while those of larger size require additional labour. Accommodation for the head labourer was provided by building a cottage on the farm lands. Other labourers were normally housed in the nearest village. Close examination of the map extract and the photograph will show examples of the different types of farm.

It may also be noted from the map that farm buildings are frequently located close to each other on adjacent properties. Thus, north-west of Nagele there are several examples of four sets of farm buildings being placed close to each other on either side of a road. The reason for this practice was partly the economies gained in providing services such as electricity, but the planners also had in mind the creation of small communities which it was hoped would be advantageous socially.

Population

Throughout the planning of the new polders the aim to produce a well balanced society has been paramount. Many farmers have claims to land in the new polders; in fact about 3,000 applications were received each year for the 150 available new farms. In the selection process attention was of course paid to hardship. Thus in the early leases priority was given to dispossessed farmers from the island of Walcheren where the floods of 1945 and subsequent reconstruction involved consolidation of previously fragmented holdings. The disastrous floods of 1953 similarly provided the polder with a number of applicants from the islands of Zeeland. Every year land is lost to agriculture in the Netherlands through the extension of towns and road building programmes. Such special hardships win much sympathy from the allocating authorities. Both professional and financial ability are also considered important. The applicant must satisfy the authority of his agricultural competence and be capable of supplying at least 25% of the financial backing himself. Of the rest, two-thirds may be borrowed from relatives or other sources, and the balance will, if necessary, be loaned to him by the co-operative farmers' credit bank. Farms are available only on leasehold since it is thought wrong that a few individuals should benefit from the great expenditure of State funds on creating the polder. The rents payable cover not only the land but also the dwelling and farm buildings. Finally, attention is paid to balance in age, religion and province of origin of the new farmers.

Village settlements

Three villages are found in the map area. The core of Urk is located on a small island which was incorporated into the North East Polder when drainage took place. This older centre can be easily recognised from the map though it will be noted that expansion has taken place to the north and north-east. Since Urk lies at the terminus of one of the main drainage and shipping canals of the polder, one may infer that the port is of some local significance, though it is doubtful if the fishing industry has the importance of earlier times. Both Nagele and Tollebeek have been carefully planned. In the centre of Nagele is a large open space serving as a village common. Along the encircling road are grouped small housing estates separated by rows of trees. The whole village is surrounded by a belt of woodland which must provide some relief, not only from the wind but also from the monotonous flatness of the polder landscape. Similar plantings of trees have been made around Tollebeek. It is noticeable that both villages have their centres away from the main roads which lead north-east to Emmeloord.

The future of the polder villages involves problems which are not uncommon in Britain. They were designed to house all agricultural labourers apart from the foremen on large farms, and in addition to serve as secondary social and supply centres. Most of the villages of the North East Polder and especially those in the west have failed to attract sufficient people. In part this has been due to mechanisation in agriculture; furthermore, many country people now demand more and better amenities than can be economically provided in a village of 800 people. The spread of car ownership has allowed these needs to be satisfied in the regional centre of Emmeloord which alone among the polder settlements has grown faster than originally planned. It is noticeable from figure 12 that the distances between villages in the more recent East Flevoland Polder, and in consequence their service areas, are much greater than in the older North East Polder.

A second series of problems seems likely to emerge as a result of the selection procedure employed. There is a high proportion of young people among the colonists (between 25 and 35 years of age), and the birth rate is far higher than average (30·8 per 1,000 compared with 21 per 1,000 for the Netherlands as a whole). Thus the age structure of the population shows a remarkably wide-based pyramid. This situation has posed difficult problems. In the early stages the schools will be overcrowded; later they may be comparatively empty. At some future date there will be a large number of school leavers seeking employment which is unlikely to materialise on the highly mechanised farms of the polder. Thus if a chronic unemployment problem is not to arise in the polder, some alternative employment must be provided. It seems likely that Emmeloord will have to develop manufacturing industries to a far greater extent than hitherto.

Exercises

1. How far can the methods applied in the North East Polder be used to alleviate problems of shortage of food and overpopulation in the under-developed regions of the world?
2. What factors determine the intensive quality of agriculture? Illustrate with examples from contrasting areas.
3. The Zuider Zee project has served only to encourage even further urbanisation of the Dutch people. Discuss.
4. Discuss with reference to contrasting areas the future of the village as a settlement unit.
5. Why is arable farming generally more profitable than dairy farming in the North East Polder?
6. Compare and contrast the landscape and economic geography of the North East Polder with those of an earlier polder such as Geestmerambacht. (Study 9.)
7. 'Proximity to sea level is a dominant theme in the geography of the Netherlands.' Discuss this statement. (Cambridge.)
8. Compare the economic developments of the Dutch polders and the English Fens, and suggest reasons for any differences noted. (Cambridge.)

Further reading

A detailed sample study of a single farm located in the area of the map extract is to be found in chapter 8 of *Case Studies in World Geography*, ed. R. M. Highsmith, Jr., Prentice-Hall, 1961.

'A Structure Plan for the Southern Ijsselmeer Polders', *Rijkswaterstaat Communication*, no. 6, Board of Zuyder Zee Works, 1965.

BURKE, G. L. *Greenheart Metropolis. Planning in the Western Netherlands*, Macmillan 1966.

CHISHOLM, M. *Rural Settlement and Land Use*, Hutchinson's University Library, 1962.

CONSTANDSE, A. K. 'Changing Human Geographical Aspects of the Netherlands: Reclamation and Colonisation of New Areas', *Tijdschrift voor Economische en Sociale Geografie*, **54**, no. 2, 1963

DUMONT, R. *Types of Rural Economy*, Methuen, 1957, chapter XIII.

From Fisherman's Paradise to Farmer's Pride, Public Relations and Information Department of the Netherlands Ministry of Transport and 'Waterstaat', Netherlands Information Service, 1953.

MONKHOUSE, F. J. *A Regional Geography of Western Europe*, 4th edn, Longman, 1974, chapter 3.

'Planning and Creation of an Environment', *Report of the Royal Institute of Netherlands Architects*, B.N.A.

SMITS, Ir. H. and WIGGERS, A. J. *Soil Survey and Land Classification as applied to Reclamation of Sea Bottom Land in the Netherlands'*, International Institute for Land Reclamation and Improvement, 1959.

Study 9
GEESTMERAM-BACHT POLDER NORTH HOLLAND NETHERLANDS

A Polder Landscape.

Extract from Map Sheets
19 West Alkmaar and
14 West Medemblik.
Dutch 1:50,000 Series.

Revised 1959.

By permission of Topografische Dienst, Delft, Netherlands.

Map 9

Photograph 11. View across
the Geestmerambacht Polder
towards the North Sea.

KLM Aerocarto, Amsterdam.

The following study is based upon extracts from the 1:25,000 and 1:50,000 maps of the Netherlands. Relief is shown by contours at 5 metre intervals on the 1:50,000 map and at 2·5 metre intervals on the 1:25,000 series. Additional information is provided by spot heights. One of the most useful features of both maps is the attention given to land use. Distinctions are made between arable and pastoral land, glasshouses and orchards, as well as between various types of woodland and heath. This presents the geographer with information that is unobtainable from the topographical maps of most other countries.

The landscape shown on photograph 11 and on maps 9 and 10 is without doubt one of the most artificial or manmade in Europe. The area is a Dutch polder landscape in the province of North Holland which lies between the North Sea in the west and the former Zuider Zee in the east. Some 4 km to the south of the map extract lies Alkmaar, an important centre for much of North Holland.

Landscape

In the south-west corner of map extract 9 lies an area of dune country. Although no spot heights are to be seen on this part of the map, the area does in fact reach heights well above sea level. (A height of 30 metres is attained at a point about 1 km west of the extract.) In this section the dune belt is comparatively wide, but further north (vide top centre and right of photograph 11) the line of dunes is much narrower and is, in fact, non-existent in the vicinity of Petten, in the top left of the photograph. The dune belt is Holland's great defence against the encroachment of the North Sea. It extends, with minor breaks as at Petten where an artificial bank has been constructed, from the Hook of Holland to Den Helder. Beyond Den Helder the line of dunes is discontinuous and forms the West Frisian Islands. The dunes are of relatively recent formation, dating from after the end of the Quaternary Ice Age at about the time of the breaching of the Straits of Dover (c. 5000 B.C.). A great offshore bar was developed by wave action, continuous, except for the mouths of the Maas and Rhine, from western Flanders to northern Germany. Upon this bar windblown sand accumulated as dunes. Behind the dune belt shallow lagoons became regions of accumulation for mud, and later plants and beds of peat. The largest of these lagoons was Lake Flevo. Subsequent invasions by the sea during historic times, and especially in the 14th century, transformed these fresh-water lagoons into salt-water areas, Lake Flevo, for example, forming the even larger Zuider Zee. Gulfs of the Zuider Zee extended westwards at this time almost to the dune rampart, notably in the Beemster and Schermer areas adjacent to Alkmaar. The polder lands of the Netherlands are the result of man's efforts to drain these low-lying regions of peat, silt and clay.

The greater part of the landscape shown on map extract 9 and photograph 11 is polder land. Examination of both maps will show the height of the floors of the polders to be well below sea level. Only in the south west, on the land between the North Holland Canal and the dune belt, are heights above sea level recorded.

The method of reclamation of the polder lands consisted of the construction of a long dyke, on the outside of which lay a peripheral canal known as a ring-vaart. The area within the ring-dyke was pumped clear of water and a close, rectilinear pattern of drainage canals ('Sloot' pl. 'Sloten') was established on the polder floor. Today, these are pumped into the ring-vaart which in turn is drained to other canals or rivers and eventually to the sea. Pumping is, of course, necessary because of the differences of levels which have been exaggerated in many areas by the shrinkage of the peat consequent upon drainage. (A similar problem is experienced in our own Fenland area.) Originally pumps were operated by wind, and the traditional Dutch windmill is still to be seen. However, in the 19th century, steam pumps, and more recently diesel and electric pumps, have largely superseded the older method.

In areas where the floors of the polders are above mean sea level the problem of drainage is easier, since less pumping needs to be done. Such an area is to be found in the south-west of map 9 as, for example, in Mangel polder, Oudburger polder and Zuurvens polder.

The greater part of the map extracts are covered by the Geestmerambacht Polder, which stretches from the North Holland Canal in the west to the canal running from 153290 to 153200 in the east. Within the main polder there are some fourteen separate smaller polders which are drained into the main canals. These in turn are drained to the Schermerboezem, which acts as a water storage area and lies to the south of Alkmaar. The most striking feature of the Geestmerambacht Polder is the very large area covered by water. Over the whole polder (5,660 hectares) about 20% is water-covered, and in the parish of Langedijk the figure is as high as 35%. The explanation is to be found in the history of the polder. Drained at an early date (14th century), the polder was important for vegetable cultivation even as early as the 16th century. Plots were improved by raising their levels with material dug out of the drainage channels. The dredged mud raised the plots, thereby securing better drainage together with improved fertility. The number and navigability of the ditches was also increased by the same process, which continued into the 20th century in response to urbanisation n the Netherlands and the growing demand for fresh vegetables.

Land use

Although farming varies from arable to pastoral (the differences in colouring on the map being borne out by comparison with differences of tone on the photograph), the dominant impression is one of intensive land use. This is understandable when the high costs of drainage and maintenance are considered. The size of the plots varies considerably; the almost minute plots of the eastern part of the Geestmerambacht Polder contrast with those in the region around Waarland in the north-east of the map area and indeed with much of the rest of Holland.

A large part of the Geestmerambacht Polder is given over to horticulture, though in contrast to the Westland district between the Hague and the New Waterway most of the cultivation is carried out on open ground rather than under glass. In the Langedijk area green vegetables and early potatoes are an important interest, as the following table shows.

Horticultural crops on the Geestmerambacht Polder: 1961
Expressed as percentages of the total horticultural area)

Parish	Green vegetables on open ground	Early potatoes	Bulbs	Onions	Remainder
Koedijk	64	29	5	1	1
Langedijk	57	32	7	3	1
St Pancras	50	36	12	1	1
Warmenhuizen	64	26	7	2	1
Polder as a whole	59	31	7	2	1

Note: The parish of St Pancras is the most southerly of the parishes. The northern part of the village is shown at 1420.)
Source for all tables: Report for the Land Development Project for Geestmerambacht, Utrecht 1964.

The farms which concentrate on horticultural work are usually small. Moreover, the farm area tends to be split into numerous small plots.

Parish	Average no of plots per farm	Average size of plot in hectares	Size of farm in hectares	Number of farms
Koedijk	7·0	0·42	0–0·5	6
Langedijk	5·5	0·42	0·5–1	23
St Pancras	4·2	0·82	1–2	161
Warmenhuizen	4·0	1·03	2–3	205
Average	5·7	0·56	3–5	187
			5–7	40 Total
			7–10	17 646
			over 10	7 farms

Farm sizes in Geestmerambacht Polder

The dominant farm size is between 1 and 5 hectares, which is not uneconomic for this type of cultivation. However, fragmentation into minute parcels of land causes difficulty. Reference to the map extract brings out very clearly the extremely small size of many of the Geestmerambacht plots compared with the more economic size of fields in the Heerhugowaard Polder which lies to the east and south.

Farms of a pastoral or arable nature producing crops such as sugar beet and wheat are much larger. In 1959 the total area occupied by the 134 farms of this type on the Geestmerambacht Polder was 1,400 hectares, which gives an average size per farm of 10·4 hectares. It is apparent from the maps that most of these farms lie in the north and west of the polder.

Much of the land west of the North Holland Canal and outside the Geestmerambacht Polder is devoted to permanent meadow or pasture. The emphasis in these areas is on dairying, with products such as cheese and butter for both home and export markets and fresh milk for nearby towns. Alkmaar, of course, is noted for its cheese market.

The only area not used for farmland lies in the south-west. Even here some return may be obtained from the pine trees, although they were originally planted with a view to stabilising the dunes.

Settlement and communications

The settlements in the area fall into two groups; those on the polders and those at the foot of the dunes. On the polder land villages are confined to higher ground along the roads which border the canals. Thus, most settlements in these areas are of a 'street-village' type, consisting of one road with little depth of housing either side. Comparison of maps and photograph will give the names of several of these linear settlements, although perhaps the most striking is Scharwoude (Nord and Zuid) which is continuous with Oudkarspel and Broek op Langedijk over a distance of more than 6 km.

On the Geestmerambacht Polder it is remarkable how dwellings are concentrated in the villages and not dispersed throughout the farmlands. The evidence of the map is confirmed by the following figures.

Population figures (1962) for the parishes of Geestmerambacht Polder

Parish	Total population	Villages	Population	% in village
Langedijk	9,278	Broek	2,500	
		Zuid Scharwoude	1,500	8,900
		Nöörd Scharwoude	3,200	
		Oudkarspel	1,700	96
St Pancras	1,728	St Pancras	1,600	93
Warmenhuizen	2,757	Warmenhuizen	2,200	80
Koedijk	2,338	Koedijk	1,100	47

The comparatively low figure of 47% for Koedijk is accounted for by the extension of the settlement alongside the road above the North Holland Canal, and by a separate nucleation south of the village of St Pancras.

BROEK OP LANGEDIJK GEESTMERAM- BACHT POLDER NORTH HOLLAND NETHERLANDS

Extract from Sheet 19 B
Alkmaar.
Dutch 1:25,000 Series.

Revised 1959.

By permission of Topografische Dienst, Delft, Netherlands.

Map 10

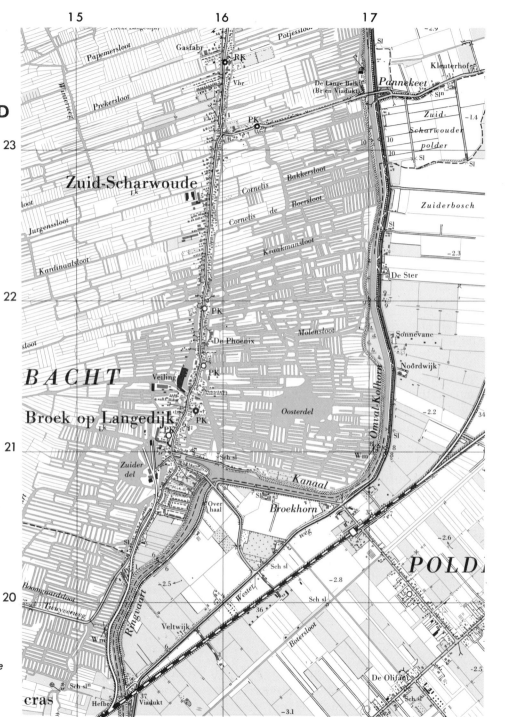

Photograph 12. Broek op Langedijk. Note the style of the houses in the village and th 'Veiling' or auction market in the foreground. Transport by boat plays an important pa in farming in this area.
KLM Aerocarto, Amsterdam.

On the higher land at the foot of the dune belt the control exerted b minor relief is not so close, and most villages, together with the town o Bergen (0820), show a less linear pattern. However, the road following th foot of the dunes from Groet (0626) is bordered by dwellings throughou most of its length. Settlement is more dispersed in this region, althoug the popular sites lie in a belt at the junction of the dunes and farmlands.

Problems of the region
The Geestmerambacht Polder is one of the economic problem areas of th Dutch polder lands. Certain points are suggested by a close study of th map and a consideration of the figures given earlier:
(a) The remarkable absence of roads in all but the most northerly parts o the Geestmerambacht Polder.
(b) The minute size of most plots of land in the area.
(c) The fragmented nature of the holdings on the Polder. As in other part

of Europe this is partly the result of the piecemeal purchase of land.

In earlier times it was of little significance if vegetable produce was conveyed by small boats and grown on very small plots. Wages were low and labour abundant for tilling the soil, transporting the produce and maintaining the intricate system of waterways. Today the position is different. With high labour costs, mechanisation becomes necessary if the farming of these areas is to be reasonably profitable. Similarly the maintenance of countless waterways and the slow and expensive transportation of produce by small boats is quite out of keeping with modern needs.

The Land Reclamation Project for Geestmerambacht Polder was published in 1964. The initial task was to lower the water table. This required the building of new and more powerful pumping stations. The main station has been constructed (1968) in the centre of the reclamation area at 126230 connected by a large open discharge with the North Holland Canal. The building of new roads has been designed to open up the area and serve the reorganised farms. Thus new dual carriageways now connect Kalverdijk with Alkmaar and Koedijk with Noord Scharwoude. Subsidiary metalled roads have been constructed to form a network at intervals of half to one kilometre. Reorganisation of farmland has been carried out west of the road from Broek op Langedijk to Noord Scharwoude. Ditches have been filled in and fields levelled. The filling material has been obtained from the subsoil, from the excavation of new major ditches and a new sand quarry at 1322. Considerable importance has been given to the achievement of a good soil profile in the new plots. A range of holdings has now been established from new dairy farms of at least 15 hectares to glasshouse units of 2 hectares, bulb farms of 5–8 hectares and vegetable farms of 8–15 hectares. The new housing has led to a more dispersed pattern of settlement and enabled many sub-standard houses to be cleared. New features of the landscape include plantations of trees, a recreation area on the site of the sand quarry and the development of certain areas, notably south east of St Pancras, as industrial centres.

Perhaps it is important to emphasise that this has been an integrated approach; only in this way can success be ensured in any regional development plan.

Exercises

1. Identify the following features shown by letters on photograph 11; (a) the water area marked A; (b) the building B; (c) the cluster of buildings at C; (d) the villages at D, E and F.

By comparing photograph 11 with the two map extracts, find (a) the direction and angle of view of the photograph; (b) the approximate observation point of the photograph.

2. Compare and contrast the landscape, land use, settlement and communication patterns of

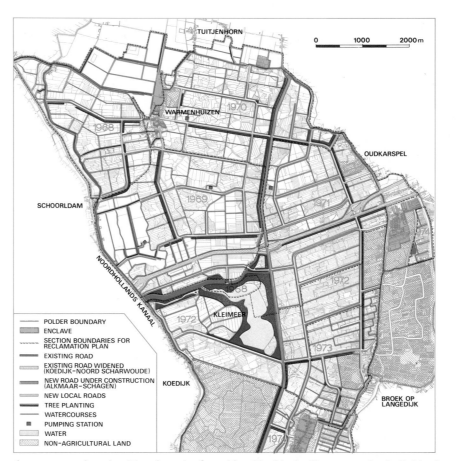

Figure 15.
The land consolidation project for Geestmerambacht Polder

POLDER BOUNDARY
ENCLAVE
SECTION BOUNDARIES FOR RECLAMATION PLAN
EXISTING ROAD
EXISTING ROAD WIDENED (KOEDIJK–NOORD SCHARWOUDE)
NEW ROAD UNDER CONSTRUCTION (ALKMAAR–SCHAGEN)
NEW LOCAL ROADS
TREE PLANTING
WATERCOURSES
PUMPING STATION
WATER
NON-AGRICULTURAL LAND

the area east of easting 15 and north of northing 26 with the Geestmerambacht Polder between the North Holland Canal and the Omval-Kolhorn Canal and south of the road from Oudkarspel to 106228.

3. What further useful information can be gained by studying the 1:25,000 map extract in addition to the 1:50,000?

4. Agricultural patterns in advanced countries are more affected by cultural, economic and political factors than by purely physical factors. Discuss.

Further reading

GRAFTDIJK, K. *Holland Rides the Sea*, World's Window Ltd, Baarn, Holland. 1964.

LAMBERT, A. 'Farm consolidation and improvement in the Netherlands', *Economic Geography* **37,** 1961.

LAMBERT, A. *The Making of the Dutch Landscape*, Seminar Press, 1971

LAWRENCE, G. R. P. *Randstad Holland*, Oxford U.P. 1973.

MONKHOUSE, F. J. *The Countries of North-western Europe*, Longmans, 1965, chapter 8.

MONKHOUSE, F. J., *A Regional Geography of Western Europe*, Longmans, 1965, chapter 3.

WAGRET, P. *Polderlands*, Methuen, 1968.

LIÈGE
BELGIUM

An Old Industrial District

Belgium produces a variety of topographical maps at scales ranging from 1:15,000 to 1:200,000. The chosen extract is from the 1:50,000 series (Type R) which is characterised by a very bold cartographic style and the inclusion of a great wealth of detail.

The position of Liège

Liège, the third city of Belgium, has a population of 440,000 and forms the centre of a conurbation with a population of over 700,000. It stands at the eastern end of the Sambre-Meuse Depression where the river Meuse is joined by the rivers Ourthe and Vesdre, which are unnamed on the map extract but enter the area from the south and south-east respectively. The Liège district forms the eastern end of the Franco-Belgian coalfield which stretches in a great crescent some 220 km long from Pas-de-Calais in France through Charleroi and Namur to the area shown on the map extract. To the north of Liège lies the more recently developed Campine (Kempen) coalfield.

The valley of the Meuse between Namur and Liège, together with that of its tributary the river Sambre, follows the axis of a synclinorium exposed by the erosion and removal of a former cover of overlying rocks. South of Namur the Meuse valley runs discordantly across a series of fold structures and has not adjusted its course to the present cover of rocks. This is usually interpreted as an example of superimposed drainage. To the south of the deeply incised Sambre-Meuse valley lies a dissected plateau known in the west as Entre-Sambre-et-Meuse and in the east as the Condroz. The map extract includes part of the northern edge of the Condroz which, on account of its similarities with the main Ardenne Plateau to the south, is known locally as the Ardenne Condrusienne.

Examination of an atlas map will reveal the importance of the position and alignment of the Sambre-Meuse Depression. The navigable river and its valley provide a natural route between two of the most densely populated and heavily industrialised regions in western Europe, namely northern France and the Ruhr, while just below Liège the Albert Canal leads from the Meuse across the Campine region to Antwerp.

Relief and drainage of the Liège district

Although very complex in detail, the area may be described in general terms as a dissected plateau cut across by the deep, steep-sided valley of the river Meuse. As T. H. Elkins remarks in describing the area, 'Everywhere the plateaux dominate, their even summits barring the horizon'. The land is highest and the plateau surface best preserved to the south of the river where resistant sandstones of Lower Devonian age outcrop at the surface. Maximum heights of over 240 metres are encountered to the south-west of Ougrée where there is a marked flattening of the hill summits. The edge of the high, heavily wooded ground between the Ourthe and Meuse is dissected by deep, narrow valleys occupied by small streams such as the Villencourt and Lize. Several of these streams are intermittent in character and none appear to reach the main river. It is impossible to say from the map evidence whether this is a result of the local geology or a lowering of the water table by excessive pumping or the diversion of the streams into underground conduits. Where the edge of the high ground is not dissected by tributary valleys the bordering slopes are extremely steep, with gradients in excess of 1 in 3 as, for example, between Ougrée and Angleur. This wooded cliff overlooking the Meuse is in fact a faultline escarpment related to the Eifel Fault which runs from the vicinity of Val-St-Lambert through the southern suburbs of Seraing and Ougrée towards Angleur.

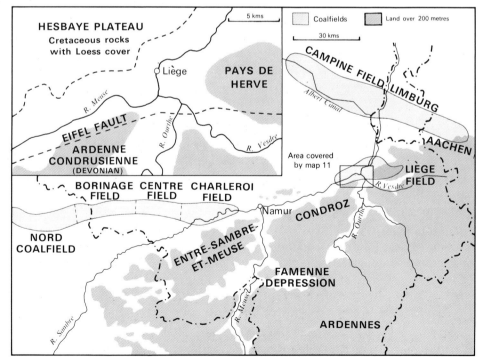

Figure 16. The coalfields of Belgium and neighbouring areas.

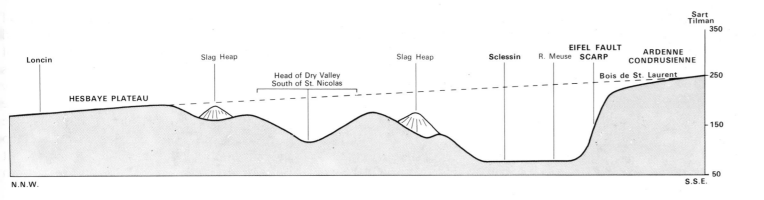

Figure 17. Section across the Meuse valley. Cross-section from Sart Tilman (South-east of Ougrée) to Loncin (North-west of Liège). Horizontal scale 1:50,000. Vertical scale 1:7,690. Notice the continuation of the surface of the Ardenne Condrusienne across the Meuse valley onto the Hesbaye Plateau which declines northwards.

The western side of the assymetrical Ourthe valley is similarly steep with cliff-like slopes where the meanders abut the valley sides. The relief of the area to the east of the Ourthe is less striking and rises more gently to heights of over 200 metres. This is the edge of the Pays de Herve, another plateau surface with dry valleys and intermittent streams.

To the north of the river Meuse the ground again rises steeply on to the Hesbaye Plateau, a dissected surface of Cretaceous rocks with a loess cover. Reference to photograph 13 shows that apart from the various slag heaps the skyline of this area is strikingly flat and even. The highest ground here is found in the vicinity of Montegnée where heights of over 190 metres are reached. A large branching valley runs from Hollogne-aux-Pierres to join the main valley at Jemeppe, while similar dry valleys penetrate the high ground from Tilleur and Liège. As is true of the map area as a whole, the district north of the Meuse is characterised by a general lack of surface drainage. Several wells are shown in the extreme north of the area and the large number of water towers indicates the need for storage of water to meet the needs of the large urban population.

The river Meuse meanders across the area in a deep, trench-like valley and has incised itself some 140 metres below the bordering uplands. The river is not shown to cross any contours on the map and it may therefore be deduced that its fall is very slight. The valley floor varies considerably in width but is very flat, and stands at a height of just under 80 metres. Liège and Seraing both stand at points where the valley floor is wider than elsewhere, and where, in the case of Liège, there is a notable embayment of low ground on the north bank of the river. Photograph 13, which is taken from the slopes above Ougrée, shows the flat ground bordering the river in the vicinity of Sclessin.

Mining and industry

Although the key for the Belgium 1:50,000 map series gives the abbreviation 'Charb' (Charbonnage) for coalmines, this does not appear on the map extract, and one must rely on the distribution of spoil heaps which are marked by hachures to obtain a picture of the location of coal-mining activity. Of course the number of such slag heaps may not correlate exactly with the actual number of collieries, since a single colliery may dispose of waste material at more than one point, and there is no means of determining how many of these spoil banks, the product of more than 160 years large scale commercial exploitation of the coal, are related to disused mines. For example, between 1965 and 1977 the number of working pits on the Sambre-Meuse coalfields fell from 47 to 5. However, it is clear that the coalfield occupies a much broader belt of ground on the northern side of the river than on the southern side. Over 30 slag heaps are shown on the Hesbaye Plateau compared with only about 7 to the south. The southern limit of mining is determined by the Eifel Fault which marks the junction between the Lower Devonian rocks of the Ardenne Condrusienne and the coal measures to the north (fig. 16).

As in other coalfield districts of the Sambre-Meuse Depression, mining in the Liège area is both difficult and expensive on account of the arrangement of the coal seams. The coal measures, lying along the margin of the Ardennes, were greatly affected by the Hercynian orogeny and are intensively folded and faulted. F. J. Monkhouse quotes an example near Mons where, as a result of faulting and overthrusting 'a single shaft 340 metres in depth passes through the same seam six times'. Furthermore the most easily mined seams have long been worked out. The Liège coalfield in fact has the lowest productivity of all the Belgian coalfields, and compares unfavourably with

LIÈGE
BELGIUM

Published 1963.
Map revised from aerial
photographs 1947. Last
complete field revision
1931-35. Rapid field
revision 1953. Roads
up-to-date 1963.
Vertical interval of contours
10 metres.

*Extract from the 1:50,000 R map
of Belgium. Liège sheet.*

Map 11

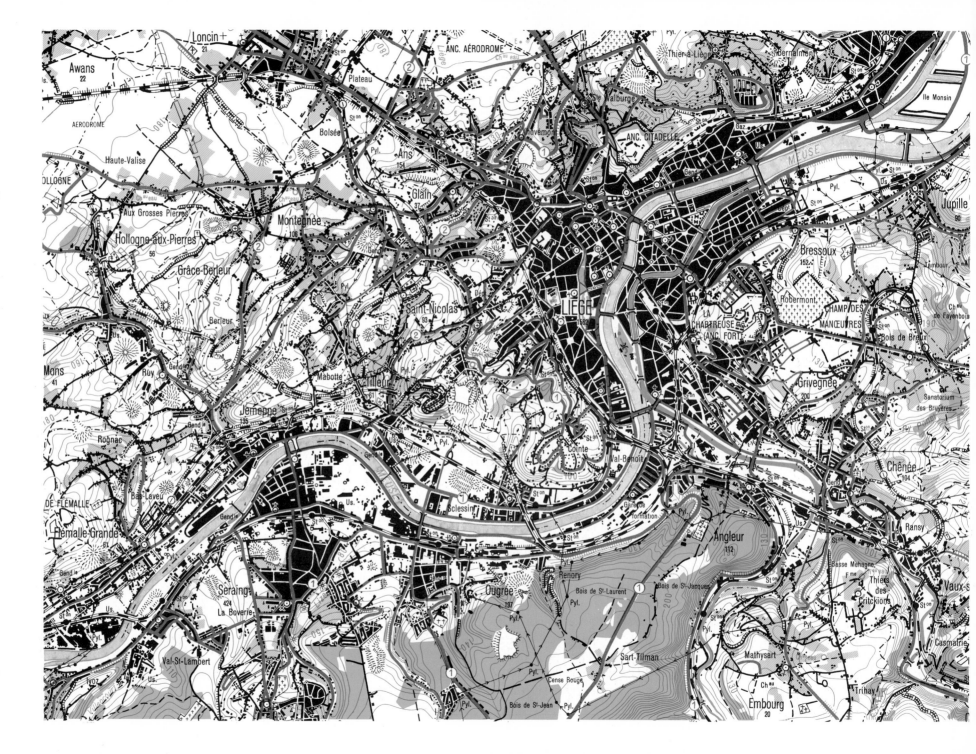

Photograph 13. The Meuse valley. View looking north-west across the Meuse valley from the slopes above Ougrée. Notice the crowding of factories and obsolete 19th century housing on the flat valley floor. In the distance is the edge of the Hesbaye Plateau with the tip-heaps from numerous collieries.

Cliché C.G.T.

the Campine coalfield to the north (see Exercise 6).

'Viewed against the wider European background, the position is more serious still. Belgium as a whole, even including the Campine, is, with its high wages and social security costs, a high cost producer, with a productivity per worker well below that of its neighbours in the European Coal and Steel Community. There is no doubt that in so far as the prosperity of Liège rests upon local coal it has an insecure foundation, and the difficulties of the industry will inevitably increase as the liberalizing measures of the Community expose it to foreign competition' (T. H. Elkins).

Fortunately the economy of Liège relies more today upon manufacturing than extractive industry. In 1977, 97,640 workers in the Liège district were employed in engineering and metal working trades compared with 5,300 in mining. However, interpretation of the industrial geography of the Liège district from the map extract is very difficult. Large industrial premises are shown in the same manner as a street block in a densely built-up area, and little or no information is given about the type of industry present. Where symbols are used to denote particular industrial premises they are largely irrelevant to the contemporary industrial scene; thus the map provides a conventional sign for water mills, as along the Lize and Villencourt valleys, but has no special symbol to denote the huge complex of iron and steel works that lie along the Meuse at Seraing and Ougrée. The abbreviation 'Us' (Usine) is shown in the key to indicate factory premises, but only a random selection appears to have been given this notation. A further guide to the industrial distribution in the area is provided by the small unshaded circles on the map, which denote large factory chimneys.

Industry in the Liège district is dominated by metal working, which was originally based on local iron ore, charcoal from the Condroz and water power from streams such as the Lize and Villencourt which join the Meuse from the bordering plateaux. At the present time the industry relies on coking coal from the Campine and Ruhr and imports of iron ore from Sweden, Luxembourg, France, Liberia, Mauritania, Brazil, etc. The origins of the modern, large-scale organisation of the iron and steel industry in the area date back to 1823, when the first Belgian blast furnace to use coke was established at Seraing by an English mechanic, John Cockerill. The industry is still centred at Seraing, and coking plants, blast furnaces, steel works and rolling mills all occupy the valley floor in the great bend of the Meuse at this point. Chemical works, using the by-products of the coking process, power stations and collieries also compete for the limited space along the banks of the waterway. At present most of the steel is produced by a small number of large integrated works. Two of the largest firms in the

Liège district, 'S. A. John Cockerill' and 'S. A. Ougrée-Marinaye' merged in 1955 to form an enormous combine 'S. A. Cockerill-Ougrée', producing about a third of Belgium's annual output of steel. Also occupying premises on both banks of the river at Jemeppe and Seraing is another of the largest iron and steel concerns in Belgium, 'S. A. Métallurgique d'Espérance-Longdoz'. These foundries and works extend east from Seraing along both banks of the river through Ougrée and Sclessin to the southern districts of Liège. Engineering industries are found in the eastern suburbs, but the main function of the city is in the organisation of commerce rather than actual industrial production. Two other important industries in the area covered by the map extract are zinc smelting, along the Ourthe and Vesdre valleys, and the manufacture of plate glass at Val-St-Lambert in the south-west.

Settlement and communications

Probably the most striking feature about the map extract is the intensive spread of settlement and the close network of communications over almost the whole area. In addition to the main urban centres, where a 'completely built up area' is indicated by solid black shading, there are extensive districts where the amount and intensity of building is lesser only in degree. In fact a whole range of settlement types may be noted. Liège stands alone in size and importance, the next largest towns being far smaller; namely Seraing, Grivegnée and Bressoux which are really suburbs of Liège, Ougrée, Jemeppe and Angleur. On the Hesbaye Plateau a number of even smaller nucleated settlements may be noted, including Montegnée, Tilleur and Loncin. The figure alongside the various town names on the map is the 1954 population total in hundreds. All of these towns have grown considerably in size and population since that date. In addition to the nucleated settlements which are linked by ribbon development along the main roads, there are many districts where a more dispersed pattern of settlement is evident, as for example in the area around St Nicholas west of Liège. Many of these areas are probably housing districts similar to the cités ouvrières of northern France. In other instances the map gives a suggestion of the incorporation of former villages into the general urban sprawl. In this district, as in many parts of Belgium, the distinction between urban and rural settlement is difficult to define. The general impression is one of unplanned, piecemeal development of housing associated with the local mining and industry. The lack of planning is particularly evident on the valley floor where residential areas lie interspersed with industrial premises.

Liège, of course, represents a different type of urban development. The original site of the city lay on the left bank slopes overlooking the flat valley floor. The Meuse formerly had a braided channel at this point, and the medieval expansion led to the occupance of a series of small islands between the various river channels. During the 18th and 19th centuries many of these shallow channels were infilled to form a number of wide boulevards through the central city. For example, the former Sauvenière meander of the river, enclosing the 'Quartier de l'Île', now forms a wide boulevard flanked by open spaces. The line of this route through the city centre on the left bank of the river is evident from the map, but a larger scale is required to reveal other correlations between the present street plan and the former channels of the river. At the present time Liège may be described as a compact settlement, confined by its valley site and with only limited extensions on to bordering plateaux.

Reference has been made to the position of Liège which occupies an important nodal position in the communications system of western Europe. On the map extract the broad pattern of valley and plateau routes which intersect in the area is obscured by the complexity and intensity of the local communications. Minor relief features, particularly the dry valleys, appear to exercise considerable control over the local road and rail pattern. Certain of the roads out of Liège are followed by tramways which suggest commuting from the outlying centres. The Albert Canal, which was opened in 1940, can be seen to branch off from the Meuse just below Liège. This allows vessels of up to 2,000 tonnes to reach the small port of Ile Monsin, but above Liège navigation is limited to vessels of a maximum of 600 tonnes capacity.

The Liège district presents the characteristic appearance and typical problems of 'old-established' areas of heavy industry on the coalfields of Europe. The industry of the area is an example of geographical inertia and is, in many respects, ill adapted to modern conditions and finds difficulty in competing with more recently established industries elsewhere. The obsolete nature of much of the building on the valley floor is apparent from the photograph. 'It is obvious that much of the southern coalfield is an *old* industrial area from its appearance. Derelict collieries, overgrown spoil banks, a chaos of pit-shafts, blast-furnaces and steel-works, chemical factories, long rows of small, drab, gardenless dwellings built in irregular rows – all these are typical of the crowded and haphazard industrial development of the 19th century' (F. J. Monkhouse). In the case of Liège active policies of urban renewal, industrial relocation and motorway building have done much to alleviate these problems, although these recent changes are not evident from either the map or photograph.

Exercises

1. Calculate the vertical exaggeration of the section included in the text. Draw a similar cross section from Sart Tilman to Jupille (east of Liège) to show the Ourthe valley and the edge of the Pays de Herve. Label the features crossed by your section line.

2. Using the population totals given on the map extract, construct a map to show the distribution of population in the area by means of proportionate circles. Comment on the inadequacies of such a method as a means of showing population distribution in this particular area. Suggest a classification of the various types of built-up area shown on the map.

3. The following terms appear in the text. Attempt a precise definition of their meaning.

(a) Fault line scarp   *(d)* Hercynian orogeny
(b) Loess   *(e)* Braided channel
(c) Superimposed drainage   *(f)* Geographical inertia.

4. Many of the most important cities in Europe lie at the foot of the Hercynian Foreland. Why should this be so?

5. With the aid of a sketch map, describe and explain the pattern of rail communications in the area covered by the map.

6. Attempt an explanation of the following figures:

Coal output per man/hour underground 1977 (kg)

West Germany	Ruhr	10,043	*Belgium*	Campine	5,141
	Saar	6,274		Sambre-Meuse	693
	Lower Saxony	4,187			
	Aachen	7,375	*U.K.*	Yorkshire	2,033
				North-East	1,813
France	Nord	2,876		North-West	1,915
	Lorraine	8,561		Midlands & Kent	2,790
	Centre-Midi	1,798		South Wales	876
				Scotland	1,945
Netherlands	Limburg	5,260			

Source: Statistical Office, European Communities, 1978.

7. On a base map, showing the main rivers and land over 100 metres, attempt to plot the distribution of industry and mining in the Liège district. Comment on the factors which determine this distribution pattern.

Further reading

CLOUT, H. D. *The Franco-Belgian Border Region*, Oxford U.P., 1975.

DICKINSON, R. E. *The West European City: A Geographical Interpretation*, 2nd edn, Routledge and Kegan Paul, 1961.

ELKINS, T. H. 'Liège and the problems of southern Belgium', *Geography*, **41**, 1956.

MERENNE-SCHOUMAKER, B. 'L'évolution économique de la province de Liège depuis 1960', *Traveaux Géographique de Liège*, **159**, 1972.

MERENNE-SCHOUMAKER, B. 'La région Liégeoise', *Traveaux Géographique de Liège*, **160**, 1973.

MINGRET, P. 'Quelques Problèmes de l'Europe; à travers l'example de Liège et de sa règion', *Revue Géographique de Lyon*, **37**, 1962.

MONKHOUSE, F. J. *A Regional Geography of Western Europe*, Longmans, 1965, chapters 8 and 18.

PATERSON, J. H. 'The population of the Ardennes. Present trends and future prospects', *Geography*, **50**, 1965.

RILEY R. C. and ASHWORTH, G. J. *Benelux: An Economic Geography of Belgium, the Netherlands and Luxembourg*, Chatto and Windus, 1975.

RILEY, R. C. *Belgium. Studies in Industrial Geography*, Hutchinson, 1978.

Study 11
KAUB
RHINELAND-
PFALZ
WEST GERMANY

A Section of the Rhine Gorge.

Extract from Sheet L.5912.
Kaub.
West German 1:50,000
Series.

Published 1960.
Vertical interval of
contours 10 metres
(Form lines at 5 metres and
2.5 metre intervals on
gentle slopes.)

*By permission of Landesvermes-
sungsamt Rheinland-Pfalz.*

Map 12

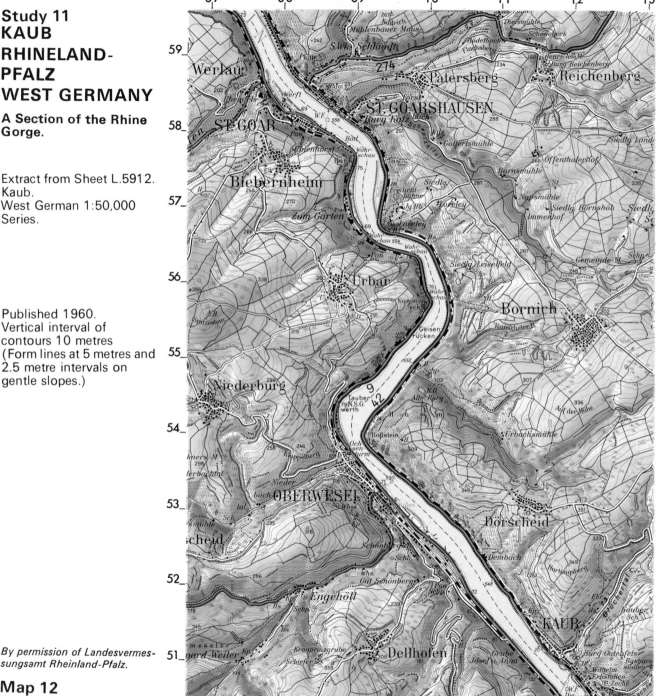

Relief

The map extract shows part of the southern end of the Rhine gorge between Bingen and Koblenz. The hill summits away from the river are rather flat and usually at heights of between 330 and 390 metres. This observation is confirmed by the photograph, where the uniformity of the even skyline is quite remarkable. Several deep and steep-sided valleys are cut into this plateau. These generally follow north-east to south-west courses, but sections at right angles to this direction are occasionally found. The course of the Urbach (1053) illustrates this point. The Rhine flows in a general south-east to north-west direction and occupies a valley which is notable for the steepness of its sides. Slopes of 1 in 1 (45°) may be calculated and confirmed on the photograph. However, the gradient of the river itself is comparatively slight. Spot heights are marked along the road on the west bank and, although one cannot be certain of the height of the road above the river, it is clear that the Rhine falls by no more than 3 metres in the 8 km from just below Kaub to St Goar, a gradient of 1 in 2666. This order of gradient is usually associated with rivers with wide floodplains, yet there is little evidence of floodplain development. Indeed, settlements are narrow and elongated, and there is often little space for the road and railway.

Reference to fig. 18 will show the abnormal character of the Rhine valley. Above Mainz, the river occupies a wide and flat valley. After a short east-north-east to west-south-west section below Mainz, it turns north-west and cuts through the Rhine Highlands in a narrow steep-sided gorge, part of which is represented in the extract. Near Bonn, the river leaves this gorge and enters another section with a wide floodplain.

The Rhine Highlands consist of the Eifel, Westerwald, Taunus and Hunsrück Uplands, and are the product of the Hercynian mountain building period. Far older than the Alps, these uplands have undergone considerable periods of erosion in the 320 million years of their history. The flat plateau tops on the extract represent a peneplain surface formed at an earlier stage of the river's history. It is thought that as this peneplain was uplifted to its present height, the river managed to cut down at a similar rate and so preserve its northward course. Thus the Rhine today flows from a plain, through a gorge, and beyond to a second plain section.

The steep-sided tributary valleys are also a consequence of incision by the Rhine. As the Rhine eroded its valley, so the tributary streams which find their base levels in the main stream also cut into the peneplain. Near the Rhine the processes of vertical corrasion have produced valleys with extremely steep sides, but further upstream the downcutting has not proceeded so far, and valley sides are more gentle. The steep gradients in the

Photograph 14. The Rhine Gorge and the Loreley.

German Tourist Information Bureau, London.

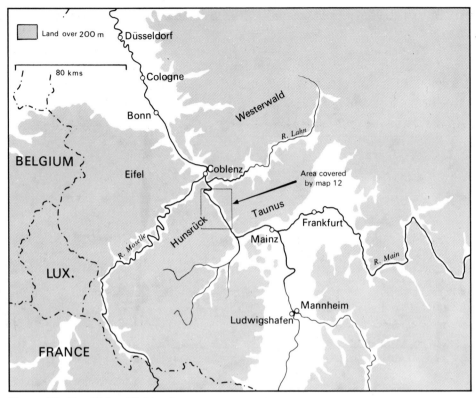

Figure 18. The Rhine Highlands.

suitable for arable farming.

The other major form of land use in the area is the growing of vines. A study of map and photograph indicates that the gradient and aspect of slopes are of considerable importance in this respect. In practically every case, vines are to be found on south, south-west, or occasionally south-east facing slopes, a particularly fine example being along the north side of the Oberbach valley in its course west of Oberwesel. Frequently these slopes reach gradients of 1 in 1, and the symbol for a bank or wall shows the necessity for terracing to hold the earth in place. Nevertheless, the advantage of the increased isolation which is necessary for the vine at 50° North more than compensates for the difficulty of working on such steep slopes.

Settlement and communications

Four villages lie along this section of the Rhine. In all cases, lack of flat land near the river has caused these settlements to assume a linear form. They are all located near to the point at which a tributary valley joins the Rhine, and usually the village has extended a short distance up the tributary valley. Settlements away from the Rhine show a complete contrast. The tributary valleys, at least in their lower parts, are far too narrow to allow space for villages. Settlements are therefore found on the plateau, and since relief is not such a controlling factor as along the banks of the Rhine, they tend to adopt a more compact shape. The dominance of the strongly nucleated form should be noted here. Study of the map extract shows remarkably few farms outside the villages. In the north-east a few hamlets and single buildings, prefixed by the word 'Siedlung' (Settlement), lie away from the villages. These isolated settlements are of recent origin, and were generally established after 1945 as a result of the influx of refugees from East Germany. High above the Rhine, and occasionally in tributary valleys, names with the suffix or prefix 'Burg' are frequently seen. These are related to defensive positions and their associated castles. In earlier times the Rhine traffic was controlled by these fortresses and tolls exacted. Today they provide an attraction for tourists.

Both map and photograph indicate the importance of the Rhine as a routeway. The valley is served by two railways and two main roads, while the river obviously carries a great amount of barge traffic. It seems unlikely that such traffic is occasioned by the villages on the map extract, which show no evidence of industrial premises of any magnitude. The harbours at Oberwesel, south of St Goarshausen, and at St Goar show little, if any, development of buildings or premises. In fact these harbours serve as refuges for barges in times of flood. The Rhine is a routeway through the highland

lower tributary valleys (Schweizertal 1 in 25) seem to have encouraged the establishment of mills although the narrowness of the valley floors precludes much settlement.

Land use

The West German 1:50,000 map series does not give the degree of detail of land use which is to be found on the corresponding Dutch sheets (see Study 9). However, certain broad distinctions can be made between various areas on the map extract. The flat tops of the plateau appear to be divided between farmland and woodland. From the close network of roads it seems clear that the non-wooded land is used for farming. Although the map does not distinguish between arable land and pasture, the photograph (top right) suggests that pasture is more common than plough. Hower, reference to *Germany* by R. E. Dickinson (map, p. 430) shows that on either side of the Rhine there are stretches of the lower part of the plateau which are covered with loess. This is of relatively recent origin, and produces a loamy soil barrier between the industrialised regions on either side, the Ruhr and Cologne areas to the north and the cities of the Rhine Rift Valley (such as Karlsruhe, Mainz, Ludwigshafen and Mannheim) to the south. An indication of its significance and of the type of traffic can be seen in the following figures.

Goods traffic on the Rhine in Rhineland-Pfalz 1976
(Rolandswerth in the north to Lingenfeld in the south)

Number of vessels	Total goods (1000 tonnes)	Outgoing	Incoming
52,293	34,059	15,278	18,781

Goods	Despatched (1000 tonnes)	Incoming (1000 tonnes)
Plant and animal products	438·7	1,316·1
Cement and building materials	675·4	255·8
Stone, gravel, sand, chalk etc	9,551·9	6,941·1
Ore and scrap metal	112·2	437·0
Coal and coke	201·9	1,753·8
Oil and products	1,817·9	5,149·7
Chemical products	1,314·5	1,869·0
Fertilisers	441·6	554·7
Iron and steel	647·0	422·5

Source: *Statistische Berichte*, Rheinland-Pfalz. 1977

Away from the Rhine, communications appear to be more difficult. There are no railways, but three 'A' class roads follow the narrow floors of tributary valleys. These ignore the considerable settlement on the plateau and appear to be part of the national road network. The plateau surface supports a dense network of local roads. These are often unmetalled, and mostly of a very minor character. Their purpose is a purely local one, serving land which is mainly under farm or wood. Connections between the plateau and the valley floor present difficulties. Most of these roads have a winding or zigzag section where they leave the Rhine or tributary valleys and ascend to the plateau.

Occupations

Map evidence for occupations is slender. The villages appear to be mainly concerned with agriculture and possibly forestry, although this latter occupation is likely to employ only small numbers. (Note the sawmill in the Hasenbachtal north of St Goarshausen.)

Along the Rhine there is some evidence of a tourist industry. The youth hostel near the Loreley, the camping-place south of St Goar and the many castles suggest a region that makes at least a part of its living from holiday-makers. Extractive industry is represented by a mine in the Volkenbachtal near Kaub, though there is no indication of the product. There is little evidence of processing and manufacturing industry, with the exception of one factory in the Bruchertal about 1 km from Kaub and the widespread

milling industry. Mills appear to be the only buildings sited on the floors of some of the valleys. In the Forstbachtal, for example, four mills are to be found in a section of five km. One must beware of assuming these are working today. As in Britain, the once widespread milling industry has been largely concentrated in a smaller number of larger premises, and no longer relies on water power.

Village	Population at 31.12.76	Village	Population at 31.12.76	Village	Population at 31.12.76
Bornich	1,002	Patersberg	504	Niederburg	697
Dörscheid	353	Reichenberg	242	St Goar (inc.	
Kaub	1,517	Sankt Goarshausen	1,844	Biebernheim and Urbar)	3,502
				Oberwesel (inc. Dellhofen)	4,598

Source: Industrie-und Handelskammer zu Koblenz. 1977.

The importance of the Rhine valley and its routeway is evident from these figures. Only Bornich of all the plateau villages reaches a population of 1,000.

The Kaub extract illustrates the geography of two worlds. The Rhine, with its barges carrying coal and oil, its railways and roads, its tourists and prosperous vineyards is very much a part of the busy commercial world of north-west Europe. A short distance away lies the contrasting world of the Taunus and Hunsrück Uplands, with life concentrated in quiet villages and concerned with farms and woods. The contrast is a consequence of isolation, an isolation brought about by the physical history of the region.

Exercises

1. The photograph is of the Loreley rock 2 kilometres south of St Goar. From which point is the photograph taken? Identify the features marked A–G on the photograph.
2. With the aid of sketch maps analyse the sites of the following villages: Bornich, Reichenberg, Oberwesel.
3. What conditions encourage the development of *(a)* strongly nucleated, and *(b)* dispersed forms of settlement?
4. How do you account for the rectilinear pattern of drainage shown on the map extract?
5. Attempt to relate the figures for goods received and exported by water from Rheinland-Pfalz to the location and types of industry found in the Land (province).
6. How far is it true to say that the Hercynian Uplands of Western Europe are repellent to cultivation and settlement?
7. Analyse the conditions under which the vine is cultivated in western Europe. Why are conditions so diverse? How is it possible for viticulture to survive in the more marginal areas?

Further reading

DICKINSON, R. E. *Germany. A General and Regional Geography*, Methuen 1961, chapter 17.
ELKINS, T. H. *Germany*, 3rd edn, Chatto & Windus, 1973, chapter 14.
FEBVRE, L. and DEMANGEON, A. *Le Rhin*, Strasbourg, 1931.
MUTTON, A., *Central Europe*, Longmans, 1968, chapter 14.
YATES, E. M. 'The Development of the Rhine' *Trans. I.B.G.*, June, 1963.

Study 12
WOLFSBURG
NIEDERSACHSEN
WEST GERMANY

An Area of Recent Industrial Development.

Extract from Sheet L.3530 Wolfsburg.
West German 1:50,000 Series.

Published 1960.
Vertical interval of contours 10 metres.
(Form lines at 5 metre and 2.5 metre intervals on gentle slopes.)

Map 13

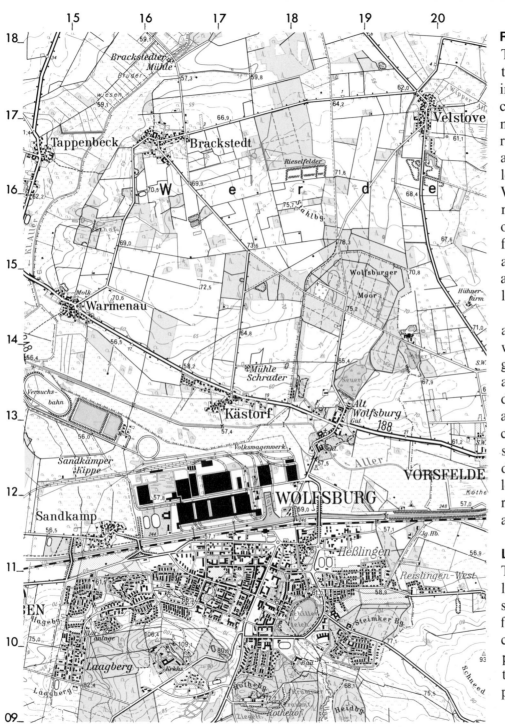

Relief

The location map, fig. 19, shows that the map extract covers a small part of the North German Plain. The landscape can be divided into three contrasting units. To the north and south lie two upland areas, while across the centre of the map runs the lowland of the Aller with an extension to the north-west along its tributary the Kleine Aller. The greatest elevations are reached in the south, where spot heights of 106·4 metres and 109·1 metres are shown near the hospital (*Krkhs* 1609). The northern upland is generally lower, usually about 65 to 70 metres, but with a maximum of 80 metres on Wolfsburger Moor (1814). Summits are rather flat, but cut into them are a number of valleys. Some of these carry streams, others are dry, notably the one lying north of Kastorf (1613). Occasionally hollows with no outlet are found; such a depression is shown by Hühner Farm at 2014. The lowland areas of the Aller and Kleine Aller valleys lie between 56 and 60 metres above sea level. These are flat and many drainage ditches have been cut to lead excess water into the straightened rivers.

The origin of this landscape lies in the Quaternary glaciation. The uplands are composed of sands and gravels known as geest. The valley of the Aller was once a glacial meltwater channel. In fact, a hint of this is given by the great width of the valley compared with the rather small river which flows along it. This part of the North German Plain was not covered with ice during the last onset of the Scandinavian ice sheets (the Weichsel glaciation) although melt-water from this stage affected the region considerably by cutting great channels, or '*urstromtäler*' from the east to the North Sea. The sands and gravels were laid down in earlier advances of the ice, particularly during the Saale glaciation. Thus erosion has been at work for a relatively long period and many of the irregularities left after deposition have been removed. Areas of bog are also to be found among the geest deposits; note the area east of Velstove (2016).

Land use

The contrasts between uplands and lowlands are reflected in the pattern of land use. Although few symbols for types of cultivation are used on this series, the density of roads suggests that much of the upland country is farmland. In addition, there are large areas of woodland, much of it of the coniferous type which might be expected on sandy or gravelly soils. The photograph confirms these conclusions. The figures overleaf (1971) show the land use situation in the parishes of the extract, though unfortunately parish boundaries are not shown on this map.

Permanent grassland accounts for roughly one third of the farmland

Photograph 15. The Volks-
wagen plant at Wolfsburg.

V.W. Press Information, London.

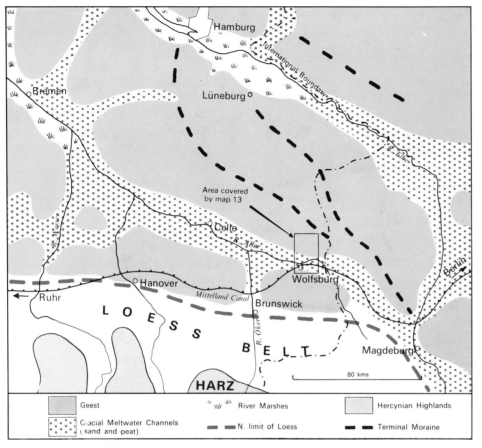

Figure 19. Part of the North German plain.

Map legend:
- Geest
- Glacial Meltwater Channels (sand and peat)
- River Marshes
- N. limit of Loess
- Hercynian Highlands
- Terminal Moraine

This consists of two types, meadow and heathland. The meadow lands lie mainly along the drained valley floors while the heathland is to be found on the geest plateau. The percentage of woodland varies widely, from

	Total land area in farms or forestry concerns in hectares	Agric. land %	Arable as % of agric.	Permt. grass as % of arable	Cereals as % of arable	Hoed crops i.e. sugar beet, potatoes, turnips as % of arable
Tappenbeck	522	84	72	28	70	28
Brackstedt	619	84	68	30	62	29
Warmenau	499	87	68	32	69	30
Kastorf	1,351	67	57	43	67	27
Velstove	740	89	64	36	70	29
Sandkamp	170	94	60	39	71	26

Source: Niedersächsisches Landesverwaltungsamt Statistik, 1971.

50% in Wolfsburg to less than 10% in Velstove and Sandkamp. The distribution of woodland seems to bear little relation to relief. Certainly the steeper slopes on Wolfsburger Moor are under woodland, but so also are large level stretches east of Brackstedt. It is likely that the soil factor is of the greater importance here; the poorer sands and gravels being left to woodland while the more fertile soils are cultivated. A surprisingly large proportion of the agricultural land is under the plough, always over 55% and around Tappenbeck 72%. By far the most important crops are cereals, mainly rye and oats, and the balance is largely given over to root crops such as potatoes. Much of this land was originally of poor quality, in contrast to the fertility of the Börde country to the south. The modern pattern of cultivation is a result of clearance of heath and forest, and painstaking effort to improve the quality of largely podsolised soils with fertiliser.

The size of farms shows a wide range from less than two hectares to over fifty hectares. The following is a breakdown of the 159 farm units in the parishes of the extract:

	Area of farms (in hectares)							
	Under 2	2–5	5–10	10–15	15–20	20–30	30–50	Over 50
No. of farms	27	17	29	14	12	17	31	12

The majority of farm units are either very small or of moderate size, but unfortunately there is no evidence to suggest how these farms are distributed or the reasons for this variation. Considering the quality of the land it is doubtful whether the smallest holdings provide an adequate livelihood for a family.

Settlements

Settlement is very largely of a nucleated type; most people live in the villages or in Wolfsburg, few live in isolated farms. The sites of the villages are very similar; all of them are above the floodplains, none of them lies on the highest parts of the uplands. The heights of the villages vary between 57·5 metres (Sandkamp) and 67·5 metres (Brackstedt). All are therefore out of reach of floods, though presumably not far above the water table. The form of the villages is usually compact, though there is some extension along roads, notably in Kastorf which assumes the shape of a street village. Alt Wolfsburg seems to have grown up around a manor house *(Gut)* and castle *(Schloss)*. However, the photograph suggests that much new development has taken place around Alt Wolfsburg since the map was published. The form of Wolfsburg suggests a town of modern growth which has expanded in an east-west direction confined by the line of the Mittelland canal to the north and by steep wooded slopes to the south. The town gives an impresion of a 'garden city' with its frequent open spaces. A notable feature is the number of large apartment blocks; both photograph and map show many of these, often arranged *en echelon*.

Occupations

Apart from the huge factory blocks of the Volkswagenwerk there is little direct evidence of occupations on the map. One may assume that most villages are concerned with agriculture, though the farm size figures suggest the possibility of labour surplus to farming requirements. Reference to the figures in Exercise 2 will show that Wolfsburg has a very large proportion of its workers in manufacturing industry (69%), the next most important categories being service occupations (over one fifth) and trade (over one tenth). The domination of the town by the Volkswagen (VW) factory is obvious, and several of the advantages of this location may be deduced.

Since the car industry is of recent growth, and space in the older industrial areas hard to find, the attraction of the flat floor of the Aller Valley must have been strong. Today, over two square miles are occupied by the VW plant and expansion appears to present few difficulties. Large areas are necessary not only for assembly lines, offices and power station, but also for the storage of completed vehicles awaiting export. North-west of the works lies a two kilometre long oval test track *(Versuchsbahn)* and adjoining it a large reservoir. The purpose of the latter is not clear; it may be related to the water requirements of the factory, to the needs of the town or even to the maintenance of water levels in the canal.

Communications are a second factor. The impressive network of railway lines within the works is linked in Fallersleben (1 km to the west) with the main line which runs east-west along the banks of the canal. Most raw materials, except for coal and oil, are handled by the railway, road transport being of far less importance. Ingots for the foundry, sheet metal, strip steel, castings, fabrics and upholstery, paints, lubricants and chemicals are brought to the works from suppliers in the Ruhr and Rhineland and from elsewhere within the Common Market. In return parts and vehicles are carried each day to other VW factories and worldwide markets. The daily turnover of railway trucks is about 1,500 including two-tiered and container wagons.

The Mittelland canal is also of advantage in this location, providing a link with the coal-producing Ruhr and the seaports of Rotterdam, Bremen and Emden. To the east it is linked with the River Elbe and Berlin, a connection of little value in the present political situation. For the VW works the canal provides cheap transport for bulk cargoes of oil, coke and coal. The photograph and map stress the significance of the canal with the power station and oil storage tanks lying next to the harbour.

A third factor in the growth of the works has been the supply of labour. The occupation tables in Exercise 2 for the surrounding villages and for Wolfsburg itself emphasize the importance of the factory. In fact about half of the employees commute daily from villages and towns up to a distance of 60 km. Being close to the East German frontier (7 km to the east), the VW works also benefited from the post-war influx of refugees. Another large group in the 50,794 employees consists of foreign workers. In July 1977 there were almost 4,000 of these (7·8% of the total labour force), the largest element being Italian. Most return home after a few years in Wolfsburg.

The 'garden city' appearance of Wolfsburg and the spaciousness of the factory site emphasize the advantages which modern industry has over the older sites usually so closely linked with coalfields (see Studies 10 and 14).

Exercises

1. Wolfsburg lies far from the sources of its raw materials and power. How then is the Volkswagen able to compete so effectively in world markets?
2. The following figures show the occupation structure (1970) of the settlements on the extract:

Settlement	Pop.	Working pop.	Farming forestry	Power and water supplies	Manuf. indust.	Building	Retail and whole-sale trade	Services and miscell.
Wolfsburg	88,655	42,783	156	304	29,432	1,396	3,674	7,821
Sandkamp	811	376	20	2	234	35	24	61
Tappenbeck	716	295	31	1	198	14	19	32
Brackstedt	399	193	48	—	97	9	12	27
Kastorf	1,780	602	72	4	196	42	47	241
Velstove	637	312	61	—	167	24	19	41
Warmenau	342	161	45	—	53	5	17	41

Source: Niedersächsisches Landesverwaltungsamt Statistik.

Draw a sketch map of the area plotting communications and the 60-metre contour. Draw circles to represent each village proportionate in size to the working population. Divide the circles into segments to represent: *(a)* farming and forestry; *(b)* manufacturing industries; *(c)* other occupations. Comment on your resulting map.
3. Identify the view from the map. What developments have taken place since the map was published?
4. Explain the meaning of the terms: podsol, urstromtäler, geest, terminal moraine.
5. Why build large apartment blocks in a district with an apparent abundance of building sites?
6. Compare and contrast the value of inland waterways in Germany with those of Britain.
7. Under what conditions are marshes or bogs formed?

Further reading

DICKINSON, R. E. *Germany, A General and Regional Geography*, Methuen, 1961, chapter 19.
ELKINS, T. H. *Germany*, 3rd edn, Chatto & Windus, 1973, chapters 2, 3 and 16.
ESTALL, R. C. and BUCHANAN, R. O. *Industrial Activity and Economic Geography*, 4th edn, Hutchinson, 1980.
SHACKLETON, M. R. *Europe*, 7th edn, Longmans, 1965, chapter 19.

Study 13
GROSS ILSEDE
NIEDERSACHSEN
WEST GERMANY

A section of the
West German Börde

Extract from Sheet L 3726.
Peine.
West German 1:50,000
Series.

Published 1958.
Vertical Interval of
Contours 10 metres. Form
lines at 2.5 and 5 metres
on gentle slopes.

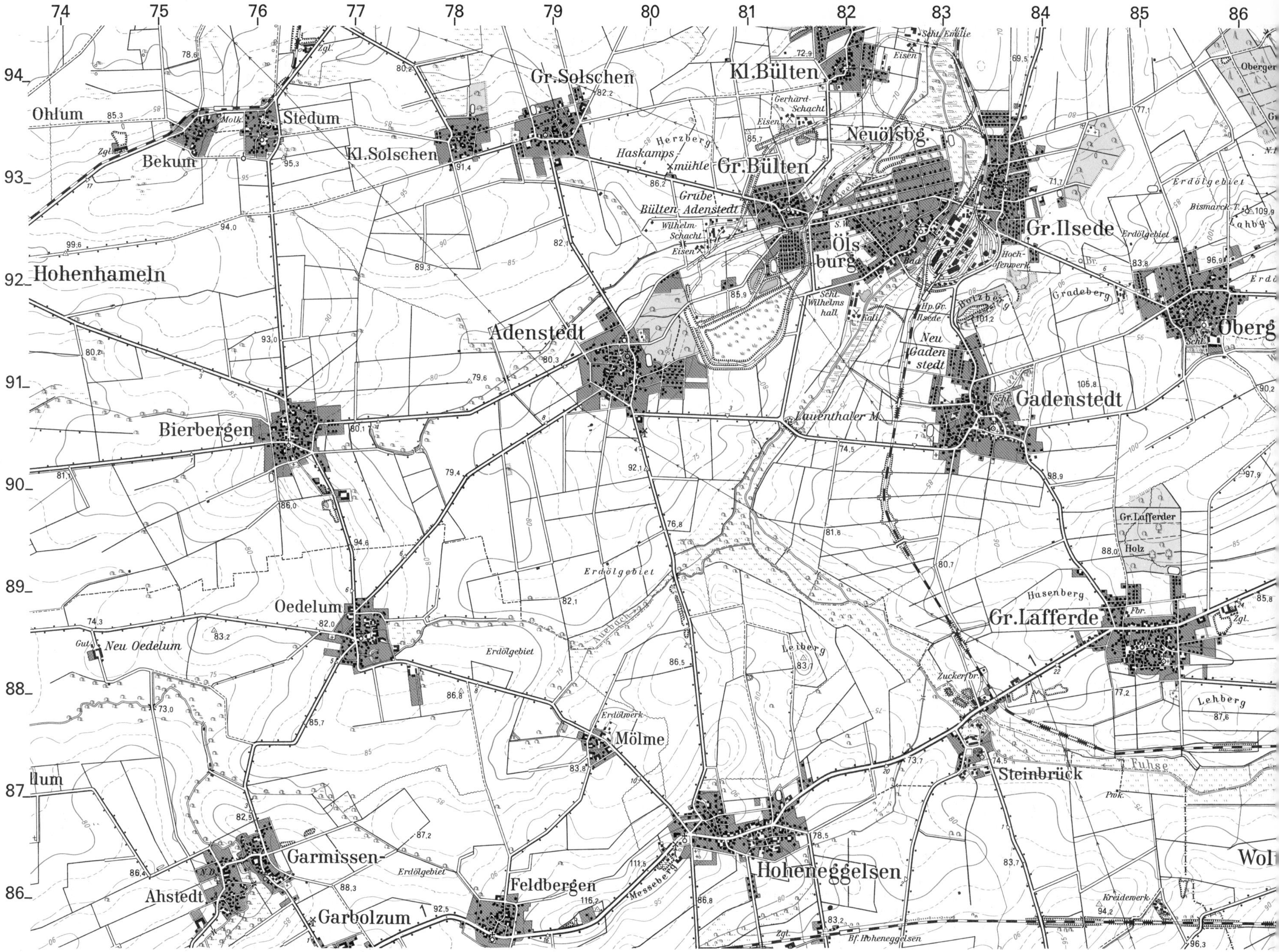

Printed by permission
of the Niedersächsisches
Landesverwaltungsamt-
Landesvermessung—9th May
1969—B4—2622 N—218/69.

Map 14

Ohlum

Stedum

Gr. Solschen

Kl. Bülten

Sch. Emilie

Eisen

Oberg

Neuölsbg.

Bekum

Molk

Kl. Solschen

Herzberg

Gerhard-Schacht

Haskamps

Gr. Bülten

Eisen

mühle

Hohenhameln

Grube
Bülten Adenstedt

Wilhelm-Schacht

Eisen

Gr. Ilsede

Erdölgebiet

Bismarck-T.

Öls burg

Hochofenwerk

Br.

Adenstedt

Neu
Gaden
stedt

Hp. Gr.
Ilsede

Kali

Sch.
Wilhelms
hall

Erdölgebiet

Gadenstedt

Bierbergen

Laurenthaler M.

Oedelum

Gut Neu Oedelum

Erdölgebiet

Leiberg

Zuckerfbr.

Gr. Lafferder
Holz

Gr. Lafferde

Hasenberg

Erdölgebiet

Mölme

Erdölwerk

Steinbrück

Fuhse

Lehberg

Garmissen-

Feldbergen

Messeberg

Hoheneggelsen

Wol

Ahstedt

Garbolzum

Kreidemerk

Bf. Hoheneggelsen

Photograph 16. Gross Ilsede. Many of the characteristics of the Börde landscape are evident in this photograph. Nucleated villages are surrounded by large fields generally cultivated in narrow strips. Notice the general absence of woods and hedges.

Hansa Luftbild. G.m.b.H., Münster

Between the geestlands of the North German Plain and the uplands of Central Germany lies a zone of loess soils renowned for its fertility. The zone is variable in width and attains its greatest extent in the Cologne bay and in the Börde of Lower Saxony. The origins of loess are generally held to lie in the immediate post-glacial period. Fine particles of silt were blown from the newly exposed surfaces of moraine and deposited to the south along the margins of the uplands. Redistribution by water often occurred so that the present pattern of these periglacial deposits is extremely complex. The resulting soil is a sandy loam rich in lime and of great fertility. Map 14 covers a small part of this loess region between Hanover and Brunswick in Lower Saxony. Relief is subdued. The lowest land on the extract, just below 70 metres, occurs along the valley of the Fuhse while the maximum heights of 105 and 111 metres are found on ridges east of Gadenstedt and west of Hoheneggelsen. Slopes are variable but never steep, and from the aerial photograph it appears that land use is hardly affected by this factor, though the flood plain is usually under permanent pasture. The drainage pattern is a simple one with two main streams carrying water to the north and west.

The most striking features of the settlement pattern shown on the map extract are its nucleated character and the regularity of village spacing. In part these features are a result of physical conditions, though the system of social organisation has probably played the dominant rôle. The lands of the Börde were amongst the earliest settled by Germanic peoples. Their fertility and ease of cultivation made them far more attractive than some of the poorer hilly lands to the south or the less fertile geestlands to the north. In the Börde country the village was surrounded by its arable lands, meadows, woodland and common pasture. The arable lands were divided into strips grouped into furlongs or *Gewanne*. The *Gewanne* were in turn grouped into three large open fields *(Zelgen)* and cultivated according to usage prescribed by the village community. The growth of population led to the extension of cultivation, again in strip form, into waste and woodland until the cultivated lands of adjacent villages were contiguous. Extension of cultivation, however, was not followed as in England, for example, by the growth of secondary settlement of a dispersed type. The nucleation of settlement in this area is therefore seen as a direct consequence of the farming system. The centralised location of the farmer's house in the village minimised the distance to the strips scattered throughout the large open fields. It is indeed hard to deduce any physical factor which could account for nucleation in this terrain: water supplies appear plentiful and the oft-quoted defensive factor seems hardly relevant if the variety of sites, from ridge crest (Hoheneggelsen) to ridge slope (Gadenstedt) and valley bottom (Steinbrück) be considered. The distance between villages may be looked upon as a direct function of the maximum distance it was economic for a farmer to journey to cultivate his strips. (An analogy might be drawn here with the regularity of spacing of market towns in, for example, East Anglia.)

An examination of the aerial photograph shows a wide variety in the size of strips. While these were originally no doubt of more regular pattern, the practice of subdivision according to the laws of equal inheritance, together with extension into waste land, have introduced a considerable variation.

The Börde today presents a picture of rich farmland. Land use can be inferred in part from the aerial photograph: note the large area devoted to arable usage, much of it for cereals, the small proportion under permanent grassland or woodland and the almost complete absence of waste land. The following figures, however, provide a more substantial basis for description.

Land use and farm size in some parishes of Landkreis Peine 1971

Gemeinde (Parish)	Area of farm and forestry concerns (hectares)	Area of forest (hectares)	Area of farmland (hectares)	Arable as % of farmland	Permanent grass as % of farmland	Cereals as % of arable	Root crops as % of arable
Bierbergen	826	—	786	94	5	70	30
Lamstedt	3,816	54	3,487	92	8	70	29
Ilsede	1,995	31	1,849	89	11	69	30
Stedum	651	2	563	87	11	71	28

	% of cereal land devoted to:			
	Wheat	Rye	Barley	Oats
Bierbergen	59	7	23	11
Lamstedt	48	10	27	14
Ilsede	44	13	29	13
Stedum	57	9	22	9

Year	Total number of farms	Under 2	2 to 4·99	5 to 9·99	10 to 14·99	15 to 19·99	20 to 29·99	30 to 49·99	50 and over
		Area in hectares							
1949	851	431	133	133	69	28	22	23	12
1960	517	193	66	57	70	52	44	22	13
1971	333	44	33	27	48	48	77	35	21

Note: In January 1964 the former parishes of Gross Solschen and Klein Solschen were amalgamated as the parish of Solschen.
In May 1966 the parish of Klein Bülten was incorporated with the parish of Bülten.
In February 1971 further reorganizations were effected. The new parish of Lamstedt included the former parishes of Adenstedt, Gadenstedt, Gross Lafferde, Munstedt and Oberg. The new parish of Ilsede incorporated the earlier parishes of Gross Bülten, Bülten, Gross Ilsede, Klein Ilsede, Ölsberg and Solschen.

Source: Niedersächsisches Landesverwaltungsamt – Statistik, Hannover.

There is an amazing uniformity about the pattern of agriculture in this region. Cereal acreages are very large and invite comparison with other areas, for example, Le Pays de Beauce (see Study 15) where a very different pattern of landscape has evolved. Maize however appears to be unimportant in this part of the Börde. The significance of sugar beet can be partly inferred from the map where a sugar beet factory is marked at Steinbrück close to a main road and railway.

The table of farm sizes shows a process of amalgamation over the past quarter century leading to an increase in the number of medium and large farms and a reduction in the number of small units. It is also clear from the aerial photograph that some larger fields are cultivated as units and not as strips. No doubt this is a response to modern mechanised cultivation in an area dominated by cereals and root crops.

Villages are of the irregular clustered type known in Germany as *haufendorfer*. The aerial photograph is instructive upon village form. None of the villages is of a simple street or cruciform pattern: all of them appear to have developed a rectilinear, triangular or more irregular road system with internal streets running in various directions. The houses are distributed along these roads with gardens adjacent to them. It is probable that there has been much infilling of houses in these settlements since medieval times. Indeed it has been suggested that many of the *haufendorfer* may originally have contained village greens. Mölme (794874) is quoted by H. Thorpe as of this type. Originally the green was of value in protecting livestock at night and in keeping animals away from the crops of the open fields. At a later stage, with the growth in population, the greens were built on or incorporated within the gardens of existing houses.

Though both map and aerial photograph give an impression of a region dominated by agriculture, analysis of occupation figures for each parish and attention to the detail of the map extract disprove this impression.

The parishes shown in the land use table had in 1970 a total working population of 9,259. Of these only 7% were engaged in farming activities though the proportions varied from 1–2% in Gross Bülten, Gross Ilsede and Ölsburg to 12% in Adenstedt and 19% in Bierbergen and Stedum. Manufacturing industry, retail trade and service occupations are certainly dominant in the densely populated area near Gross Ilsede. One aspect of manufacturing is shown clearly on the map extract and in the aerial photograph; namely, iron manufacture. The works occupy a large site on the floor of the valley of the Fuhse. They are served by a number of railway tracks which are linked to the main line from Peine (5 kilometres north of the map area) and to Brunswick and Salzgitter to the east and south. The ore for these works was produced locally at three mines near Klein Bülten and Gross Bülten. Production here has now ceased and ore supplies are now drawn from abroad. The sources of coal and coke are not evident from the map but since a harbour on the Mittelland Canal lies only 4·5 kilometres to the north of the blast furnaces it might reasonably be suggested that the Ruhr is the source of these materials. Evidence of mining activities is also found elsewhere on the map. A disused mine with the word *Kali* (potash) beside it lies on the southern outskirts of Ölsburg, while near Oberg and Mölme the words *Erdölgebiet* (oil field) and *Erdölwerk* (oil works) are printed. This is a very minor oil-producing area and production ceased at Oberg in 1968. The Mölme field produced 2,000 tonnes of oil in 1977. Examination of the map will produce further evidence of industry in Gross Lafferde, Bekum and Ölsburg.

The Börde is perhaps the most productive farming region of Western Germany. However, it would be wrong to take either map or photographic evidence as reliable indicators of the significance of farming activities in the life of the people. The field patterns, the morphology and distribution of most of the villages date from earlier times—times when techniques of land usage were very different from those of today. At the present time the non-agricultural population of the district of Peine numbers about 37,000 while the farming population is a minority of less than 3,000. Commerce and manufacturing assume importance in even the smallest settlements.

Exercises

1. Comment on the morphology of the villages of Gadenstedt and Oberg.
2. Discuss the factors responsible for the growth of iron and steel industries in Lower Saxony.
3. Describe and comment on field patterns around the village of Oberg.
4. What evidence can you deduce from the map and the photograph of a growth in population over the last 50 years?
5. Using the figures given in the text, construct histograms to show frequency of farms of different sizes for 1949, 1960 and 1971. Comment on your result.

Further reading

CHISHOLM, M. D. *Rural Settlement and Land Use*, Hutchinson, 1962.
DICKINSON, R. E. *Germany*, Methuen, 1961, especially chapters 6, 9 and 19.
DICKINSON, R. E. 'Rural Settlement in the German Lands', *A.A.A.G.* **39**, 1949.
ELKINS, T. H. *Germany*, 3rd edn, Chatto & Windus, 1973.
EVERSON, J. A. and FITZGERALD, B. P. *Settlement Patterns*, Longman, 1969.
Geografiska Annaler, **43**, 1961, contains a number of articles on village form and field systems.
THORPE, H. 'The Green Village as a Distinctive Form of Settlement on the North European Plain', *Société Belge d'Etudes Géographiques*, **30**, 1961.

DUISBURG-RUHRORT
NORDRHEIN-WESTFALEN
WEST GERMANY

A Section of the Ruhr Conurbation.

Extract from Sheet L.4506 Duisburg.
West German 1:50,000 Series.

Published 1952.
Revised 1966.
Vertical interval of contours 10 metres.
(Form lines at 5 metre and 2.5 metre intervals on gentle slopes)

By permission of Landesvermessungsamt, Nordrhein-Westfalen of 27.11.67 Control No. 2616 reproduced by Longmans, Green & Co. London, W.1.

Map 15

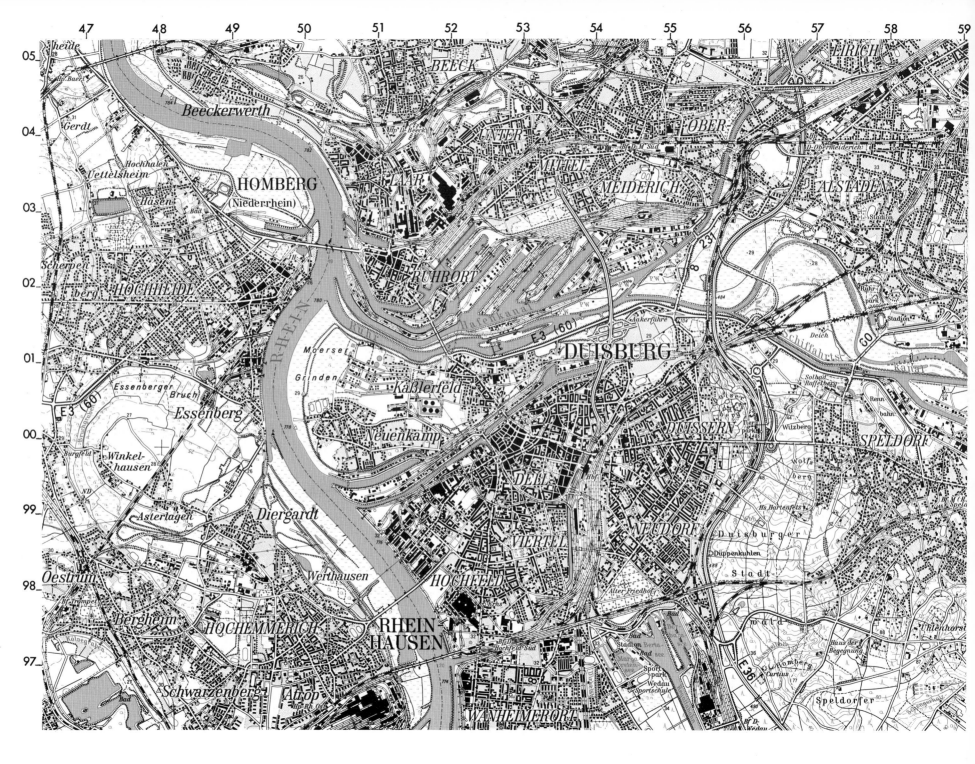

Photograph 17. The docks at
Duisburg-Ruhrort.

German Tourist Information Bureau, London.

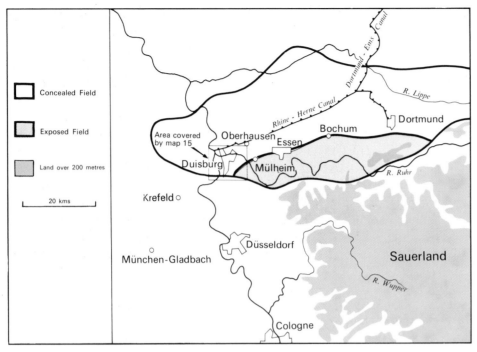

Figure 20. The Ruhr.

either side of the Rhine shows considerable evidence of liability to flooding and of changes of channel. West of the Rhine between Essenberg (4800) and Hochemmerich (4897) lies a loop of land followed by the Bruchgraben. This is seamed with drainage channels and is covered with bushes and reeds. The shape of the loop suggests an abandoned meander. Along both sides of the Rhine and Ruhr the frequency of banks or dykes indicates the need to protect settlements from flooding. Quite wide stretches of land are shown to be covered only with reeds. This, in an area of dense settlement and high land values, suggests that flooding is a very real possibility.

Land use

Both map and photographs show a landscape dominated by industry and commerce, Photograph 17 is of the docks at Duisburg-Ruhrort, while photograph 18 shows the Rhine at Duisburg with a multitude of factories and chimneys clustering along the river's right bank.

Duisburg lies at the eastern end of the Ruhr, undoubtedly the most industrialised region of Germany and possibly of Europe. To the south of

Photograph 18. The Rhine front at Duisburg.

German Tourist Information Bureau, London.

Studies 11, 12, 13 and 14 are based on the West German 1:50,000 series. The style of these maps shows slight variations, according to the Land (province) in which they are published. Relief is expressed by contours or form lines which may have an interval of as little as 2·5 metres on gentle slopes but 10 metres on steeper slopes. Oblique hill shading is employed on the Kaub sheet.

The landscape shown on map 15 is part of the Rhine valley where it is joined by the River Ruhr from the east. The Rhine at this point is about 25 metres above sea level. Areas of higher land at about 30 metres occur both west of the river, at Hochheide (4702), Oestrum (4798) and Schwarzenberg (4896), and east of the Rhine at Hochfeld and Dellviertal (5298). Further to the east there is an abrupt rise to summit heights of about 75 to 80 metres on the Kaiserberg, Wolfsberg and Homberg (5500, 5699, 5697). These summits are at similar levels, but the sides of the hill masses are steep and deeply dissected by small streams. Although the actual map evidence is not abundant, the relief suggests a flood plain with terraces above it which relate to various phases of the Rhine's history (see Study 11). The plain on

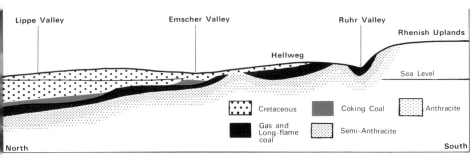

Figure 21. Generalised section across the Ruhr coalfield *(after T. H. Elkins.)*

The legend for the figure reads:
- Cretaceous
- Coking Coal
- Anthracite
- Gas and Long-flame coal
- Semi-Anthracite

the Ruhr lie the Hercynian mountains of Germany (Sauerland, Westerwald); to the north are the infertile gravels, sands and marshes of the North German Plain (see Study 12). Between the two lies the loess belt, with its light and porous soils which have proved attractive to farmers over many centuries. In the Middle Ages this belt constituted an important routeway between France and Belgium to the west and Saxony and Silesia to the east. To the south of Duisburg the Rhine provided the most important routeway through the Hercynian uplands. Thus the area has long been important as a cross-roads. Cologne first arose under the Romans, whilst Duisburg, Essen and Dortmund, lying on this east to west route (the Hellweg), had some significance as Hanse cities in the 14th and 15th centuries.

The tradition of manufacturing can likewise be traced back to medieval times. The Siegerland hills to the south, with their supplies of iron ore, their woods to provide charcoal and their water power from fast flowing streams, have a long history of metal working. Indeed, in 1800 this hill region was one of the most important iron working centres in Europe. The advent of the blast-furnace, using coke, heralded the development of the Ruhr region itself as a major metal working area.

The Ruhr coalfield consists of a series of basins with a north-east strike. To the south, on the flanks of the hill country, the coal measures are exposed, but north of a line from Duisburg to Bochum they are overlain by Cretaceous strata (to a depth of 1,400 metres near Münster). There are some 57 workable seams within the field having a total thickness of 61 metres. Two-thirds of the production is best coking coal, one-fifth is gas coal, and less than one-twentieth is poor quality coal. Though seams are faulted and sometimes difficult to work, nevertheless the wide variety of coal, the thickness of seams and the enormous reserves have given the region an excellent base for manufacturing industry. A few mines are shown in operation near Duisburg, including the Diergardt (489983), and Altstaden (580018 and 571041) mines which produce anthracite. However, most coal is now produced in mines much further to the north. Indeed evidence for the decline in mining is shown on the map near Hochheide, where two disused mines are depicted (488015 and 477011).

The first blast furnace was built in the Ruhr at Mülheim (2 km east of the map extract) in 1849. Although home supplies of ore were at first sufficient (principally from the Lahn, Dill and Siegerland districts south of the Ruhr), foreign supplies became more important after 1860. With the invention of the Gilchrist-Thomas basic process in 1879 for using phosphoric ores, the Ruhr was able to make use of the Minette ores of Lorraine, which was at that time part of Germany. However, by 1913 Swedish ores had become of greater importance: transport from Lorraine was difficult and the Minette ores were of low grade. Smelting in Lorraine using Ruhr coke became more profitable than moving Lorraine ore for smelting to the Ruhr. In 1902 the Narvik railway was constructed, reducing the cost of Lapland ore. Thus a connection was established between Sweden and the Ruhr which has persisted to the present day (see Study 4).

Imports of iron ore into Western Germany 1975 (1,000 tonnes)

Country of origin		Country of origin		Total imports 1975
Brazil	11,023	Canada	4,065	
Oceania (Australia)	6,412	France	2,623	
Liberia	6,196	Venezuela	1,873	44,322
Sweden	5,762	Norway	1,160	

Source: 1977 *Iron and Steel Statistical Bulletin*, Statistical Office, European Communities

The above figures stress the reliance that West Germany places upon imported supplies of ore. In the same year her own domestic production amounted to 4,273 thousand tonnes. This situation has tended to attract the industries towards the routes along which the ore travels. The largest plants in the Ruhr region are to be found in Duisburg-Hamborn-Ruhrort-Meiderich, Mülheim, Oberhausen and Essen. All except Essen are served by the Rhine and the canals which lead from it. Greater Duisburg is on the Rhine itself; Mülheim is linked to the Rhine by the ship canal marked on the eastern side of the map extract; Oberhausen lies adjacent to the Rhein-Herne canal which leaves the map in the north-east. The eastern area is typified by Dortmund; this is connected to the sea at Emden by the Dortmund-Ems canal, but is rather less important than the western region based on the Rhine. The map shows several iron and steel producing works. Their names and distribution can be ascertained by reference to fig. 22. Significantly, all of them lie close to navigable waterways and indeed they sometimes possess their own private docks. In comparison with much British plant, they are large and usually of an integrated type, i.e. blastfurnaces, steel furnaces and finishing plant lie adjacent to each other within the same works area. In the case of the Phoenix works in Ruhrort, the coal and coke producing plant is on the same site, but for other works coke has to come from further afield.

The coke works also provide the basis for an important chemical industry. In Meiderich, for example, coal tar distillation plant produces a wide range of products including pitch, oil, creosote, sulphate of ammonia, dyestuffs and raw materials for explosives and pharmaceutical products. The locations of many chemical works are shown on fig. 22 and the importance of a location near to waterways or railways for the transport of bulky goods is again apparent. The petrochemical industry has shown spectacular growth in recent years, and it is significant that since 1961 a large area of land has been taken over for this purpose south of the mouth of the Ruhr river.

In addition to the basic manufacture of coke, iron, steel and chemicals, there is a wide range of other industries in this region, many of which draw their raw materials from the iron and steel industries. Particularly important are the metal, construction and engineering industries. A comparison between fig. 22 and the map extract will reveal at least some of the reasons behind their locations.

Settlement and communications
Settlement in the area of the map extract appears to be almost continuous except for the difficult areas of the river flood plains and the steep wooded hills of the south-east. Greater Duisburg includes Ruhrort, Meiderich and Hamborn (to the north of Ruhrort) and had a population of 445,000 in 1972. Duisburg itself originated as a fortress at a crossing point of the Rhine about A.D. 700. In medieval times it grew to considerable importance as a trading town on the important east-west route known as the Hellweg. The old town can be recognised at 5300 on the south side of the Innenhafen. In those days the Rhine pursued a more easterly course and the town benefited from its proximity. The extension of Duisburg was rapid in the 19th century when industrialisation became important, but its growth was limited to the east by the hills of the Kaiserberg. Today there is a marked zoning of function which is easily seen on the map. Along the banks of the Rhine, by the harbours, and by the side of the railways leading to the Rhine lies an area mainly given over to industry. Photograph 18 shows the vast extent of the waterside industry by the Rhine. To the east of the main railway

in Duissern and Neudorf and to the south of the old city lie the main residential areas. Duisburg, however, does not seem to be without its amenities. In contrast to some of the older industrial cities of Britain, a large amount of open space still persists. In practically all the residential districts the symbol for a garden is widely shown, while in the south a large Sports Park is to be found with a stadium, swimming and boating and other facilities.

Ruhrort is of later growth. Its beginnings lay in the 14th century when a castle on an island in the Rhine exacted tolls on river traffic. A nearby fishing village became associated with the castle, and eventually walls were built.

Figure 22. Duisburg: Industrial location.   (Drawn at half the scale of Map 15)

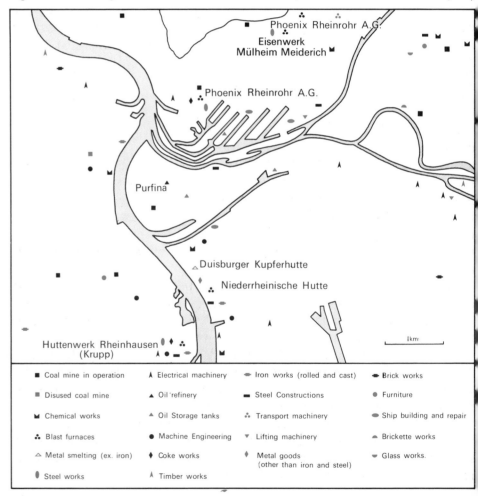

■ Coal mine in operation	▲ Electrical machinery	⊢ Iron works (rolled and cast)	⊢ Brick works
■ Disused coal mine	▲ Oil refinery	▬ Steel Constructions	● Furniture
⋓ Chemical works	▲ Oil Storage tanks	⁂ Transport machinery	⊸ Ship building and repair
⁂ Blast furnaces	● Machine Engineering	▼ Lifting machinery	▲ Brickette works
△ Metal smelting (ex. iron)	◆ Coke works	◆ Metal goods (other than iron and steel)	⊸ Glass works
◗ Steel works	▲ Timber works		

This formed the Altstadt (510018). To the north the Neustadt was laid out in the latter part of the 19th century. This followed the improvement of navigation on the River Ruhr which allowed coal traffic to reach the Rhine from mines in the south.

The growth of Duisburg and Ruhrort has been largely a result of improvements in communications, many of which date from the 19th century. The complex of harbours, railway lines, canals and roads has enabled the area to become a major transport centre for much of the industrialised Ruhr region. The construction of docks was obviously facilitated by the soft stretches of alluvium found in the flood plains. Though most of these were built in the 19th century, the three harbours north of the Hafenkanal were completed only in 1908. The linkage of the port to its hinterland in the Ruhr was effected by the construction of the Rhein-Herne canal in 1914 and of a canalised channel to Mülheim. The growth of traffic through the ports of Duisburg-Ruhrort was particularly marked from 1880 onwards.

Total Goods Traffic (1000 tonnes)

1875	1895	1905	1927	1937
2,935	7,416	19,462	33,567	34,297

(These figures refer to the entire Duisburg harbours including Schwelgern in the north and Huckingen in the south. The figures in Ex. 5 refer solely to the Duisburg-Ruhrort harbours on the extract).

During the 1939–45 war many of the harbour installations were badly damaged but after a long period of recovery the figure reached 30 million tonnes in 1957, and in 1976 stood at 54 million tonnes.

Photograph 17 shows the vast spread of the docks at the mouth of the River Ruhr. At the top right-hand corner the lock entrances can be seen to both the canalised River Ruhr and the Rhein-Herne canal. The docks are mainly concerned with bulky products of generally low value. Ruhrort dominates the coal export trade and imports large quantities of iron ore. There is also evidence on the photograph of a third important cargo, namely oil.

The docks in Duisburg, significantly, have no connection with the Ruhr and the Rhein-Herne canals. Timber, cotton, wool and grain are important cargoes. Their destination may be factories in Duisburg or distribution to the rest of Germany by rail.

Communication by railway is of great significance in the Duisburg area. A close network of lines links the dock, warehouse and factory area with cities in the Ruhr and beyond. The pattern follows the ancient east-west lines of communication and the north-south Rhine route. In T. H. Elkins's words: 'At the mouth of the Ruhr river, the Hercynian foreland and the Rhine routeways intersect: there could not possibly be a more favourable situation for the development of a coalfield and the growth of an industrial region than at this crossroads of Europe'.

Exercises

1. Examine the changing significance of factors in the location of the iron and steel industries of West Germany and Britain.
2. Calculate the length of docking space in Duisburg-Ruhrort on the map extract, and compare with that of Marseilles (map 22). Comment on your result, relating it to the types of traffic entering and leaving the ports.
3. Construct a flow diagram for iron ore movement to West Germany. Comment on sources and scale of movement.
4. 'In the Ruhr region the road system is antiquated, tortuous and frequently congested by tram lines, this being neither convenient nor important for anything but local traffic' (A. Mutton). Comment on this quotation in relation to the map extract.

5. *Total goods traffic (1,000 tonnes)*

	1936	1960	1976
Total	17,366	18,100	22,044
Coal	12,092	4,663	4,095
Ore	1,092	4,656	7,429
Mineral oil	209	2,438	4,551
Iron and steel	364	1,360 }	2,217
Non-ferrous metals	43	190 }	
Scrap	384	1,135	595
Foodstuffs, grain, fodder	465	315	356
Chemicals	36 }	572	430 }
Fertilisers	194 }		60 }
Rock, minerals and construction materials	1,884	1,813 }	1,816
Salt	153	381 }	
Other goods	316	131	52
Local traffic	134	446	443

Source: Duisburg-Ruhrorter- Häfen AG

The above figures show imports and exports for the Duisburg-Ruhrort harbours. Construct a suitable diagram to express these figures and comment upon the changes in trade patterns that they reveal.

6. Give an account of the industrial geography of the Ruhr. (W.J.E.C.)
7. Examine the influence of water transport on the industrial development of the Ruhr. (J.M.B.)

Further reading

BARR, J. 'Planning for the Ruhr', *Geographical Magazine*, **40**, 1970.
BURTENSHAW, D. *Economic Geography of West Germany*, Macmillan, 1974.
DICKINSON, R. E. *Germany: A General and Regional Geography*, Methuen, 1961, chapter 18.
ELKINS, T. H. *Germany*, 3rd edn, Chatto & Windus, 1973, chapter 15.
HALL, P. *The World Cities*, World University Library, 2nd edn, Weidenfeld and Nicolson, 1977, chapter 5.
HARRIS, C. D. 'The Ruhr coal mining district', *Geographical Review* **36**, 1946.
HELLEN, J. A. *North-Rhine Westphalia*, Oxford U.P., 1973.
POUNDS, N. J. G. *The Geography of Iron and Steel*, Hutchinson's University Library, 1966.
POUNDS, N. J. G. *The Ruhr: A Study in Historical and Economic Geography*, Faber, 1952.
POUNDS, N. J. G. and PARKER, W. N. *Coal and Steel in Western Europe*, Faber, 1957.

BEAUCE, BRIE, CHAMPAGNE AND NORMANDY.

Agricultural
Contrasts in the
Paris Basin

The four map extracts which illustrate this study are taken from various parts of the Paris Basin, the core or heartland of France. The definition of the Paris Basin is beset with difficulties. As H. Ormsby remarks, 'the nucleus at the centre is a much more definite feature than the vague line of the cell wall'. Most writers consider the basin to lie between the Armorican Massif on the west, the Massif Central on the south and the ancient blocks of the Vosges and Ardennes on the east, with the sea forming the northern boundary. However, for physical, human and economic reasons, Lorraine is usually excluded.

The unity of the Paris Basin seems to be mainly a result of its drainage pattern, the Seine and its tributaries imparting to Paris a nodality which extends particularly to the east and south-east as far as the uplands overlooking the Saône and Meuse Basins. The central Loire valley provides something of a problem, since in this section the Loire cuts across the sedimentary rocks of the Paris Basin from its upper course in the Massif Central to its lower course across the Armorican Massif. Furthermore, along the coast of the English Channel the drainage is direct to the sea via rivers such as the Somme and Bresle. In both cases, however, the divides from the Seine system are so low and traversed so easily that both areas appear to belong to the major region of the Paris Basin.

Within the broad unity of the Paris Basin considerable diversity exists, and the selection of map extracts and photographs is designed to emphasise this point. This diversity is in the main a consequence of differences in rock and soil although location and distance from Paris also play a part. The Paris Basin, at least in outline, is geologically simple. The basin corresponds to a structural depression in the Hercynian zone which permitted the accumulation of Secondary and Tertiary rocks while the surrounding massifs were raised. Subsidence continued longest in the centre, and it is here that the greatest thicknesses of Tertiary strata are to be found. Figure 23 shows in outline the main geological divisions of the region. The Jurassic series of limestones and clays are most prominent in the east and the south, though they can be traced in the west from Normandy to the south of the basin. The scarps of Lorraine and the south-east arise from the resistant qualities of the Portland, Corallian and Oolitic limestones while the intervening vales are developed on the Kimmeridge, Oxford and Lias clays. The Cretaceous rocks are the most widespread and ring the basin completely. The most important rock in this group is the chalk. The heart of the basin is a plateau of Tertiary rocks including limestones, clays, sandstones and marls, although the limestones (*Calcaire de Beauce, Calcaire de Brie, Calcaire Grossier*) form the dominant surface rock throughout most of the area. Further diversity of

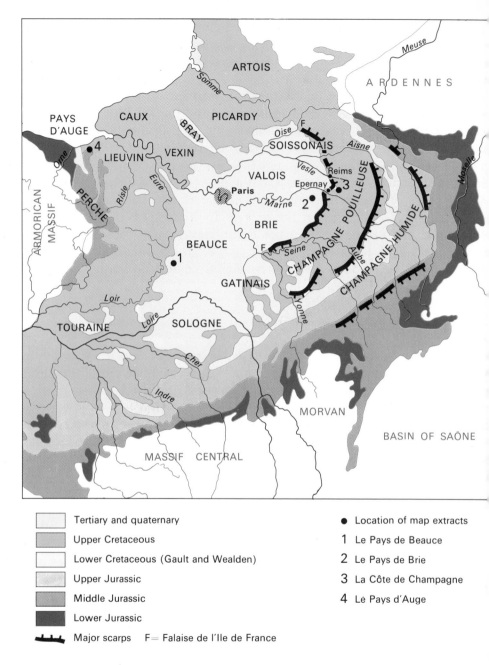

☐	Tertiary and quaternary	● Location of map extracts
▨	Upper Cretaceous	1 Le Pays de Beauce
☐	Lower Cretaceous (Gault and Wealden)	2 Le Pays de Brie
▨	Upper Jurassic	3 La Côte de Champagne
▨	Middle Jurassic	4 Le Pays d'Auge
▨	Lower Jurassic	

⊢⊣⊣⊣ Major scarps   F= Falaise de l'Ile de France

Figure 23. The Paris basin showing geology, drainage and the location of some of the most important *pays*.

landscape arises from the variety and frequency of superficial deposits, especially those of clay-with-flints and limon. The alluvia of river valleys such as the Seine and Loire should also be noted. Subsidence of a gentle nature associated with the Alpine folding to the south imparted a basin-like structure to these sediments and the concentration of rivers towards the Paris area was determined largely by this movement. It is worth noting that in the east, where stability reigned for a much longer time, drainage lines are from south to north (Meuse, Moselle) and independent of the centre. Generally the patterns of drainage were initiated in Pliocene times and the resultant differential erosion produced a variety of landforms, often of a scarp and vale character, although low, dissected plateau blocks are also common.

Landforms and land use are thus closely related to rock type in the Paris Basin. The individuality of the various parts of the region is reflected in a series of widely used *pays* names. These correspond to no administrative divisions and delimitation is often uncertain. Nevertheless, they do appear to correspond to certain unities based on similarities of relief and soil.

Le Pays de Beauce

A small part of the Pays de Beauce is represented in map 16. An impression of a very level surface is clearly given by the accompanying photograph which looks east-south-eastwards from the village of Aigneville in the foreground. No indication of surface water is found. The water towers *(Ch.^{au} d'eau)* are a constant reminder of the need for water storage in this apparently dry land. Beauce is founded on limestone, the youngest of the Tertiary limestones of the Paris Basin. Its fertility, however, is largely derived from a superficial covering of limon, which originated as a windblown dust in interglacial or immediate postglacial times.

Beauce Dunoise 1967: agricultural land use

	hectares		Size of farms (agricultural land)	Number of farms
Total agricultural land	67,500		less than 2 ha	120
Wheat	21,700	32%	2– 4·99 ha	70
Barley	20,100	30%	5– 9·99 ha	70
Maize	19,400	29%	10– 19·99 ha	90
Other cereals	1,000	1%	20– 29·99 ha	90
Forage crops	2,300	3%	30– 49·99 ha	230
Natural pasture	600	1%	50– 69·99 ha	110
			70– 99·99 ha	140
			over 100 ha	220
			Average size of farms in Beauce Dunoise: 59 ha	

Source: Direction Départementale de l'Agriculture. Section Statistique. Eure-et-Loir 1968.

The above figures refer to Beauce Dunoise, which forms the south-eastern part of the department of Eure-et-Loir and includes the map area.

The outstanding characteristic of land use in Beauce is the almost complete utilisation of the land for agriculture. Woodland and wasteland of any type are rare. Agriculture in Beauce Dunoise is today concerned with crops; seldom do animal products make a large contribution to farm income; though in the past sheep were grazed on the stubble of cereals. In 1975 91% of the agricultural land in Beauce Dunoise was devoted to cereals, a figure which it would be difficult to exceed in France, or indeed in Western Europe. Between 1955 and 1975 cereal acreage in Beauce Dunoise increased by over 50%. Much of this extension has been in the cultivation of maize, a crop in which considerable advances have been made by agronomists.

Farms in Beauce are today highly mechanised. Since 1955 an increase of 83% has been recorded in the number of tractors with corresponding increases in the number of combine harvesters and other machines. Certainly the natural conditions of the land, with its uniform relief and fertility, have encouraged these developments. Even the man-made problem of *parcellement* or scattered holdings has long been solved in Beauce, unlike most other regions of France. No doubt the obvious advantages of having large fields adjacent to each other were of greater value in Beauce than in other less uniform landscapes and economies. Farm sizes are varied but the average for Beauce Dunoise is 59 hectares. Most farms are worked by the farmer and his family, though some of the larger ones employ additional labour. Generally there is a tendency for the average farm size to grow. Between 1955 and 1967 the total number of farms in Beauce Dunoise was reduced by 19%, the result of a diminution in the number of holdings below 50 hectares and an increase in the number above that size.

Settlement in Beauce is strongly conditioned by the need for water. There is plenty of ground water in the limestone at a depth of about 50 metres, but the construction of wells of such a depth has in the past proved a costly undertaking. Thus there tends to be a strong nucleation of dwellings in large villages. Outside these settlements only the most wealthy farmers could afford to bore their own wells. The isolated dwellings shown on the map are, therefore, usually the buildings of very large farms. Recently, with a high standard of productivity and affluence, new wells have been constructed, frequently for sprinkler irrigation of maize which is prone to damage in the dry summers so often experienced in Beauce.

Beauce today presents a landscape of progress. The high standards of living, the willingness to experiment with new methods, represent a radical change in attitudes in recent years.

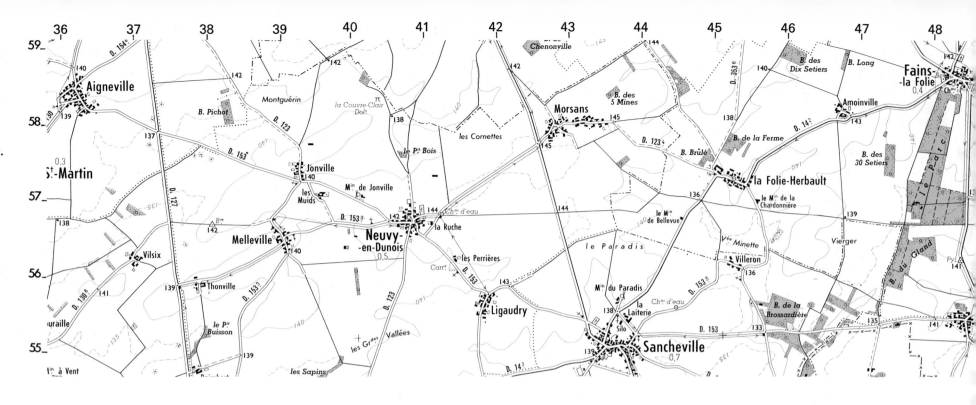

LE PAYS DE BEAUCE EURE-ET-LOIRE FRANCE

Extract from Sheet XXI-18.
Orgères-En-Beauce.
French 1:50,000 Series.

Published 1959.
Vertical Interval of
Contours 10 metres. Form
lines at 5 metres on gentle
slopes.

*Reproduced from a map
published by the Institut
Geographique National, Paris.*

Map 16

Photograph 19. The village
of Aigneville, Beauce.

Alain Perceval

Le Pays de Brie

Brie lies east and south-east of Paris between the valleys of the Seine and Marne (see figure 23). A distinct boundary is provided to the east and south-east by the Tertiary scarp (Falaise de l'Ile de France) which overlooks the lands of Champagne (see map 18). Superficially Brie is similar to Beauce. Both are founded on Tertiary limestones, both are level; but here the similarities end. The Brie limestone is thinner than that of Beauce and the surface layers contain bands of tough millstones *(meulières)* which form large fragments in residual clay deposits. These are particularly abundant in the north and north-east. Limon is to be found, though in most areas its thickness is far less than in Beauce. Perhaps the greatest contrast to conditions in Beauce lies in the matter of drainage. Though drier conditions exist in the south, where clay deposits are notably absent, most of central and north-eastern Brie has abundant surface water. The thin layers of Brie limestone lie immediately above waterholding marls while the clay and *meulières* lead to impermeability at the surface. Thus the higher northern parts of Brie were long covered with dense woodland and lakes and marshes were common. A further contrast between the two *pays* lies in the valleys.

Photograph 20. Viels Maisons, Brie.   *Institut Géographique National, Paris.*

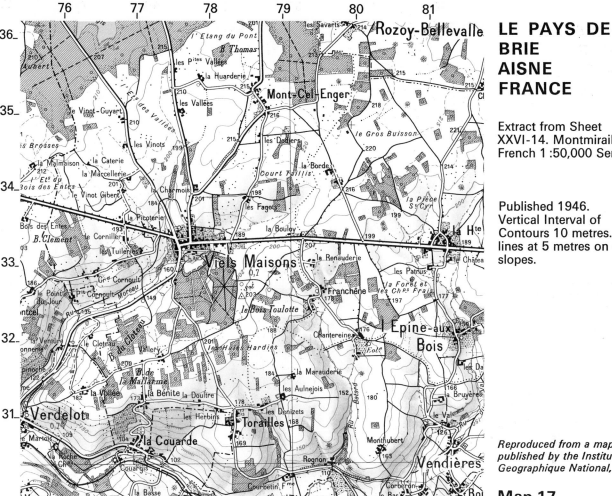

LE PAYS DE BRIE AISNE FRANCE

Extract from Sheet XXVI-14. Montmirail. French 1:50,000 Series.

Published 1946. Vertical Interval of Contours 10 metres. Form lines at 5 metres on gentle slopes.

Reproduced from a map published by the Institut Geographique National, Paris.

Map 17

While Beauce is a rolling plateau with but minor undulations, Brie is carved into a series of level blocks by river valleys such as the Petit and Grand Morin, which are deeply incised into the plateau.

Consideration of the map extract and photograph amplifies many of the points made above. The plateau around Viels Maisons is seen to lie mainly between 185 and 215 metres, with the greatest altitudes in the north and north-east. The valleys of the Petit Morin (in the south-west of the map) and its tributaries Ru. Moreau, Ru. Batard and Ru. du Val *(Ruisseau* abb. *Ru.*—a stream) are steep sided and cut down to about 95 metres, giving a maximum depth of nearly 100 metres. Water is abundant at lower levels while even on the plateau there are several streams of at least an ephemeral nature. In the north two lakes and several marshy areas denote an impermeable surface. Evidently the water table seldom lies far below the plateau.

The presence of water and the variations in relief and soil result in a more varied land use compared with Beauce. Examination of the aerial photograph shows considerable variation; the white fields suggest arable farming, probably for cereals; the dark grey fields are most likely to contain some fodder crop or are quite possibly devoted to permanent pasture; the dark patches of woodland are unmistakeable and their distribution accords with that on the topographical map. The existence of isolated trees in some of the dark grey fields strongly suggests that these contain permanent pasture rather than an arable crop. Perhaps these are fruit trees: apples are commonly found in such situations, although the topographical map is not entirely in agreement with the aerial photograph in its distribution of black dots. However, it should be borne in mind that the aerial photograph was taken in 1967 while the last revision of the map was in 1943. The shape and size of fields vary considerably. On the valley slopes of the Petit Morin fields are narrow rectangles with their long axes lying along the slope. On the plateau small fields of varied shapes occur around the villages of Viels Maisons and Mont-Cel-Enger, but larger fields are to be found, especially on the borders of the forest land to the north, possibly as a result of comparatively late clearance.

Some indication of land use is given by the following statistics:

Land use expressed as a percentage of total area 1970–71

Canton	Commune	Agricultural land	Woodland	Other (water, roads, buildings, wasteland)
Charly	L'Epine-aux-Bois	72	8	20
	Vendières	77	12	11
	Viels Maison	60	35	5
Condé-en-Brie	Rozoy Bellevalle	77	20	3

Use of agricultural land in the Canton de Charly (%) 1970–71

Arable 55·2 including Fodder crops 11·1
　　　　　　　　　　　Cereals 37·1 of which Wheat 18·9, Barley 12·1
Permanent pasture 40·9
Vines 3·5

Source: Chambre d'Agriculture de l'Aisne

The mixed character of agriculture in this part of Brie is substantiated by these figures. Cereals are of great importance on the higher lands of Brie while sugar beet is a minor crop. Maize is rarely cultivated here, no doubt because of the less favourable conditions of climate and soil as compared with Beauce. Cattle and sheep provide an important income for the farmer and the reputations of Brie butter and cheese are international.

Farm size in the four communes of Rozoy Bellevalle, Viels Maisons, Epine aux Bois and Vendières

	less than 10 ha	10–19·99 ha	20–49·99 ha	50–99·99 ha	over 100 ha
Number of farms	16	10	47	17	5
% of total number	17	11	49	18	5

Source: Chambre de l'Agriculture de l'Aisne. 1964/67.

Farm sizes are given in the table above. It is apparent that small and medium farms are dominant in number, though if figures representing the proportion of the total area covered by each size group are plotted the larger farms are seen to be of greater significance. An interesting point that emerges from a study of farm size and population is that a distinct correlation exists between size of farm and age of the farmer. Thus over 48% of all the farms of less than 20 hectares are occupied by farmers of over 55 years of age, while for farms of over 50 hectares the corresponding figure is 18%.

Settlement is dispersed to a far greater extent than in Beauce. The larger villages of Verdelot, Viels Maisons, L'Epine aux Bois and Vendières are placed on the slopes or floors of valleys. While Verdelot is compact, possibly because of the limitations of its site, Viels Maisons assumes a linear, almost cruciform shape through the influence of important roads. Elsewhere hamlets and isolated farms are common throughout the plateau.

La Côte de Champagne

The heartland of the Paris Basin consisting of Tertiary rocks is bounded to the east and south-east by the Falaise de l'Ile de France. In the neighbourhood of Epernay and Reims this scarp is particularly well formed though not continuous since the rivers Aisne, Vesle and Marne have all cut important gaps through it. Furthermore, minor flexures of folding have produced projections and embayments along the scarp. Lying to the north-east of Epernay the greatest of these projections is known as the Montagne de Reims and appears on the map extract north of Bouzy and Trépail. The most striking features of this upland area are the well-developed systems of dry valleys and the lack of any surface water, with an almost continuous cover of forest. To the south and east the steep slope of the scarp falls to the lowlands bordering the river Marne. Heights in the south reach only 90 metres above sea level and the land is for the most part gently rolling. Nearer to the scarp gradients increase and the occasional outlier of limestone such as Mont Tournant (208 metres) at 3659 adds variety to the landscape. Like the higher land to the north, most of the plain lacks surface water, apart from the river Marne in the south and an intermittent stream which has its source near Trépail. This lowland is part of Dry Champagne or La Champagne Pouilleuse, a landscape based on chalk and resembling Salisbury Plain in much of its scenery.

The following statistics refer to land use in the communes of Bouzy and Trépail. It should be noted that the whole of the commune of Trépail is shown on the map extract, but only part of that of Bouzy.

Commune of Bouzy 1970

	hectares		
Arable	468	Including	
		Cereals	281 ha
		Sugar beet	44 ha
		Fodder crops	83 ha
		Colza	10 ha
Permanent pasture	18		
Vines	283		
Other land	20		
Total agricultural land	779		

Commune of Trépail 1970

Total area of commune 836 hectares including Forests 359 ha

Vines 247 ha

of the remainder 167 hectares belongs to a single farm growing cereals, beets, and oil seeds and raising cattle.

Source: Le Comité Interprofessionel du Vin de Champagne.

From a study of map, photograph and statistics it is clear that there are great contrasts between land use on the plain and that on the scarp. The growth of vines in small fields (note the road pattern) dominates the scarp slope, while more general farming, often of an arable nature in much larger fields, is characteristic of the plain.

The reasons for the persistence of vine growing at such a northerly latitude are diverse. Certain physical conditions for the vine are good. The chalk on the scarp slope is covered with 20 to 30 centimetres of gravelly loam which promotes aeration and drainage yet allows warmth to penetrate early in the year. Climatic conditions might best be described as marginal. Low winter temperatures, cloudy and rather cool summers are hardly the conditions normally associated with viticulture. However, the location of the vineyards on south-east or south-facing slopes maximises the limited insolation while the slopes give some protection against late frosts which are more common on the lowland. Furthermore, the chalky soil acts as a reflector of light and exerts a beneficial effect on the maturation of the grapes. The most important reason for the success of viticulture in this region is undoubtedly the human factor. In medieval times the episcopal cities of Reims and Châlons-sur-Marne fostered the development of vine growing and through the fairs of Champagne (one of the great crossroads of medieval Europe) the reputations of local wines spread throughout France. The international reputation of the wines of Champagne grew from the late seventeenth century and in particular as a result of the activities of one man, Dom Perignon, appointed cellarer of the Benedictine Abbey of Hautvilliers in 1688. Champagne wines are today produced in a similar manner to that perfected by Dom Perignon. The process involves the blending of wines from many vineyards and the development of a sparkling wine through a series of two fermentations. The time involved is often three or four years. This fact is important, since considerable capital resources become necessary and the manufacturing process is, therefore, mainly the prerogative of large firms which buy most of their grapes from small farmers. Altogether 30,000 hectares of vine growing land are allowed to use the official name Champagne. The invasion of the vineyards by the *phylloxera* epidemic at the end of the nineteenth century resulted in complete destruction and only 11,000 hectares of the original 30,000 hectares had been replanted by the beginning of the 1939–45 war. Since then the area has been extended to reach 24,000 hectares largely in response to an increased demand from abroad. The greater part of the vine-growing land is cultivated by small holders. Thus 87% 20,300 ha) is divided amongst 17,000 vine-growers while the other 13% (3,700 ha) is owned by the manufacturing firms (*Maisons dé Champagne*). The average size of farm is therefore extremely small. The following figures relate to a sample of 14,000 vine-growers.

Percentage of farms	Size of farms
39·7	less than 0·5 ha
18·5	from 0·5 to 1 ha
20·2	from 1 to 2 ha
11·3	from 2 to 3 ha
7·3	from 3 to 5 ha
3·0	over 5 ha

Source: Le Comité Interprofessionel du Vin de Champagne.

LA CÔTE DE CHAMPAGNE MARNE FRANCE

Extract from Sheet XXVII-13. Avize. French 1:50,000 Series.

Published 1949. Partial Revision 1959. Vertical Interval of Contours 10 metres.

Reproduced from a map published by the Institut Geographique National, Paris

Map 18

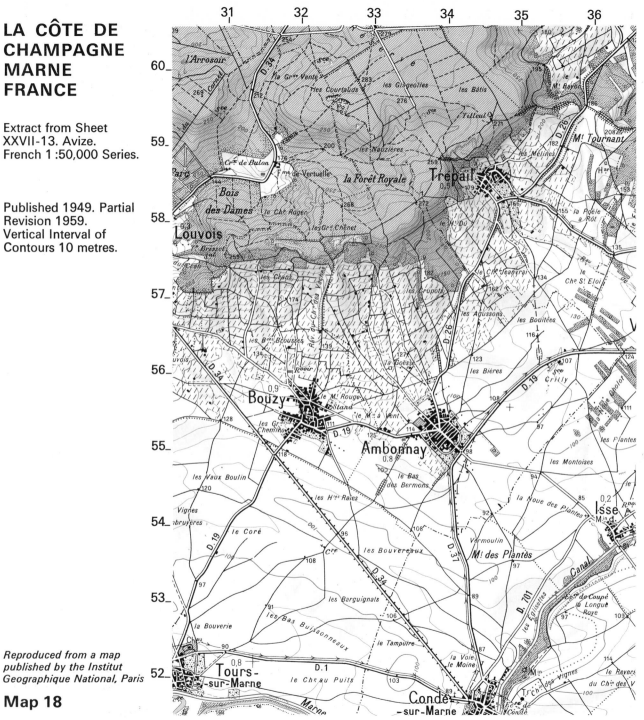

Photograph 21.   Part of the Côte de Champagne near Trépail.

Alain Perceval

A similar point can be elucidated from figures for the commune of Trépail, where the 247 hectares of vines are divided between 182 growers. The lands belonging to the *Maisons de Champagne*, though only 13% of the total, represent the best of the vine-growing land. The total holding is normally between 200 and 300 hectares per firm, though it is usually scattered over several communes and composed of many small plots. The cultivation of these plots is in the hands of tenants who work for the *Maisons de Champagne*.

Careful regulation governs both the growth and processing of grapes. The vines are set in long rows about 1 metre apart, each plant lying between 60 and 80 centimetres from its neighbour. The shoots are trained each year on wires. Altogether about 10,000 vines are planted to the hectare and a strict limitation of 3,000 litres is placed on the amount of wine officially designated Champagne which may be produced from each hectare. The main varieties grown are the black and grey Pinots in the better soils and the Pinot Meunier in poorer areas, while in the south white grapes of the variety known as Chardonnay are planted along the Côte des Blancs (the escarpment south of the river Marne). Though there is no season in which attention is not required to the plants, the harvesting of the grapes imposes heavy demands upon the labour force and temporary workers are then recruited from nearby provinces, particularly Lorraine. It should be emphasised that

Photograph 22. Bocage country around Clarbec.

Institut Géographique National, Paris

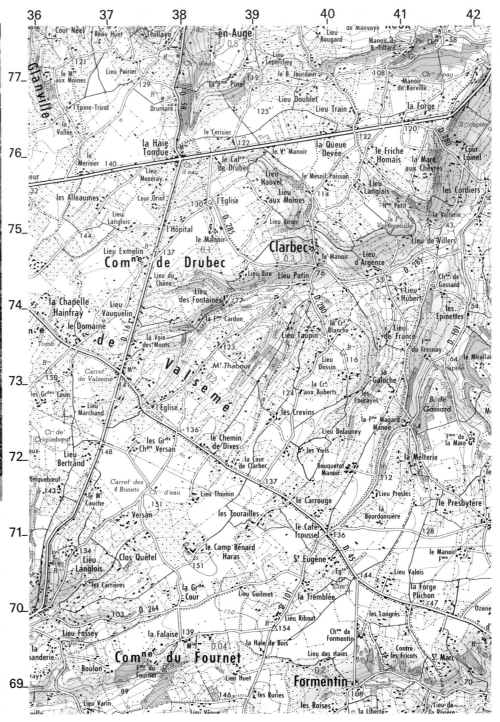

LE PAYS
D'AUGE
CALVADOS
FRANCE

Extract from Sheet XVII-12.
Lisieux.
French 1:50,000 Series.

Published 1959.
Vertical Interval of
Contours 10 metres.

Reproduced from a map
published by the Institut
Géographique National, Paris.

Map 19

Champagne is a manufactured product, the result of the blending of wines from several sources; thus there are no vintage champagnes designated with the names of the vineyards of origin (as in the case of the wines of Bordeaux and Burgundy). Instead, marketing is carried out under the name of the firm responsible for manufacture—Pommery, Heidsieck, Clicquot, Bollinger and many others—located chiefly in Epernay and Reims.

The problems of this small area are an inevitable result of both geographical position and the organisation of the industry. Lying in an area only marginally favourable to the vine, there is a sad frequency of years in which too much rain, too little sun or late frosts result in poor yields. The large firms remain comparatively unaffected, since they carry large stocks of wine, but the small independent grower is more vulnerable, for he relies heavily upon the return from each year's harvest. Since 1945 co-operation has increased amongst the small producers, and in 1975 there were 125 wine co-operatives. These are an important development since they give the small producer a stronger bargaining position *vis-à-vis* the firms who buy his grapes. It might be argued that a complete reorganisation along vertical lines would be economically and socially desirable. The greatest difficulties seem to lie in the considerable capital and expertise required for manufacturing and in the hold over the market exerted by the famous names of the *Maisons de Champagne*. However production by co-operatives and small independent growers outside the *Maisons de Champagne* had increased to 31% of the total in 1977.

Le Pays d'Auge

To the west there is a gradual transition from the Paris Basin to Brittany and Normandy. As with so many geographical regions, it is difficult to draw firm boundary lines, yet the Pays d'Auge illustrated in map 19 and photograph 22 is generally deemed to be a part of the Paris Basin. It consists of two parts, a lower region in the west drained by the river Dives and a higher plateau country in the east into which is cut the valley of the river Touques. Between the two a serrated scarp slope descends over 100 metres. Clarbec and its neighbourhood lie on the plateau. Examination of the map shows a surface between 110 and 150 metres which is dissected by a considerable number of valleys, most of them tributary to the valley of the river Touques which is reached 3 kilometres north-east of the map extract at Pont l'Evêque. It is noticeable that the upper parts of the streams occupying these valleys are marked as ephemeral while the surface of the plateau is dry except for a number of ponds, probably artificial. The drainage characteristics, therefore, point to a permeable rock. Indeed the plateau of the Pays d'Auge is composed of chalk with some superficial clay and limon deposits. Underneath the chalk lie deposits of Oxford clay of Upper Jurassic age: these form the country rock of much of the lowland of the Dives valley to the west. It is probable that the valleys of the major streams dissecting the plateau have cut down to these clays: this may account for the stream flow in the Yvie valley in the north-east.

Unlike the *pays* of Beauce and Brie, the Pays d'Auge is a landscape of small hedged fields with many trees and very largely devoted to pasture. This is *bocage* country. The following land use figures for 1970 refer to the canton of Pont l'Evêque which includes the commune of Clarbec.

(expressed as a percentage of total agricultural land, excluding woodland)

Arable 5·5 including fodder crops 3·0 (maize 2·2)
cereals 2·1
Permanent grass 92·8

Land use in the commune of Clarbec in 1970 was as follows:

(expressed as a percentage of total area)

Arable 5·9 including fodder crops 1·8
cereals 3·7
Permanent grass 93·1

Source: Direction Départementale de l'Agriculture de Calvados. 1971.

The figures serve to emphasise the importance of permanent grassland and the very subsidiary rôle of arable cultivation in this area. The Pays d'Auge produces milk, beef, veal and many other animal products. Both the climate, with its oceanic mildness, the moisture-retaining soils based on limon and superficial clays, and the demands of the cities of Paris and Rouen exert an influence on the pattern of farming. Indeed the products of these areas are well known outside France. Local factories, frequently on a co-operative basis, furnish quantities of Camembert and Livarot cheeses as well as butter for export. One important product is evident from the map and the photograph, but not from the statistics. Permanent pasture fields are frequently used for the growth of apple trees and the traditional cider and calvados are in a sense a by-product of the pastoral industries.

Land holdings are not large in this plateau country. The figures for Clarbec (1971) are as follows:

Size in hectares	less than 1	1–1·99	2–4·99	5–9·99	10–19·99	20–34·99	35–49·99	50 and over
No. of farms	0	0	3	6	7	10	2	6

Source: Direction Départementale de l'Agriculture de Calvados. 1971.

For the larger area of the canton of Pont l'Evêque the average size of farm in 1970 was 24 hectares with an average of eight plots of land per farm. Settlement is dispersed with no single, well-defined nucleus.

Conclusion

The description of the four areas presents a series of contrasts from the extremes of Beauce and the Pays d'Auge to the intermediate Briard type and the specialised viticulture of the Côte de Champagne. It would be a mistake, however, to conclude this study without reference to the tendencies towards change over much of the Paris Basin. In former times the influence of soil and other purely physical factors was much greater than now. Today, with efficient transport networks and an increasingly scientific approach, farm economies can be radically altered. Nowhere is this more evident than in Champagne Pouilleuse which was always considered to be amongst the poorest of the *pays* of the Paris Basin. Today, mainly because of the use of chemical fertilisers, this region has become an important cereal producer.

The influence of the rapidly growing metropolitan area of Greater Paris has shown itself in two ways. Firstly it demands an increasing quantity of food for its inhabitants. Secondly it has been a magnet for agricultural workers in search of a high standard of living. The response of agriculture has been twofold: firstly to make do with less labour, secondly to increase efficiency so as to be able to compete with other producers further afield. A mechanical revolution is occurring in French agriculture, not only in Beauce but also in the more remote pastoral districts of the west. An important side effect of this trend towards mechanisation and greater efficiency has been the reorganisation of land holdings or *remembrement*. The division of farm land amongst a large number of farmers *(morcellement)* and the frequent division of a single holding into many scattered plots *(parcellement)* are inimical to efficiency. Thus, especially in the lands devoted to cereals, there has been a move towards reorganisation into more economically sized and shaped plots. The tendency is far less pronounced in the pastoral areas (Pays d'Auge) or in the fruit and viticulture regions where mechanisation and size of field are not so important. Similarly there has also been a tendency towards regrouping into larger farm units, especially in the cereal areas. Perhaps the most telling index of change lies in population density. Over most of the Paris Basin the agricultural population averages about 0·1 per hectare: this is between four and five times less than in Brittany and three times less than in much of Aquitaine. At least in the Paris Basin the traditional view of a French agriculture involving peasants with an almost mystical attachment to their plots of land is out of date. An efficient, mechanised and scientific agriculture is increasingly manifest.

Exercises

1. The four map extracts show considerable contrasts in settlement pattern. Describe and explain these contrasts.

2. What information is required (statistical and otherwise) in order to delimit major geographical regions?

3. With reference to a range of examples, show how and why major changes may occur in patterns of crop production.

4. 'There is no such thing as a typical chalk landscape.' Discuss.

5. Discuss the pattern of roads and tracks revealed by a study of the aerial photographs and maps of Brie and Le Pays d'Auge.

6. 'Specialization in agriculture will take place irrespective of physical environment.' Discuss this statement. (O. and C.)

7. Either *(a)* comment on the relationship between rocks and relief in the Paris Basin or *(b)* explain what is meant by the French term *pays* and illustrate your answer with examples. (Cambridge.)

8. The following statistics refer to departments in the Paris Basin. Represent these in diagram or graph form and comment on the information revealed:

Total population (T.P.) and working agricultural population (W.A.P.) in thousands

	1946 T.P.	1946 W.A.P.	1962 T.P.	1962 W.A.P.	1975 T.P.	1975 W.A.P.		1946 T.P.	1946 W.A.P.	1962 T.P.	1962 W.A.P.	1975 T.P.	1975 W.A.P.
Seine-et-Marne	399	187	524	23	756	13	Orne	269	151	281	54	294	31
Eure-et-Loir	255	127	278	30	335	16	Calvados	393	207	481	56	561	31
Oise	389	181	481	30	606	17	Eure	311	159	362	38	423	20
Marne	385	185	442	39	530	27	Seine Maritime	832	411	1,037	55	1,173	30
Aube	234	121	255	21	285	13	Somme	437	209	488	45	538	25
Loiret	342	174	390	38	490	20	Aisne	452	202	513	39	534	23
Loir-et-Cher	241	127	251	39	284	19							

9. The following statistics (in 1,000 hectares) refer to total agricultural land and land reorganised under the Service du Remembrement in 1966. Construct a distribution map and comment on the pattern revealed.

Department	Total agricultural land	Land reorganised	Department	Total agricultural land	Land reorganised
Calvados	569	86	Oise	589	257
Orne	614	81	Seine-et-Oise	566	205
Sarthe	624	37	Seine	48	—
Loir-et-Cher	642	120	Seine-et-Marne	593	292
Loiret	681	197	Yonne	746	263
Eure-et-Loir	594	367	Aisne	743	289
Eure	604	248	Marne	821	345
Seine Maritime	634	42	Aube	600	171

Source of Statistics for Exercises 8 and 9: Ministère de l'Agriculture, Paris.

Further reading

BAKER, A. R. H. 'Le Remembrement Rural en France', *Geography*, **46**, 1961.

BAKER, A. R. H. 'A Modern French Revolution', *Geographical Magazine*, February, 1968.

CHABOT, G. *Géographie Régionale de la France*, 3rd edn, Masson et Cie, 1975, section III.

DEFFONTAINES, P. and DELAMARRE, M. J. *Atlas Aérien de France*, Volume IV, Paris, 1962.

GEORGE, P. and RANDET, P. *La Région Parisienne. La France de Demain*, Presses Universitaires de France, Paris, 1964.

LE LANNOU, M. *Les Régions Géographiques de la France*, Paris, 1964, Volume I.

MONKHOUSE, F. J. *A Regional Geography of Western Europe*, 4th edn, Longman, 1974

ORMSBY, H. *France. A Regional and Economic Geography*, Methuen, 1950, chapter IV.

SCARGILL, D. I. *Economic Geography of France*, Macmillan, 1968.

SHACKLETON, M. R. *Europe: A Regional Geography*, 7th edn, Longman, 1965, chapter X.

THOMPSON, I. B. *The Paris Basin*, Oxford U.P., 1973.

Extract from Sheet XXXIII-
46. Toulon.
French 1:50,000 Series.

Published 1953.
Partial Revision 1958.
Vertical interval of
contours 10 metres.

Reproduced from a map published
by Institut Géographique
National, Paris.

Map 20

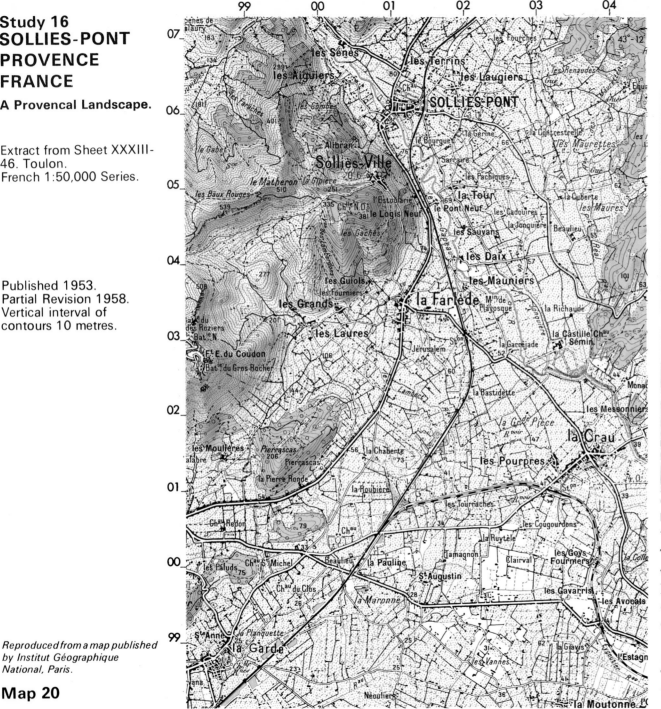

Photograph 23. Solliès-Pont. Plain of the Gapeau.
Aerofilms Ltd., London.

The location of the map extract is shown in fig. 24. To the north and north-west lie the most southerly of the Alpine chains; to the east lie the Massifs of Les Maures and L'Esterel. Between the two, the map shows part of the plain of Hyères, one of the largest areas of lowland on the French Mediterranean coast east of Marseilles.

Relief and drainage

The landscape shown on the map and photograph falls naturally into two types, hills and plain. The plain slopes gently from 70 to 80 metres in the north to under 30 metres in the south. The relief of the plain is diversified by several knolls, notably at 0101 and 0398. On either side there is a gentle rise to the foot of the hills, then a marked break of slope where the steep-sided uplands are reached. The hills reach their greatest height and are at their steepest (1 in 3) in the west (Massif du Coudon 702 metres). Several steep-sided valleys dissect the hills and the upland is often thereby reduced to a series of ridges. In the south-west, erosion appears to have led to the severance of several outliers from the main hill mass. In the east less of the upland area is shown on the extract and slopes are less steep (1 in 10), but a number of short valleys appear to cut into the hills.

Over much of the plain, drainage is artificially directed. The main stream is the Gapeau which runs south-east close to La Crau. A low watershed separates the Gapeau basin from that of the Eygoutier which drains the southern area. The western hills show no evidence of permanent drainage except in the deep valley in the extreme north. In several cases valleys are completely dry, in others a seasonal flow may be assumed from the pecked blue lines. The eastern hills appear to be better watered, though even here streams are ephemeral. From the evidence of the dry valleys, the extremely steep slopes (notably near Les Baux Rouges at 9805, and the Massif du Coudon), and the general absence of any vegetation cover more luxuriant than brushwood, one can assume that the western highlands are probably composed of limestone. The eastern hills, with their less arid and rocky slopes covered with a much denser woodland, appear to be formed of a less permeable, though still resistant, rock.

The location map shows that the plain is part of a broad depression separating the limestones of the Provence Alps behind Toulon and Marseilles from the older crystalline highlands which reach the coast between Toulon and Cannes.

Land use

Both the map and photograph show a marked contrast in land usage between the hill country and the plain.

The hill masses of Le Coudon and Le Matheron (9905) appear to be of little agricultural use. The steep slopes (often reaching gradients of 1 in 3 or more), the absence of water and the presence of a poor brushwood vegetation *(garrigue)* over the greater part offer difficulties to arable cultivation. Reference to the photograph will substantiate these conclusions. Indeed, these hills appear to be only fit for the sheep or the goat to graze. In the lower parts of the two valleys which dissect this hill mass, the symbol for meadow or grassland is shown, together with a considerable number of

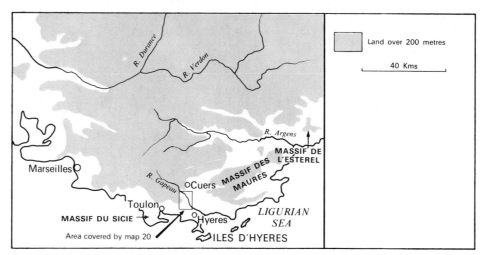

Figure 24. Provence.

buildings connected by footpaths. One may assume that these are farms, though it is doubtful if their standard of living is very high in such difficult surroundings.

The eastern hill masses, together with the three isolated knolls in the south-west, are almost devoid of settlement.

The plain is a different world. Slopes are gentle, water seems plentiful, and no doubt soils are of a thickness and fertility unknown in the hills. The map gives a fair amount of information about land use. Over a great part of the region the vine is dominant, but it is frequently associated with the growth of fruit trees. Orchards without vines occur in a discontinuous belt along the gently sloping land at the foot of the western hills and along either side of the Gapeau River between Les Sénès (0006) and Les Mauniers (0103). The most notable absence is that of land devoted to arable cultivation for cereals or similar field crops.

Fig. 26 is based on studies issued by the agricultural authorities for the Department of Var, and shows the situation in the neighbourhood of Solliès Pont in greater detail than on the topographical map. The boundary of the region surveyed coincides with the edge of the steep slopes of the hill masses (about 150 metres in the west and 100 metres in the east). On the south it follows the boundary between the communes of Solliès Ville and La Farlède. The figures stress the importance of fruit and the vine. Either on their own or with the vine, fruit trees cover 57% of this low-lying land. The evidence of the topographical map concerning the lack of arable cultivation is also confirmed; only 28 hectares (4%) are given to cereals and

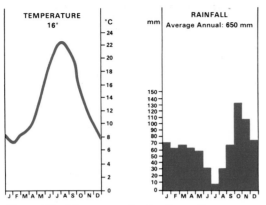

TEMPERATURE 16°

RAINFALL Average Annual: 650 mm

Figure 25. Climate graphs for Cuers. Provence.

fodder.

The reasons for this pattern of land use are partly revealed by the map extract. The inference of thick, fertile, possibly alluvial soils has already been made, but a study of the watercourses shows an additional reason for their fertility. The Gapeau is a permanent stream and feeds many small canals from two main points, one just south of Les Sénès, the other west of La Tour. The eastern part of the region is insufficiently irrigated largely because its watercourse, le Petit Réal, carries little volume compared with the Gapeau. It is significant that this area is largely given over to the vine, a plant which survives happily with little water. A third important factor is not revealed by the map. This is climatic. Graphs from the nearest recording station, at Cuers, indicate some important advantages, particularly for fruit and market garden produce. The warm springs, the hot summers and the absence of really low temperatures are all significant. The insolation figure for Cuers is 2,882 hours and for Toulon 2,915 hours. (Eastbourne on the coast of Sussex experiences 1,809 hours per year.) Thus the area is one of the most favoured in France—the problems are mainly those of water supply in the dry summer months. Paradoxically an additional problem of excess water occurs in spring and autumn when rain-storms frequently produce floods on the plain, particularly east of La Garde, where the Eygoutier stream normally floods 800 hectares of land each year. A fourth factor in the development of this fruit and vegetable economy is the existence of transport facilities to the great markets in Paris and Lyons. Thus the traditional Mediterranean pattern of farming involving cereal, olive, vine and sheep or goats has been superseded by a far more specialised type.

The following figures refer to size of farms and fields in relation to crops in the section of the plain delimited in fig. 26.

Size of farm (in ha.)	No. of farms	Total areas of farms (in ha.)	% of total area	Fields No.	Av. size (in ha.)	Use of land (in ha.) Waste or Fallow	Vines	Veg.	Orchard and orchard with vines	Cereals and orchard and fodder
Under 2	163	127	17	236	0·5	19	47	11	46	4·2
2– 4·99	55	174	25	97	1·8	24	29	7·6	107	6·3
5–13·99	33	226	31	61	3·7	2	18	0·2	195	11
Over 14	7	193	27	20	9·7	50	57	21	58	7
	Total 258	Total 720		Total 414	1·7	95	151	40	406	28

Source: Société du Canal de Provence et d'Aménagement de la Région Provençale. Étude Générale des Régions Desservies. Secteur 14. Solliès-Pont.

63% of the farms are of less than 2 hectares and generally consist of small fields (average ½ hectare in size). Upon these farms the vine is the dominant crop. Fruit production seems to be of the greatest importance on farms of moderate size (2–14 hectares), and the size of fields shows a marked increase to an average of 2 hectares or more.

The labour situation upon these farms is of interest.

Size of farm (in ha.)	No. of farms	Family Working on farm	Working off farm	No. of employees	Density per farm
Under 2	163	244	93	4	1·5
2– 4·99	55	73	19	12	1·5
5–13·99	33	62	3	16	2·4
Over 14	7	24	0	64	12

Source: Société du Canal de Provence et d'Aménagement de la Région Provençale. Étude Générale des Régions Desservies. Secteur 14. Solliès-Pont.

The small farms are obviously not capable of supporting the families who live on them. Thus almost one person in two travels outside the farm to work, possibly in the local town or even further afield, in Toulon.

The origin of the problems of small fields and small farms lies in such factors as the traditional French inheritance laws. This, together with the piecemeal buying of small patches of land, leads to fragmentation or *morcellement*. With an intensive type of agriculture producing fruit and vegetables the problem seems less acute than in other parts of France, where cereals and livestock are of greater importance and larger fields more economical.

The pattern of farming in the more southerly part of the plain appears to be similar to the north. The following statistics refer to the commune of La Farlède, the boundary of which may be traced on the map. Unlike the area of fig. 26, this commune includes both plain and hill country.

Crop production (area in hectares)

No. of Farms	Land under cultivation	Arable including	Cereals	Vegetables	Vines	Orchards	Market gardens (veg. and flowers)
174	398	37	1	8	206	62	69

Livestock (numbers)

Cattle including	Milking cows	Sheep	Pigs	including Sows
138	9	4	347	14

Source: Recensement Générale de l'Agriculture 1970.

Settlement and communications

Examination of map and photograph shows two types of settlement. Over most of the plain a dispersed pattern is the rule. The density of this varies; it is at its greatest to the south-east of Solliès Pont along the left bank of the Gapeau, and again north of Solliès Pont. This may well relate to the greater intensity of cultivation possible with irrigation. On the other hand, east of La Garde the number of farms seems to decrease—possibly due to the flooding hazard mentioned previously.

The second type of plain settlement is strongly nucleated. The growth of these settlements (Solliès Pont, La Farlède, La Crau, La Garde), is closely related to the physical geography and communications, and can be deduced easily from the map.

The future of farming in this area, as indeed over most of Mediterranean France, appears to be bound up with irrigation. The crops which produce the greatest return per hectare are vegetables and flowers. Thus we may well see an extension of this type of land use at the expense of the vine and tree crops. This is only possible with better water supplies, probably from the Durance basin to the north.

Exercises

1. Describe and account for the distribution of woodland in the area.
2. Explain the distribution of the various types of land use shown in fig. 26.
3. Why has Solliès Pont become the largest settlement in the area, while Solliès Ville has remained relatively small?
4. Explain the facts shown in the temperature and rainfall graphs for Cuers. How do these graphs depart from the characteristic 'Mediterranean' climate? Explain these differences.
5. What do you understand by the term 'river régime'? Discuss the importance of an understanding of river régimes in human geography, drawing your examples from contrasting rivers.
6. What additional information can be obtained about the Provençal landscape by using the photograph as well as the map?
7. Construct a rectangle 11 centimetres high and the same width as the map extract. Divide into 5 horizontal sections, the top one of 3 cm, the other four of 2 cm, height. In the top section draw an east–west section across the map through le Matheron (9905) and Solliès Ville (scale 1 cm to 200 metres). In the other four sections, draw accurate maps of (a) drainage features; (b) land use; (c) settlements; and (d) communications in the strip of land lying between northings 05 and 06. Comment on the geographical relationships revealed by your transects.

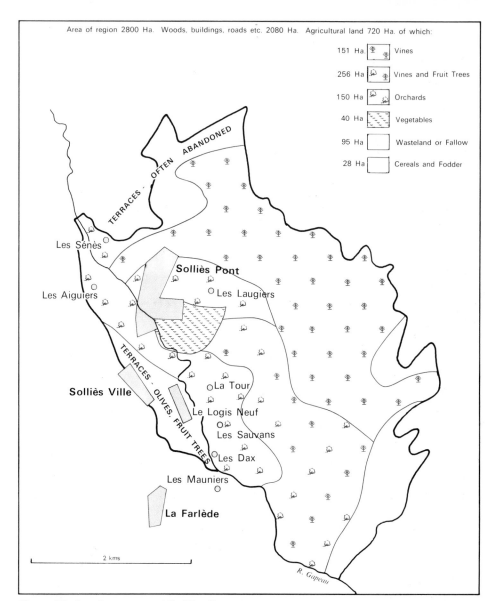

Figure 26. Land use around Solliès-Pont.

Further reading

EVANS, E. E. France, Chatto and Windus, 1960, chapters 4, 5 and 20.
LAMBERT, A. 'Farm consolidation in Western Europe', Geography, 47, 1963.
MARTONNE, E. DE. Geographical Regions of France, 2nd edn, Heinemann, 1948, chapter 14.
MONKHOUSE, F. J. A Regional Geography of Western Europe, 4th edn, Longman, 1974, chapter 15.
ORMSBY, H. France, Methuen, 1950, chapter 10.

Study 17
HAGONDANGE
MOSELLE
FRANCE

An iron and steel works in the Moselle Valley

Extracts from Sheets Uckange 1-2 and 5-6. French 1:25,000 Series.

Published 1954. Vertical Interval of Contours 5 metres. Form lines at 1.25 and 2.5 metres on gentle slopes.

Reproduced from maps published by the Institut Géographique National, Paris.

Map 21

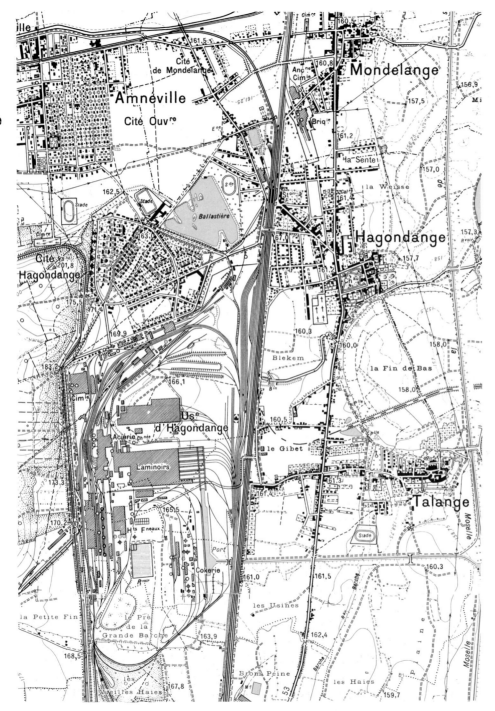

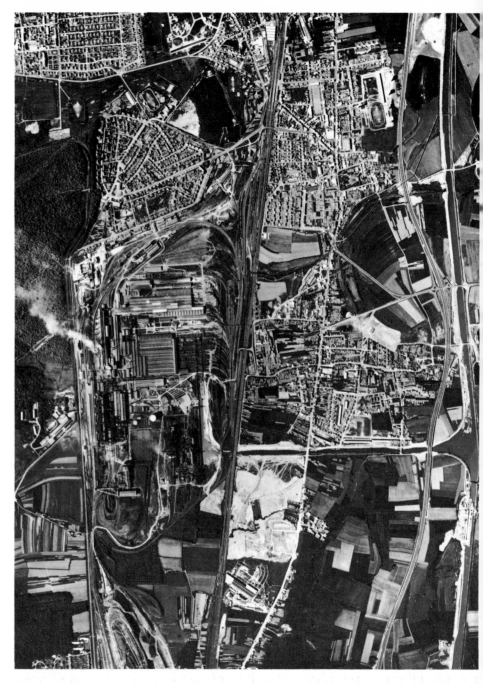

Photograph 24. Iron and steel works at Hagondange

Institut Géographique National, Paris

The iron and steel industry of Lorraine is often quoted as the classic example of the significance of iron ore as a locational factor. The 1:25,000 map extract and photograph 24 show the site and layout of one of the larger works in this region, that of the Sacilor group at Hagondange in the Moselle valley. The site of the works is on a level stretch of land at about 165 metres, a little above the height of the Moselle floodplain. To the west rises the Bois de Coulange, part of the north-south Jurassic escarpment which is cut by the valley of the River Orne to the north of Amnéville.

The Hagondange works form an integrated unit; that is, they carry out the full range of production processes from the manufacture of coke and pig iron to the making of steel products. The details of layout shown on the map and photograph are amplified in the annotated plan (figure 27).

Any iron and steel plant may be best thought of as an assembly point. The raw materials are bulky and of relatively low value; thus the costs of assembling the raw materials at the plant and of despatching the finished products form a considerable part of the costs of production. The raw materials for the blast furnaces are iron ore, coke, and in some cases limestone. The iron ore for the Hagondange works is derived from the lean Jurassic *(minette)* ores of Lorraine. These occur at the base of the Oolite which forms the scarps overlooking the Liassic clay vales of the Moselle valley and Luxemburg. The importance of these ores to both France and the European Economic Community can be gauged from the following figures:

Production of iron ore (million tonnes) 1976

Eastern France	43·3
France	45·5
E.E.C.	55·9

Source: Chambre Syndicate de la Sidérurgie Française.

Although the ores average only 31% iron content, their quantity and accessibility are such that mining is economically justified. The iron-bearing formations have a maximum thickness of about 50 metres, include 12 workable beds and dip gently westwards with few faults. Large-scale mechanised mining is therefore favoured although extraction today is largely from underground mines rather than opencast workings. The works at Hagondange are supplied with ore largely from concessions owned by the manufacturers. In 1960 the blast furnaces consumed 2·86 million tonnes of ore and of this figure 1·98 million tonnes were supplied by the mines at Roncourt (11 kilometres to the south-west) and those at Algrange, 10 kilometres west of Thionville. The two suppliers provide different types of ore. Thus 83% of that from Roncourt is silicious (chamosite) while 99% of the Algrange ore is calcareous (siderite). The

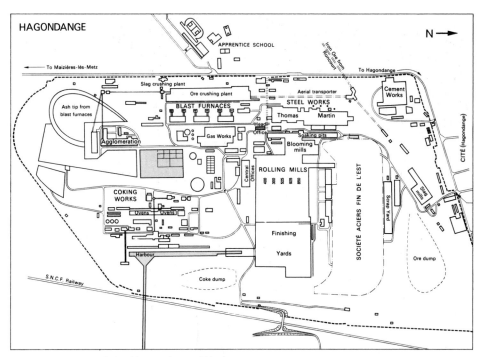

Figure 27. Plan of the Hagondange Works
Source: Wendel-Sidelor

calcareous ores are self-fluxing while the silicious ores require either limestone to be added to the charge or mixing with calcareous ore. Transport from mine to works is carried out either by railway or by overhead cable. The cable linking Hagondange with Roncourt may be noted leaving the map extract in a south-westerly direction.

The second important raw material for the blast furnaces is coke. About half of the requirements for the works are manufactured on the site although before 1929, when the first coke ovens were installed, supplies were brought from the Nord and Ruhr coalfields. The stocks of coal are maintained in huge piles by the harbour, which is served both by the canal and by the railway. Two conflicting influences are at present affecting coal and coke supplies. The canalisation of the Moselle in 1964 was followed by lower freight rates (by railway as well as by canal) between the Ruhr and Lorraine. Furthermore, since 1954 the Sacilor group has controlled about 5% of the coal output and 10% of the coke production of the Ruhr through its acquisition of the Harpener-Bergbau collieries and cokeries near Dortmund. On the other hand, the development of new coke-oven techniques in the late 1950s meant that the coal of the Moselle and Saarland fields with its inferior coking qualities can be used on an increasing scale. Orthodox methods, when used with these coals, required an admixture of 70% of good coking coal from other fields, usually the Ruhr or Nord. The position is now reversed and a mixture containing 70% or more Saar-Moselle coal can now produce good metallurgical coke. Ninety coke ovens are equipped for this process at Hagondange. The effect on Lorraine as a whole is of an increasing reliance upon Moselle coal and coke. In 1967 the coke ovens at Hagondange produced 528,123 tonnes of coke of which the greatest part was of metallurgical quality. In addition a wide range of by-products was secured, including 30,887 tonnes of tar, 6,633 tonnes of benzole, 3,827 tonnes of sulphate and 216 million cubic metres of gas. The latter is of great importance as a source of heat to the coke ovens and steel furnaces. In addition, some is delivered to the Lorgaz company for transmission to the Ardennes and Paris regions for industrial and domestic uses.

The manufacture of iron at Hagondange consists of two principal operations, the treatment of the ore and the smelting process. The ore arrives from the mines in large pieces unsuitable for the charging machinery. It is therefore crushed, sorted and put through a further process of agglomeration to provide a standard-sized enriched (32–41% iron content) material for the furnaces. The agglomeration process also has the desirable effect of reducing the need for coke (519 kilogrammes per tonne of iron in 1976 compared with 972 kilogrammes in 1960). The quality of the end product can be varied by changing the proportions of calcareous and silicious ores placed in the furnaces. Total production capacity of the five blast furnaces is about 750,000 tonnes per year. In addition they supply gas to the electrical power station in the works, to the steel furnaces, to the coke ovens and to the giant power station at Richemont, near the confluence of the rivers Orne and Moselle. In return Richemont provides additional electricity for the works. A second by-product is slag, the result of the impurities in the ore *(gangue)*. This is used as a raw material, together with local limestone, in the cement factory at the north-western end of the site.

Steel production at Hagondange is carried out in works adjacent to the blast furnaces, thus avoiding the costs of transporting and reheating the pig iron. Formerly two processes were employed: the basic Bessemer process invented by Gilchrist and Thomas in 1879, and the Siemens-Martin open hearth process dating from 1864. The Gilchrist-Thomas, or basic Bessemer process, was the key which opened the riches of the vast Lorraine ore deposits. Before this date no satisfactory method of making steel from these phosphoric ores had been invented. A lining of crushed dolomite was added to the older

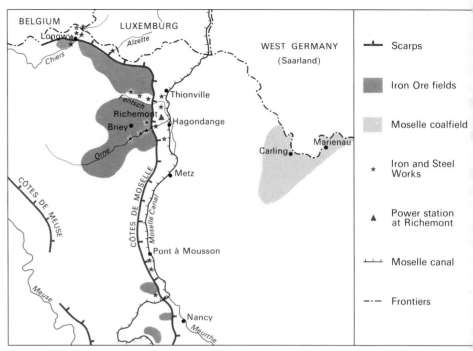

Figure 28. The Moselle Valley
Based on maps by J. E. Martin

Bessemer converter which produced a basic slag absorbent of the phosphoric oxides. The Siemens-Martin open hearth furnace was adapted in a similar way. In recent years the oxygen converter has gained rapidly in importance. Both in initial capital costs and in running costs this process has proved cheaper than the older processes. Thus in 1975 of a total Lorraine production of 10·2 million tonnes, 3·3 million tonnes were produced by the Thomas process, 0·5 million tonnes by Martin, 0·7 million tonnes in electric furnaces and 5·7 million tonnes in oxygen converters. At Hagondange the Martin process was discontinued in 1971 and there remain three oxygen converters with an annual capacity of 700,000 tonnes.

Finishing processes are carried out in the same area of the works in a series of rolling mills. These take steel ingots and by a process of hot rolling turn out sections of steel to the required pattern. Adjoining the rolling mills of the Sacilor group is another steel works belonging to the Société Aciers Fins de l'Est (S.A.F.E.) which is linked to the Renault automobile organization. This works contains two electric arc furnaces and produces rolled bars, plate, forged and stamped pieces destined chiefly for the automobile industry.

Transport is of vital importance in this industry. Both internal and external traffic are moved largely by railway. The internal system with its many kilometres of track is linked to the Metz-Thionville SNCF line by junctions at Hagondange and Maizières-lès-Metz (just south of the map extract). In recent years the waterway system has been radically improved. Boats of 1,500 tons can now use the harbour (extended since the publication of the map by a new section just east of the main railway line) and its linkages to the north with the canalised Moselle.

A striking feature of the map extract is the contrast in settlement form between the old village nucleii of Mondelange, Hagondange and Talange and the modern *cités ouvrières* with their symmetrical and planned layout as in the Cité Ouvrière of Amnéville and the Cité d'Hagondange. The industrial growth of Lorraine has not led to any spectacular expansion of pre-existing settlements. Instead a new industrial world has been created apart from rural Lorraine. 'Les centres industriels sont anonymes, nés de rien, pas même de la campagne lorraine . . . Villes neuves, trop neuves, non assimilés par la paysage, calquées artificiellement, comme un décor.' (R. Nistri and C. Prêcheur). On the other hand, the poor living and housing conditions of the Nord region, for example, are avoided in these enterprises. Indeed the industrial groups of Lorraine take some pride in providing their workers with good amenities. In part this has been a result of an earlier shortage of labour for the needs of industry, which was alleviated only by the recruitment of workers from other parts of France, Italy, Algeria, Poland and Spain. Thus along the Moselle valley and in the valleys of the Orne and Fentsch has grown a series of new towns linked with the very rapid and recent development of the iron and steel industry. In recent years the adoption of methods yielding higher productivity has led to some labour redundancy. Both in the ore mines and in the iron and steel works the labour force has been reduced. Lorraine is now one of the specially favoured areas for regional planning and various grants and State loans are available.

The production of iron and steel in Lorraine is today dominated by large firms. This process was in evidence even before 1939 but has been carried still further in recent years. Thus Wendel-Sidelor was formed in 1968 by the fusion of the three most important firms in Lorraine (La Société Mosellane de Sidérurgie, l'Union Sidérurgique Lorraine and Wendel et Cie, S.A.). Later still the Sacilor-Sollac group was created in 1975. This is now one of the largest European steel makers and its activities cover a considerable part of Lorraine including the Moselle valley between Metz and Thionville, the tributary valleys of the Orne and the Fentsch, and the basin of Longwy to the north. Along with this process of amalgamation has come the closing down of smaller, less economic works.

The economic future of Hagondange itself is now threatened by the recent slump in the fortunes of the steel industry. Plans are in hand to discontinue both the coke and blast furnace works at Hagondange. Both are old and less productive than more modern works. It is likely that 2,200 jobs will be lost at Hagondange and a similar number at Rombas in the Orne valley.

Exercises

1. What advantages of site for an iron and steel works can be deduced from the 1 : 25,000 map extract and the aerial photograph?
2. It is conceivable that through waterways might be constructed from the Rhône to Rotterdam via either the Meuse, the Rhine or the Moselle valleys. *(a)* What justification is there for such a connection between the Mediterranean and the North Sea? *(b)* What relative advantages are possessed by each of these possible routes?
3. What similarities and contrasts are there between the exploitation of the French and British Jurassic iron ores?
4. Compare the sites of the older village nucleii of Mondelange, Hagondange and Talange with those of the newer settlements of Cité d'Hagondange and Amnéville. *(Cité Ouvrière.)*
5. Analyse the significance of the use of scrap metal in the modern steel industry.
6. Using detailed examples, describe and explain the differences between horizontally and vertically organised industries.
7. Examine the geographical basis of one major area of steel production within North-western Europe. (London.)

Further reading

CHABOT, G. *Géographie Régionale de la France*, 3rd edn, Masson et Cie, 1975.

LE LANNOU, M. *Les Régions Géographiques de la France*, Paris, 1964.

MARTIN, J. E. 'Location Factors in the Lorraine Iron and Steel Industry', *Trans. I.B.G.* **23**, 1957.

MARTIN, J. E. 'Recent Trends in the Lorraine Iron and Steel Industry', *Geography*, **43**, 1958.

MARTIN, J. E. 'Developments in the Lorraine Iron and Steel Industry', *Geography*, **46**, 1961.

MARTIN, J. E. 'New Trends in the Lorraine Iron Region', *Geography*, **53**, 1968.

MICHEL, A. A. 'The Canalization of the Moselle and West European Integration', *Geographical Review*, **52**, 1962.

MONKHOUSE, F. J. *A Regional Geography of Western Europe*, 4th edn, Longman, 1974.

NISTRI, R. and PRÊCHEUR, C. *La Région du Nord et du Nord-Est. La France de Demain*, Presses Universitaires de France, Paris, 1959.

POUNDS, N. J. G. 'Lorraine and the Ruhr', *Economic Geography*, **33**, 1957.

POUNDS, N. J. G. *The Geography of Iron and Steel*, Hutchinson's University Library, 1966.

SCHOLFIELD, G. 'The Canalization of the Moselle', *Geography*, **50**, 1965.

WARREN. K. 'The Changing Steel Industry of the European Common Market', *Economic Geography*, **43**, 1967.

Study 18
MARSEILLES
BOUCHE-DU-RHONE
FRANCE

A Study of Port Growth.

Extract from Sheet XXXI-45. Marseille.
French 1:50,000 Series.
(Type 1922)

Based on a survey of 1900–04.
Revised 1933–36.
Published 1941.
Partial revision 1966.
Vertical interval of contours 10 metres.

Reproduced from a map published by Institut Géographique National, Paris.

Map 22

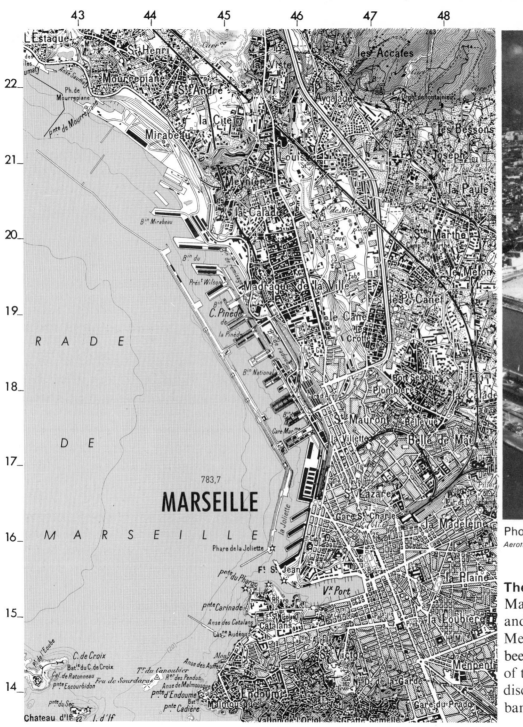

Photograph 25. Marseilles. 19th century dock extensions.
Aerofilms Ltd., London.

The site and position of Marseilles

Marseilles, with a population of 1,071,000 in 1975, is the second largest city and first port of France and the most important and busiest port on the Mediterranean. One of the key factors enabling it to achieve this status has been its position near the southern end of the **Rhône-Saône Corridor**, one of the chief routeways in western Europe. However, the fact that the Rhône discharges into the Mediterranean by means of a delta with shifting sand banks and a shallow offshore gradient long precluded the development of a large seaport at the actual mouth of the river. To the west of the delta, longshore drifting has created a coast of sandbars and lagoons, so that until recently the only place near the mouth of the river where a harbour might be created was to the east where a series of limestone hills, a continuation of the Pyreneean system, approaches the coast.

The site of the original settlement was around the shore of a small inlet on this deep water, virtually tideless and silt-free coast where some shelter is afforded by the surrounding hills and a group of small offshore islands, including the Ile Pomègues, Ile Rattoneau (just beyond the limits of the extract) and the Ile d'If. Around the original harbour, the present Vieux Port, is a belt of undulating ground with a series of steep-sided hills beyond. To the north, east and south of Marseilles respectively lie the hills of the Chaîne de l'Estaque, Chaîne de l'Etoile and the Montagne Marseilleveyre (fig. 29). The city thus lies on a generally low plain surrounded by a semi-circle of hills and the Mediterranean. The site is in many ways an ideal one for a

small settlement, but for a city of the size of Marseilles the steep bordering hills limit the space for the circulation of traffic and the expansion of industry and housing, so that very high building densities have resulted in the districts of the inner town. The surrounding hills are not evident from the map extract except in the north-east where the land rises to 263 metres in the district of les Accates and in the extreme south where a spot height of 162 metres is shown on the well-known sea mark of Notre Dame de la Garde (465142). A minor site element, but one which has played an important role in the development of the city, is the small limestone hill of St Laurent (unnamed on the extract) which lies to the immediate north of the Vieux Port (463158). It was on this hill, which protected the harbour at its foot from the *Mistral*, that the settlement had its beginnings.

The growth of Marseilles

The earliest settlement, Massilia, was founded about 600 B.C. by Greek merchants who recognised the advantages of the position of the small harbour, or Lacydon as it was named. Both the Greco-Roman and the medieval settlement occupied the same position on the St Laurent hill overlooking the port. The town subsequently expanded to the east and was enclosed by a wall at the end of the 14th century (fig. 30). Until the end of the 17th century Marseilles remained within the limits of this wall, crowded with narrow streets and alleys running down the hill to the waterfront. Despite much recent demolition many of these narrow streets still remain to the south-east of the cathedral (460160). Following plans by Colbert for the development of the town, new walls were constructed between 1670 and 1690. These took in large areas to the east and south of the existing settlement and involved the construction of a number of wide boulevards and streets, often laid out in a rectilinear plan. This pattern of streets persists to the present time and is clearly seen on the extract to the immediate east and south-east of the Vieux Port. Demolition of the outer walls began in 1790, but even before that date it had proved impossible to restrain buildings within the fortifications and the town had already spread along the routes to Aix and Toulon.

However, Marseilles's greatest period of expansion came in the 19th century. The French settlement of Algeria which began in 1830 led to an expansion of trade between the two shores of the Mediterranean. The port traffic of Marseilles increased from 800,000 tonnes in 1827 to over 3 million tonnes in 1847, and increasingly in the 19th century Marseilles became the centre from which trade with North Africa was organised. In 1869 the

Figure 29. The position of Marseilles.

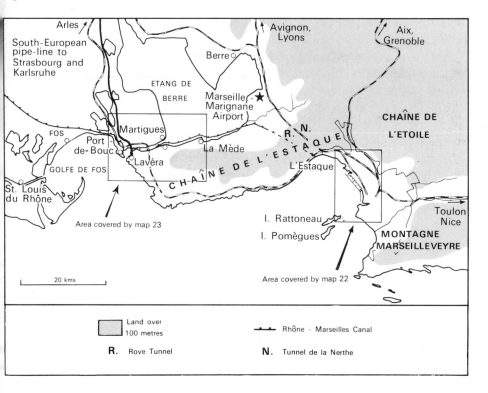

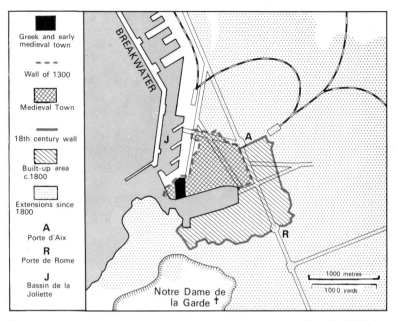

Figure 30. The growth elements of central Marseilles, *(after R. E. Dickinson)*

Legend:
- Greek and early medieval town
- Wall of 1300
- Medieval Town
- 18th century wall
- Built-up area c.1800
- Extensions since 1800
- A Porte d'Aix
- R Porte de Rome
- J Bassin de la Joliette

BREAKWATER

Notre Dame de la Garde †

1000 metres
1000 yards

opening of the Suez Canal placed the town in a strong position for trade with the Far East and provided access to new sources of raw materials for the industrial development of the city. The trade of Marseilles has always been very closely connected with developments in Algeria. For example, Algerian independence led to a 60 per cent reduction in trade between Marseilles and North Africa, although another interesting result of this development was an influx of about 100,000 returning French to boost the population of the city from 784,000 in 1962 to 930,000 in 1964.

The 19th century growth of maritime trade necessitated extensions to the port. A small annexe to the Vieux Port was cut out of solid limestone on the south side of the natural harbour (460151), but this provided only a small addition to the existing docking space. The eventual solution took the form of major harbour works to the north of the Vieux Port. The shore of the Rade de Marseille was evened out and a great protective breakwater built some 500 metres out from the straightened shore in 10–15 metres of water. A series of projecting moles was constructed from the new shore to create a series of interconnected dock basins within the shelter of the breakwater. The first of these, the Bassin de la Joliette, was opened in 1853 and others followed to the north in rapid succession. At the same time the

warehouses, silos, stations, sidings and harbour installations which are clearly seen on the map and photograph 25 were developed. Communications inland were also improved to deal with the increasing volume of trade. The Tunnel de la Nerthe was cut through the Chaîne de l'Estaque to carry a railway to Avignon and Lyons in 1852. This was followed by lines to Toulon and Grenoble in 1859 and 1877. In 1915 the Corniche line was constructed westwards along the rocky coast to Port-de-Bouc at the entrance to the Etang de Berre. In 1927 the seven-kilometre-long Rove Tunnel through the Chaîne de l'Estaque was opened to carry the Marseilles-Rhône Canal northwards from l'Estaque to the Etang de Berre where it runs along the southern shore to Martigues. From there the navigation leads through the Etang de Caronte to Port-de-Bouc to connect with the Arles-Bouc Canal which runs northwestwards to join the Rhône (see fig. 29 and map 23, showing the entrance to the Etang de Berre).

During the 19th and present centuries the city has expanded north and west on the low ground at the foot of the hills, although this naturally marshy ground, with its numerous streams such as the Ruisseau de Plombières and Ruisseau des Aygalades (not named on the map), was far from an ideal site for urban development. As can be seen from the extract, the buildings and streets of the town are now climbing the heights of the Massif de la Garde and les Accates.

Many of the present day industries of Marseilles date back to the 19th century, especially those based on the processing of raw materials from Africa and the Far East. Within this group mention should be made of sugar-refining and the processing of fats and oils to produce soap, margarine and various edible oils. Other food industries include flour-milling and the manufacture of chocolate, jams, biscuits, semolina, etc. As in all large ports ship-repairing, marine-engineering and metal-working employ large numbers. Up to about 1920 the industry of Marseilles consisted almost entirely of these types, but in recent decades there has been a marked growth of a wide range of generally light industries, a trend which relates in part to the development of hydro-electric power resources in south-eastern France and partly to the government policy of decentralisation of industry, which makes a peripheral area such as Marseilles attractive for such developments. The chief industrial districts of the central town shown on the extract include St Lazare (4616), St Mauron (4617), Belle de Mai, Bellevue and Plombières (4717), and la Viste (4522).

From these remarks it is clear that the growth of Marseilles can be divided into two phases: a long initial period of development up to *c.* 1850 in which the growing town shows a submission to the conditions of its site, and secondly the modern growth after 1850, which has involved ambitious engineering projects (harbour works, tunnelling, land drainage, etc.) to overcome, in part at least, the natural limitations of the site and to enable the potential strength of the town's position to be realised.

The port of Marseilles

As mentioned above, the modern port of Marseilles lies within the shelter of the breakwater which has been progressively extended until it now exceeds 7 km in length. On the inner side of the breakwater a number of moles have been built out from the straightened shore to create a series of interconnected dock basins and a total length of over 30 km of quays. The virtually tideless nature of the Mediterranean means that ships can enter and leave at all times and no locks are needed at the dock entrances. The various quays are all connected by railway tracks to an elaborate system of sidings and the principal station serving the port, the Gare d'Arenc. The Gare de la Joliette serves the southern part of the harbour. The form of the harbour is well illustrated on photograph 25, which shows the Bassin du Président Wilson and Bassin de la Pinède in the foreground. Beyond the bascule bridge which links the breakwater with the shore can be seen the Bassin Nationale. The intensive use of the various jetties and the shore bordering the harbour is evident from the photograph. A striking cluster of silos, storage tanks and other buildings can be seen on the slightly higher ground of the former Cap Pinède. It is interesting to note that the Bassin de remisage, a former ship repairing basin, which is shown on the map extract, has been infilled and is in the process of being built upon. During

Details of the docks of Marseilles

Name of docks	Date of opening	Depth in metres	Cargoes handled	Chief trading connections	Other remarks
1. Le Bassin de la Joliette	1853	8-9	Fruit and *Primeurs*	Algeria, Tunisia, Morocco, Corsica, Israel, Senegal.	Largest of the dock basins. Quayside installations include fruit and vegetable markets, grain silos, wine stores and the harbour operations office. Gare de la Joliette deals almost exclusively with the fruit and vegetable trade.
2. Le Bassin de la Gare Maritime	1859	9	Ground nuts, copra, palm kernels, coal, sulphur, china clay.	Algeria, W. Africa, Greece, Turkey.	Takes name from maritime station formerly on one of the moles. Shown on map extract but now disused. Storage premises for bananas.
3. Le Bassin Nationale	1863	9	Varied cargoes— vegetable oils, grain, coal, etc.	Middle East, Greece, Turkey.	Vegetable oil storage installations on the quayside.
4. Le Bassin de Radoub	1863	9	None.	None.	This section of the harbour consists of 7 dry docks for ship repairing. (70% of all French ship repairing work is done in Marseilles.)
5. Le Bassin de la Pinède	1900	9.5	Varied cargoes— oil, tropical produce, grain, etc.	Malagasie, Réunion, Spain, Argentina, Italy.	Separated from the Bassin Nationale by a bascule bridge which carries a railway to the outer breakwater. (Not shown on the map). Grain silos, oil storage tanks.
6. Le Bassin du Président Wilson	1909	9-12	Imports of sugar, etc. Much passenger traffic.	Far East, S. America, Australia, W. Indies.	New storage premises under construction for storage of sugar and bauxite.
Le Bassin de remisage			A former ship repairing basin, now infilled. (See Photograph 25).		
7. Le Bassin Mirabeau	1940	9–18.3	Varied cargoes— much passenger traffic.	N. America, Central America, S. Africa, Australia, etc.	Greatest depths here. Largest liners operate from these northern docks. Floating docks for ship repairing.

Marseilles: port traffic 1975

Imports	*Tonnes*
Crude oil and petroleum products	70,001,700
Metal ores and scrap metal	3,999,500
Foodstuffs (fruit, vegetables, cereals, raw sugar, molasses, coffee, wine, etc.)	1,519,200
Vegetable oils	652,800
Fertilisers	400,100
Timber, cork	360,700
Chemicals	334,100
Manufactured goods (machinery, textiles, paper, etc.)	332,700
Iron and steel, and non-ferrous metals	165,200
Coal	120,600
Rubber	75,300
Other goods	1,299,900
Total Imports	79,261,800

of which total 75,298,000 tonnes (95%) was handled by the port annexes (almost entirely crude oil).

Exports	
Refined petroleum products	11,509,200
Manufactured goods (machinery, textiles, glass, etc.)	1,148,200
Chemical products (plastics, soap, detergents)	1,210,100
Foodstuffs (wine, sugar, flour, semolina)	991,800
Iron and steel, and non-ferrous metals	539,100
Building materials (cement, bricks, tiles)	330,600
Coal	24,300
Other goods	766,400
Total Exports	16,519,700

of which total 12,885,000 (78%) was handled by the port annexes.

Source: Annuaire Statistique de la France, 1977.

THE ENTRANCE TO THE ETANG DE BERRE

BOUCHES-DU-RHONE

FRANCE

A Zone of New Industrial and Harbour Developments.

Extracts from Sheets XXX-44 & 45 Istres, XXXI-44 Martigues and XXXI-45 Marseilles.
French 1:50,000 Series.

Revisions.
Istres. Full Revision 1960
Martigues. Full Revision 1960
Partial Revision 1963.
Marseilles. Partial Revision 1966.
Vertical interval of contours 10 metres.

Reproduced from maps published by Institut Géographique National, Paris.

Map 23

Photograph 26. The Lavéra oil refinery, tanker terminal and petro-chemical plant.

British Petroleum Ltd., London.

the last 10 years many changes have taken place at the northern end of the harbour. The breakwater has been extended to the north-west to create a new dock basin. In the Mirabeau district an extensive area has recently been reclaimed from the sea and now includes quays, warehouses, dry docks, railway sidings etc. Building is continuing here at the present time. Details of the various dock basins are given in tabular form.

In 1975 Marseilles and its annexes ranked second among the ports of Europe (after Rotterdam) in terms of tonnage of goods loaded and unloaded, and handled 32% of French maritime trade. In that year the port handled almost 96 million tonnes of goods, dealt with 885,000 passengers and had over 24,000 arrivals and departures of vessels. Details of the export/import trade are shown on page 101.

A striking point about these figures is the fact that the port annexes of Marseilles (Port-de-Bouc, Lavéra, Martigues, La Mède, Berre, Fos and Port St Louis du Rhône) now handle more than ten times the tonnage of Marseilles itself. Part of this area of relatively new harbour installations and industry is shown on the second map extract of the Marseilles region.

The entrance to the Etang de Berre

The exact location of the map area which lies 40 kilometres to the north-west of Marseilles is shown on fig. 29. It should be noted that the extract is composed of sections of map from three different sheets of the 1:50,000 series, each with varying dates of revision. Thus, certain discrepancies occur along the north-south line 188 as, for example, the break in the road west of St. Pierre (188223).

Relief and drainage of the area bordering the entrance to the Etang de Berre

The southern part of the map extract shows the western end of the limestone hills of the Chaîne de l'Estaque. The pervious nature of the rocks in this area is indicated by the temporary and interrupted nature of most of the stream courses, the large number of dry valleys and the need for numerous reservoirs for the storage of water. The hills gradually decline in elevation westwards, but drop steeply northwards to the Etang de Berre and the Chenal de Caronte. This northern edge is dissected by a series of short dry valleys, as to the south of Martigues. The summits of the Plaine d'Escourillon and the Plaine de Boutier, where a maximum elevation of 201 metres is attained (253242), show a marked flattening. In the extreme south the large valley of St Pierre runs eastwards into the hills for over 5 km, but of greater interest is the unusual form and drainage pattern of the smaller

vallon (abb. *von*) which lies high above the level of the main valley and runs east-west approximately along the level of grid line 23. The higher parts of the Chaîne de l'Estaque are heavily wooded apart from the Plaine de Boutier which, like the western slopes, has a cover of *garrigue* vegetation. To the north of the Chenal de Caronte is another area of hilly ground, although in this instance the relief is generally lower and more subdued, and rarely rises above 100 metres. In the north-west two depressions lie just below sea level and are occupied by the lagoons of Engrenier and Pourra. The margins of the latter are subject to wide seasonal fluctuations. In the area north of the Chenal de Caronte the woodland is more broken and interspersed with areas of vines and olives. The shores of the channel linking the Etang de Berre and the Mediterranean are flanked by low, marshy ground which reaches almost 1 km in width to the north-west of Lavéra.

The map extract provides little information about navigation channels in this area. The Mediterranean is shown to have a fairly gentle offshore profile, while the Etang de Berre is uniformly shallow at a depth of 5–10 metres. The map fails to reveal the fact that the Chenal de Caronte has had a channel over 10 metres deep dredged through it, while a similar channel has been made across the Etang de Berre continuing the line of the marker buoys east of Martigues. This enables tankers to reach the terminal at Berre on the north-eastern shore of the lagoon.

Settlement and industrial development

Away from the coast settlement is scattered. In the south the higher parts of the limestone hills are virtually devoid of settlement. The two largest settlements are Martigues and Port-de-Bouc at either end of the Chenal de Caronte. Martigues, which occupies land on either side of the channel together with the Ile Jonquières is shown to have a population of 21,500, but this has increased since the publication of the map to almost 40,000. Similarly the population of Port-de-Bouc is now almost double the 12,500 indicated on the map. La Mède occupies a quite steeply sloping site at the mouth of a large valley which penetrates west into the hills. Lavéra is a vast complex of industrial developments, but the actual settlement to the east of the railway remains quite small.

The industrial and port developments of the Etang de Berre were due to the impossibility of extending the port of Marseilles beyond l'Estaque, and also the lack of extensive sites in the city for expanding industry, especially the petrochemical industry which, as can be seen from photograph 26, requires a vast area of ground. First developments around the lagoon began in the early 1920s; the first oil refinery was introduced in 1931 and this industry has shown a phenomenal growth since the war. Imports of crude oil to the refineries of the Etang de Berre totalled over 70 million tonnes in 1975 compared with 3 million tonnes in 1948. Three refineries now operate around the shores of the lagoon, at Lavéra (Sté Française des Petroles B.P.), La Mède (Cie Française de Raffinage) and Berre (Sté Shell-Berre). In addition to these, a refinery (Esso) was opened in 1965 at Fos-sur-Mer some 2 km to the north-west of the map extract. This latter development was in fact the beginning of an enormous project which has created new tanker terminals and a vast industrial zone on the shore of the Golfe de Fos. The Fos development includes oil refineries, gas treatment plants, steel foundries, and chemical plants as well as a tanker terminal and container terminal able to receive vessels up to 500,000 tonnes d.w.t. The Lavéra terminal, constructed in 1952, can accommodate tankers of up to 100,000 tonnes. In 1962 a pipe-line (Le Pipe-Line Sud-Européan) was opened between Lavéra and Strasbourg and Karlsruhe, thus shortening the route for oil to that area by 1,500 km compared with the route via the North Sea and Rotterdam.

In 1975 the four refineries imported 70 million tonnes of crude oil chiefly from the Saharan and Middle East Oilfields, 44 million tonnes of which was piped directly to the Rhine valley and 26 million tonnes refined locally.

Sources of crude oil 1975		Output of refineries 1975	
Saudi Arabia	38%	La Mède	7·5 M. tonnes
Iran	14%	Berre	7·0 M. tonnes
Iraq	11%	Lavéra	6·4 M. tonnes
Algeria	8%	Fos-s-Mer	5·1 M. tonnes
Libya	8%		
Tunisia	7%		26·0 M. tonnes
Syria	6%		(24% of French refined production)
Nigeria	6%		
Other sources	2%		

Source: *Port de Marseille 1975.* Direction du Port Autonome de Marseille 1976.

The industrial developments of the district are basically concerned with oil refining, but an impressive range of ancillary petrochemical industries has also developed. These include the manufacture of carbon black for the paint and rubber industries, ethylene, propylene and other plastics, captane, acetones, detergents, insecticides etc. These industries are found on the north bank of the Chenal de Caronte and also in close proximity to the refineries of Lavéra and La Mède. On photograph 26 the oil refinery is shown in the centre of the view, while the extensive plant in the lower left of the photograph consists of the associated chemical industry. These complex industrial developments represent the present stage reached in a long and continuous evolution of harbour works and industries in the Marseilles region, an evolution which has its beginnings in the Greek trading post established on the St Laurent Hill more than 2,500 years ago. The future of Marseilles lies in the establishment of efficient communications with its hinterland. Already the South European Pipe-Line enables it to serve the Rhine Rift Valley. The development of a complete waterway link with the Rhine would strengthen this connection and enable Marseilles to compete with Rotterdam and Europort in serving this interior part of Europe.

Exercises

1. Amplify the statement that Marseilles occupies a poor site but an excellent position for a modern seaport.
2. Examine the effects of the following on the development of Marseilles:
(a) the opening of the Suez Canal; *(b)* the history of French settlement in Algeria; *(c)* the opening of trans-Alpine railway routes.
3. It has been pointed out that Marseilles has a similar site, position and history of development as Genoa. Examine the truth of this statement.
4. Compare the new industrial and harbour developments in the Marseilles region with the Europort developments of Rotterdam.
5. What criteria may be used to classify ports?
6. Examine the conditions necessary for the establishment of large scale oil refining and petrochemical industries.
7. With reference to the map of the Etang de Berre, draw an annotated contour sketch map of the area in the south west bounded by easting 21 and northing 25. In what ways is the drainage pattern of this area unusual? Suggest how it may have evolved.

Further reading

BOYLE, P. S. 'Le Nouveau Port Petrolier de Lavéra: Expansion Portuaire de Marseille.' *Review de Géographie Alpine.* Vol. 48. no 3. 1960.
DICKINSON, R. E. *The West European City,* 2nd edn, Routledge and Kegan Paul 1961, chapter 18.
HOYLE, B. S. Recent Port Expansion and Associated Industrial Development at Marseilles, *Tijdschrift Voor Economische en Sociale Geografie.* no 3. March 1960.
JONES, H. D. 'Marseilles Looks Ahead', *Geographical Magazine* xxv, May 1952.
MONKHOUSE, F. J. *A Regional Geography of Western Europe,* 4th edn, Longman, 1974, chapter 15.
MORGAN, F. W. and BIRD, J. *Ports and Harbours,* 2nd edn, Hutchinson, 1958.
ORMSBY, H. *France,* 2nd edn, Methuen 1950, chapter 10.
PIERREIN, L. 'Les Constants de l'Evolution Economique et les Problèmes d'Avenir', *La Revue de la Chambre de Commerce de Marseille,* **756,** 1965.
PIERREIN, L. 'Sur l'Expansion Economique de Marseille et sa Région', *Bulletin de Géographie d'Aix-Marseille,* **66,** 1955.
SIEGFRIED, A. *The Mediterranean,* Cape, 1948.
THOMPSON, I. B. *The Lower Rhône and Marseille,* Oxford U.P., 1975.
TOMKINSON, D. 'The Marseilles Experiment', *Town Planning Review,* **24,** 1953.
TUPPEN, J. 'Fos: Europort of the South?' *Geography,* **60,** 1975.

Pamphlets issued by the Petroleum Information Bureau.
The Port of Lavéra. October 1963.
From Mediterranean to Rhine. December 1963.

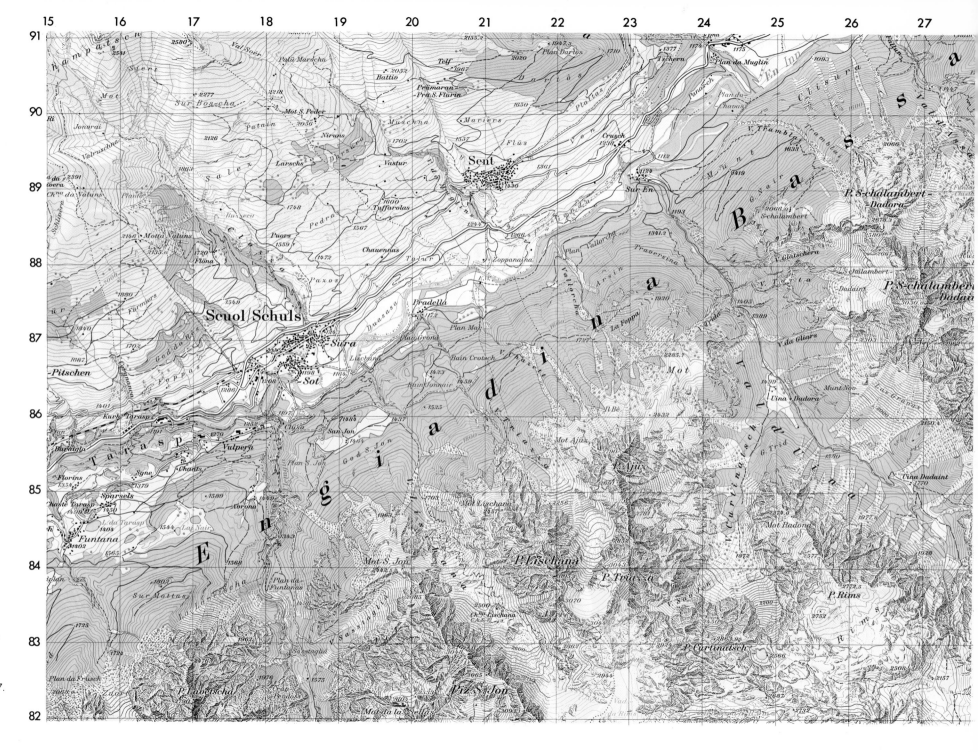

Study 19
THE ENGADINE GRISONS SWITZERLAND

An Alpine Valley.

Extract from Sheet 249.
Tarasp.
Swiss 1:50,000 Series.

Map Published 1951.
Revised 1964.
Vertical interval of
contours 20 metres.

Extract from the Swiss National Map 1:50,000 reproduced with the permission of the Topographical Survey of Switzerland of 5 December, 1967.

Map 24

Photograph 27. Part of the Engadine valley. Notice the cultivated terraces, the forested north-facing slopes and the incised river.

Swiss National Tourist Office, London.

The map extracts of the Gorner Glacier and the Lower Engadine are taken from the Swiss 1:50,000 series. These maps, like their companion series at 1:25,000 and 1:100,000 are distinguished by very fine draughtsmanship and in particular by the excellent manner in which relief is shown. Contours are normally drawn at a 20 metre vertical interval, but on parts of the Gorner Glacier a 10 metre interval is used to give a clearer impression of relief. On steep rocky slopes a fine rock drawing technique is employed, and over the whole map a system of oblique hill shading emphasises the general pattern of relief. The combination of these three methods gives a clear impression of landscapes which are complicated and which have a considerable range of altitude within short distances.

The map extract shows a section of the Engadine region which is located in the eastern part of Switzerland and is drained by the River Inn in an easterly direction towards Austria. A comparison of the map and photograph will illustrate many of the essential geographical features common to a large number of Alpine valleys.

Relief

The southern peaks show many characteristics of recent glacial and frost action. In fact, small ice-patches, hardly large enough to be designated glaciers, still occupy the higher parts (c. 2,800 metres) of the Val da Lischana (2282) and Val Triazza (2283). The heads of these valleys are rounded in plan with steep back and side walls and are separated from each other and from the adjacent Val Curtinatsch by steep-sided ridges or arêtes.

Further down, both valleys show evidence of recent ice extension to lower levels. Melt-water from the small corrie glaciers loses itself in piles or morainic material only to issue $1\frac{1}{2}$ to 2 km away and some 900 metres lower down the valleys.

The peaks are represented on the map by a combination of contours, rock shading and oblique hill shading. These convey an impression of ruggedness and steepness which is borne out when reference is made to the photograph. For much of the year crevices and hollows contain snow and ice, and alternate freezing and melting in response to wide diurnal ranges of temperature is responsible for the weathering of the bare slopes, thus producing a rough and angular surface with scree lower down. Deep gullies are cut in the lower slopes by melt-water armed with angular debris.

Evidence that ice once extended to much lower levels is afforded by the appearance of both main and tributary valleys. Both the Clemgia and Val d'Uina streams show a longitudinal profile which hangs into the main valley. The upper parts of each of these valleys have gentle gradients, and in the case of the Val d'Uina a width sufficient for habitation and possibly cultivation (2486 and 2685). Lower down, each valley narrows and reaches the floor of the Inn trench through steep-sided gorges of considerable gradient, which were cut in post-glacial times by river action. (Note especially the stream in squares 1884 and 1885.)

The Inn valley has a flat floor which contrasts strongly with the steepness of its sides. This fact, together with the absence of spurs extending into the valley, supports the theory that a large valley glacier once occupied the Inn trench. At higher levels, discontinuous benches are observable along the valley which probably represent the remains of the pre-glacial valley sides before over-deepening took place. Parts of these benches are visible in the photograph, notably in the centre where a small clearing (San Jon 1,464 metres) is to be seen. Similarly on the northern side in the village of Sent a bench can be noted at 1,430 metres. Since glacial times a considerable amount of erosion has been accomplished. The river now flows some 80 metres below the level of the low terrace (1786), although further downstream the entrenchment of the river is much less. Some widening at the present river level has taken place, notably by Scuol-Sot (1886), Duasasa (1987) and in square 2389.

Land use

The most remarkable feature of the land use on both the map and photograph is the contrast between the two sides of the Inn trench. On the southern side of the valley the greater part of the land is forested with larch and fir up to the treeline at about 2,000 metres. On the northern side forests are far less common, being limited to the steep sides of the tributary valley north of Scuol and a few patches on the slopes north of Sent. Instead, most of this northern side is covered by pasture land, though not always of the highest quality. Marshy ground is shown at intervals and loose rock is occasionally in evidence. The low terrace of the Inn valley is shown in the photograph to be intensively cultivated on the northern side. A variety of cropping is carried out to the very edge of the terrace and for a short distance up the slopes of the north side. On the south side of the valley there seems to be little evidence of farming. A few clearings with buildings occur in the woodland, and also further up the tributary valleys as at Uina Dadora (2486), but these are probably for hay and grazing rather than cropping. (Note the San Jon clearing on the photograph.) On the upper slopes north of the Inn there are far more of these isolated buildings; twenty-nine north of the Inn valley above 1,500 metres compared with eleven south of the valley. It seems probable that these pasturelands are for use during the summer only and correspond to the mayens of Central Switzerland. In comparison, the height of the mayen in the Val d'Anniviers in Valais is at 1,970 metres, and the highest pasture or alp occurs between 2,200 and 2,800 metres.

The contrast in land use between the north-facing and south-facing slopes can be directly attributed to differences in insolation rather than to differences of slope. The proximity of peaks such as Piz Ajûz, Piz Lisehana and Piz S. Jon considerably reduces the hours of sunlight on the north-facing slopes during much of the year. This is particularly important during the spring and autumn seasons, when the sun is at a moderate angle of elevation and when crops and pasture are at the beginning or climax of their growth cycle. For a full discussion of these problems and for an explanation of the methods of calculating the duration and intensity of insolation, reference should be made to the work on alpine valleys by A. Garnett.

Settlement and communications

Both major settlements, Scuol and Sent, owe their position to the availability of land for cropping and pasture. Their actual siting on the northern side of the valley is dictated by the suitability of slopes for building. An examination of the map will show that Scuol has two nuclei: Scuol-Sura is built on gently sloping land at a point where the stream issuing from the valley of La Clozza has built up an alluvial fan, while Scuol-Sot is on a terrace close to the entrenched River Inn. Both settlements were originally agricultural centres, but tourism has stimulated their growth in recent decades, particularly along the roads leading out of the town. Sent is considerably higher than Scuol (1,430 metres compared with 1,200 metres at Scuol) and is sited on a fairly level bench some 300 metres above the floor of the valley. The factor of insolation to which reference has already been made probably has an influence here. Tarasp-Vulpera owes its development mainly to its reputation as a health resort based on mineral waters, the Kurhaus being a hotel in which a mineral water treatment may be taken.

Lines of communication inevitably follow the river valley. Scuol is the terminus of a single track railway which runs north-east from St Moritz and links with Italian and Swiss railways through the Bernina and Albula Passes. The growth of Scuol and Tarasp as tourist resorts is connected with this development. Roads follow the sides of the valley at two distinct levels on the northern side and link the larger settlements. It is noteworthy that there is no continuous road connection on the southern side of the valley, and the section of road that does exist merely serves the tourist centres of Tarasp and Vulpera. The hills are served only by tracks which frequently take tortuous hairpin courses to link the higher pasturelands with the valley.

Until the late 19th century the Engadine was one of the most isolated parts of the Alps. Communications up the Inn valley to the rest of Switzerland and to Italy entailed difficult crossings of the Maloja, Bernina or Julier Passes, while downstream the route to Austria was made hazardous by the Finstermunz Gorge. This area has preserved its own language of Romansch, although some of the more important features also have German names, for example, Romansch—Scuol, German—Schuls. The following Romansch terms frequently occur on the map extract, and a knowledge of their meaning aids interpretation:

Plan Terrace, plateau
Piz Peak
Mot A summit of the ridge culminating in the peak of that name.
Vadret abb. Vad. Glacier
Lai Lake

The combination of valley cultivation, upland pasture, forestry and tourism is today characteristic of many Alpine valleys, not only in Switzerland but also in Austria and France. Interesting comparisons can be made with the Rhône valley near Sion and with many Austrian examples. Seldom though is the distinction so clear between sunny, cultivated, south-facing slopes (*adret* or *sonnenseite*) and the shaded, forested, north-facing slopes (*ubac* or *schattenseite*).

Exercises

1. The large settlement on the lefthand side of the photograph is Scuol. Give a map reference for the point from which the photograph was taken. What is the direction and angle of view of the photograph?
2. Construct a longitudinal profile of the stream in Val d'Uina from the spot height 2157 metres (2782) to its confluence with the River Inn. Try to explain any peculiarities of its course.
3. Plot on a sheet of tracing paper the settlements on the map extract. Comment on their distribution in relation to *(a)* relief; *(b)* land use; *(c)* communications.
4. Note the height of each settlement on the map above 1500 metres. Construct a frequency curve for settlement distribution by plotting on graph paper the number of settlements at different heights. What conclusions can you draw from your graph?
5. With reference to a wide range of examples, discuss the influence of slopes on agriculture and settlement.

Further reading

EVANS, E. E. 'Transhumance in Europe', *Geography*, **25**, 1940.
GARNETT, A. 'Insolation, topography and settlement in the Alps', *Geographical Review*, **25**, 1935, p. 601.
GARNETT, A. 'Insolation and Relief', *Trans. of the Institute of British Geographers*, **5**, 1937.
MUTTON, A. F. A. *Central Europe*, Longmans, 1968, chapters 5 and 6.
PEATTIE, R. 'Limits of mountain economies', *Geographical Review* **21**, 1931.
PEATTIE, R. *Mountain Geography*, Harvard U.P., 1936.

**A commercial and
industrial centre on
the Swiss plateau**

Extract from Sheet 225.
Zürich.
Swiss 1:50,000 Series.

Published 1962.
Vertical Interval of
Contours 20 metres.

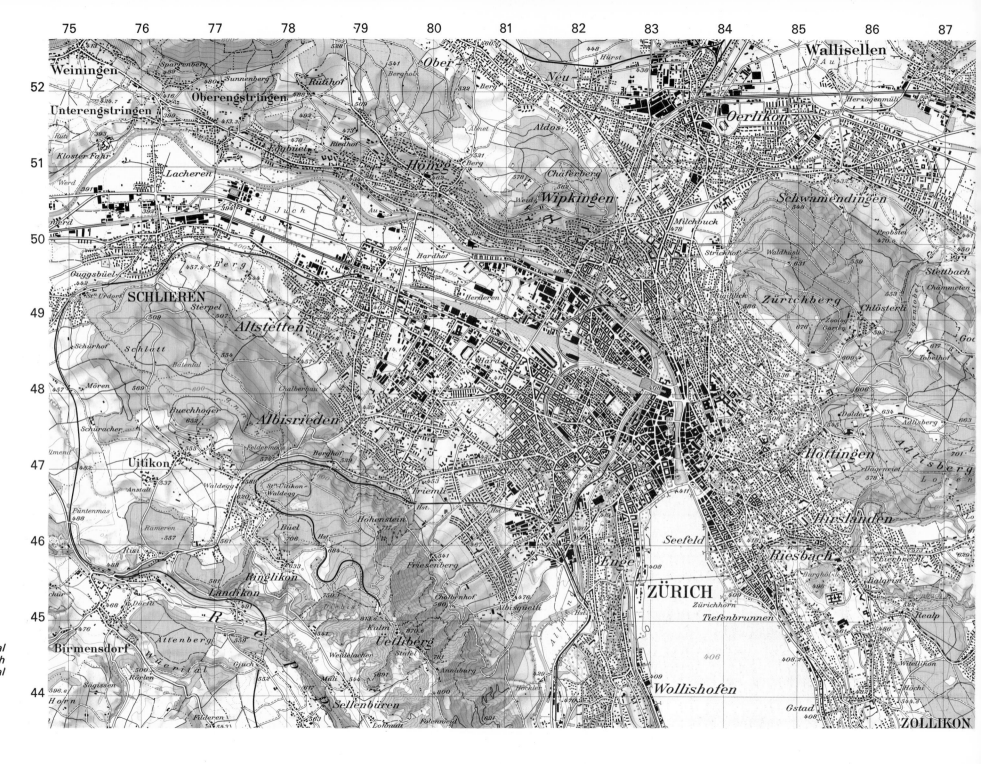

*Extract from the Swiss National
Map 1:50,000, reproduced with
permission of the Topographical
Survey of Switzerland of 18th
September, 1968.*

Map 25

Photograph 28. Central Zürich. View north-north-west across central Zürich towards Chäferberg and the northern suburbs. Various features of the inner town which are numbered on the photograph are indicated in the key below.

1. Lindenhof.
2. Central Station (Hauptbahnhof).
3. Swiss National Museum. (Schweizerisches Landesmuseum.)
4. Bahnhofstrasse.
5. Stadhaus.
6. Grossmunster Cathedral.
7. University.
8. Federal Institute of Technology.
9. Fine Arts Museum (Kunsthaus).
10. City Hall (Rathaus).
11. Bellevue Platz.

Aerofilms Ltd.

Physical factors exercise a vital influence on the distribution of urban settlements in Switzerland. Zürich, capital of the Canton of Zürich and the largest city of the country, is located, like all the other major Swiss towns, in the region of the Mittelland or Central Plateau. The city, with a population of 379,635 in 1977, is sited at the northern end of Lake Zürich and forms the centre of one of the most densely populated and most highly urbanised parts of the country. The Zürich agglomeration as defined by the Swiss Census Authority had a population of 706,454 in 1977.

Zürich is favourably placed for movement across the Mittelland to Bern, Lausanne, Geneva and Basle as well as to Munich and the other cities of southern Germany. It also has connections via the St Gotthard Pass to Milan and the Arlberg Pass to Innsbruck and Vienna. It is the centre of the Swiss Federal Railways system, and its airport at Zürich-Kloten, just north of the map area, is the base of Swissair and the largest in Switzerland.

Lake Zürich has a surface level of 406 metres and is drained by the River Limmat (unnamed on the map extract) which later joins the River Aar. On discharging from the lake the river first flows north, and then having been joined by the River Sihl from the south, swings west in a series of gentle meanders which occupy the floor of a broad valley bounded by wooded hills. The hills to the south and west reach a maximum height of 871 metres at Uetliberg (796448) below which is a steep face overlooking the Limmat valley. The hills to the north and east which include Chäferberg (see photograph 28), Zürichberg and Adlisberg are rather lower and more rounded and cut by a broad col with a floor height of 478 metres between Wipkingen and Schwamendingen through which the northern districts of Zürich have spread to join the built-up area of Oerlikon which occupies a depression with a floor level of 420–30 metres.

Growth of Zürich

The earliest known settlement in the area occupied the small Lindenhof Hill (833475) on the west bank of the Limmat. This minor site element which rises a mere 20 metres above the level of the nearby river is both unnamed on the map extract and barely discernible from the contour pattern. The settlement on the Lindenhof Hill was termed Turicum during the Roman period of domination, but following its fall to the Alemanni in the fifth century the town declined until the eighth century when the Grossmünster Cathedral (835472) is reputed to have been founded by Charlemagne on the east bank of the Limmat (see photograph 28). Zürich became an imperial city in 1218 and in 1351 joined the Swiss Confederation. During the sixteenth century the city emerged as one of the great cultural and academic centres of Europe, a tradition which it maintains at the present time with its university (838480), the largest in Switzerland, and its famous Federal Institute of Technology (838479). However, even by 1800 the city's population was still a mere 21,500 and it had spread only little beyond its earlier compact form within fortifications at the head of the lake. The modern rapid growth of Zürich really dates from the mid-nineteenth century when the city's numbers increased from 41,585 in 1850 to 168,021 in 1900, followed by further rapid growth in the present century to reach 390,020 in 1950.

Aspects of the urban morphology

The historic core of the city lies on the west bank of the Limmat between the main river and its tributary the Sihl. The early town was bounded in the west by an artificial channel cut between Lake Zürich and the Sihl to complete the encirclement of the settlement by water. This part of the town now contains the principal shopping streets and squares of the city as well as the main offices, banks and commercial premises. Particularly well known is the Bahnhofstrasse which runs between the central station (832480) and the shore of Lake Zürich (833467). This main thoroughfare, which can be picked out on both the map and photograph, is flanked by the city's most handsome stores and many of the biggest banking houses in Europe. On the east bank of the Limmat and linked by six bridges to this district is another part of the historic town which contains the university, the Federal Institute of Technology, libraries, art galleries and the main entertainments district of the city around Bellevue Platz (836468). Reference to photograph 28 provides considerable information about the central area of the town. An obvious point is the extremely high density of building and the irregular pattern of streets in the core area. Considerable redevelopment appears to have recently taken place towards the western side of the central area where a number of modern blocks are seen interspersed within the city core. By contrast the part of the central area which lies east of the Limmat and on the slopes below the university appears to have been less redeveloped and contains older, smaller, and generally lower and more closely packed buildings. These historic buildings include the cathedral, the city hall and a number of old guildhalls along the Limmat Quay. The central area of Zürich thus described and shown on the map extract by street blocks in solid black covers an area of 182 hectares, or 2% of the total area of the city, and corresponds to Kreis 1 in the population table.

Early nineteenth century growth took place on the flat ground to the west of the Sihl in the districts of Gewerbeschule, Langstrasse and Werd as well as in the Seefeld and Enge districts along the shores of Lake Zürich (see figure 31). Neither the map nor the photograph provide much indication of the present function of these areas. From their rather indeterminate nature it seems possible that these may be former areas of large houses into which central area functions are spreading from the historic core of the city at the head of the lake. These districts would thus correspond with the 'zone of assimilation' of R. E. Murphy and J. E. Vance (see Further Reading). In recent years the Enge district, for example, has been chosen for the head offices of many of Zürich's numerous insurance companies.

Factors of relief and gradient appear to have exercised a significant influence on residential developments. In many districts roads run parallel to the contours and are interconnected by short steep transverse roads which in some instances even assume a zig-zag form (839489). Such an arrangement can be seen on the south-western slopes of Zürichberg and in the residential areas of Höngg and Wipkingen on the south side of Chäferberg. On the slopes below Uetliberg modern apartment blocks are aligned almost perfectly with the 480-metre contour (8045 and 8046). Apart from the districts to the immediate west and north-west of the central area which show a tendency towards a rectilinear arrangement of streets, the map gives an impression of generally dispersed housing developments with moderately low building densities over most of the city. The city planners appear to have allowed the city to spread outwards along the Limmat valley, through the northern col or along the shores of the lake rather than increase densities and produce a more compact city structure. The extensive areas of woodland and other types of open space are also in large part the result of the nature of the terrain within the urban boundary. Housing densities are lowest in the fashionable districts of Enge and Wollishofen which contain many large detached villas in spacious grounds overlooking the lake. In order to build up a more detailed picture of the distribution of housing and residential population in Zürich the map extract may be profitably studied in connection with the information provided in the population table and figures 31 and 32. From the sixteenth century onwards Zürich established itself as the commercial centre for the scattered domestic spinning and weaving industry of eastern Switzerland. With the growth of factory industry in the nineteenth century it is not surprising that textile mills should be established in the city which had long played a vital rôle in the organisation of the industry. As H. Carol remarks 'Zürich was the place where capital had been accumulated and where financial and commercial enterprises had the greatest chance of success.' In any case, there was a tradition of silk working, dating from a sixteenth century influx of Italian refugees. The nineteenth century cotton mills were built chiefly on the flat floor of the Limmat valley and close to the

Zürich: residential and working population by districts 1977

	Total area (hectares)	Area ex. wood and water areas	Population	Population density[1]	Employed population	Employment Density[2]	Intensity[3]	% Change in population 1960–75
Kreis 1								
Rathus	36·8	27·3	3,802	139	8,269	303	217	−26·3
Hochschulen	49·6	42·5	1,084	25	8,801	207	814	−25·2
Lindenhof	29·2	22·8	1,451	64	12,779	560	881	−25·9
City	66·8	61·2	949	15	33,063	540	3,484	−36·5
Kreis 2								
Wollishofen	579·9	347·8	16,971	49	6,511	19	38	− 6·6
Leimbach	294·7	158·7	4,496	28	520	3	12	+26·9
Enge	240·3	179·7	9,178	51	26,780	149	292	−17·2
Kreis 3								
Alt-Wiedikon	207·8	199·5	14,305	72	13,205	66	92	− 7·0
Friesenberg	482·2	211·0	10,782	51	3,299	16	31	+17·3
Sihlfeld	164·7	163·9	22,154	134	9,318	57	42	− 9·0
Kreis 4								
Werd	30·7	28·2	4,068	146	8,682	308	213	−25·0
Langstrasse	107·1	102·3	12,360	121	16,785	164	136	−16·4
Hard	132·1	132·1	12,547	95	6,787	51	54	− 5·7
Kreis 5								
Gewerbeschule	80·1	72·4	9,105	126	11,389	157	125	− 9·6
Escher-Wyss	137·2	132·0	1,551	12	13,186	100	850	−13·4
Kreis 6								
Unterstrass	244·3	240·3	22,867	95	12,601	52	55	−14·4
Oberstrass	263·5	159·0	11,233	71	6,049	38	54	−14·0
Kreis 7								
Fluntern	284·5	209·9	8,243	39	8,067	38	98	− 7·5
Hottingen	513·2	256·9	11,618	45	8,661	34	74	−14·9
Hirslanden	220·0	94·2	7,695	82	3,382	36	44	−10·6
Witikon	484·1	290·4	8,951	31	1,435	5	16	+56·1
Kreis 8								
Seefeld	246·1	69·6	6,234	90	8,717	125	140	−20·6
Mühlebach	63·3	63·2	5,970	95	7,563	120	127	−13·5
Weinegg	172·8	157·4	6,167	39	4,393	28	71	− 4·0
Kreis 9								
Albisrieden	462·9	266·2	18,553	70	8,596	32	46	+ 5·9
Altstetten	744·0	562·2	28,496	51	18,591	33	65	+ 9·9
Kreis 10								
Höngg	699·5	464·6	17,556	38	3,552	8	20	+16·5
Wipkingen	212·2	152·9	16,926	111	5,362	35	32	− 7·8
Kreis 11								
Affoltern	603·0	494·2	18,122	37	3,895	8	21	+22·7
Oerlikon	268·8	266·6	16,783	63	19,100	72	114	− 9·6
Seebach	471·9	428·5	19,075	44	10,515	24	55	+17·5
Kreis 12								
Saatlen	106·1	102·8	6,823	67	1,126	11	16	+ 3·1
Schwamendingen	285·9	139·6	11,243	81	2,930	21	26	+ 2·9
Hirzenbach	205·6	178·1	12,277	70	1,219	7	10	+ 2·7
Total	9,090·9	6,478·0	379,635	59	315,128	49	83	− 4·0

Source: *Statistisches Jahrbuch der Stadt Zürich 1977*. Statistisches Amt der Stadt Zürich 1978.
Compiled from various tables.
1 Residential population per hectare } Calculated for areas given in second column
2 Working population per hectare
3 Working population per 100 residential population

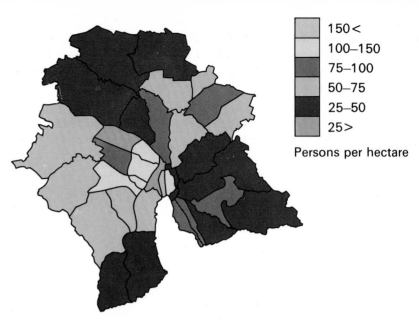

Figure 31. Zürich. Censal Districts and Kreis Boundaries
Note that parts of Wollishofen, Liembach, Witikon, Affoltern and Seebach are not shown on Map 25. Note also that not all districts are named on the map extract.

Figure 32. Zürich. Density of Residential Population 1977
Note the same class intervals are used on figs 32 and 33

1	Rathaus	18	Fluntern
2	Hochschulen	19	Hottingen
3	Lindenhof	20	Hirslanden
4	City	21	Witikon
5	Wollishofen	22	Seefeld
6	Liembach	23	Mühlebach
7	Enge	24	Weinegg
8	Alt Wiedikon	25	Albisrieden
9	Friesenbert	26	Altstretten
10	Sihlfeld	27	Höngg
11	Werd	28	Wipkingen
12	Langstrasse	29	Affoltern
13	Hard	30	Oerlikon
14	Gewerbeschule	31	Seebach
15	Escher-Wyss	32	Saatlen
16	Uberstrass	33	Schwamendingen
17	Oberstrass	34	Hirzenbach

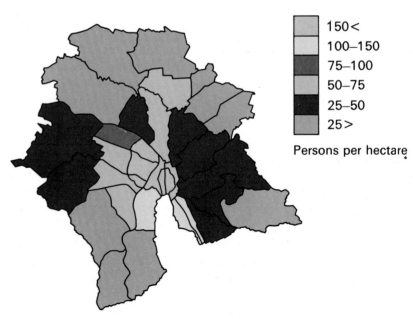

Kreis boundaries are shown in brown and correspond to the groupings of districts in the table on p. 113.

Figure 33. Zürich. Density of Working Population 1977
Source for figs 31, 32, 33: *Statistisches Jahrbuch der Stadt Zürich* 1977

railway leading west from the city. Sponsored by the mill owners, factories producing textile machinery were also established in the same area and later, from this specialised field of engineering, there evolved a varied range of metallurgical, engineering and other industries including the production of machine tools, diesel engines, armaments, chemicals and synthetic textile fibres. The latter are now chiefly found in the districts of Altstetten and Oerlikon, and at Schlieren to the west of the city. The original textile industries have declined in relative importance and now employ only a small proportion of the industrial population. Close to the central area, in the districts of Werd, Langstrasse and Gewerbeschule are light industries which cater for the needs of the urban population and include paper, printing, food and clothing industries.

Occupation structure of Zürich 1975

Primary industry		Tertiary industry (Services)	Total 202,994
Agriculture, horticulture	1,338		
		Commerce (retail and wholesale)	53,439
Secondary industry		Banking and insurance	27,734
(Manufacturing) Total	64,566	Professional services (health, education, etc.)	26,720
Engineering	24,690	Transport and communications	18,222
Paper and printing	11,502	Building and construction	16,650
Metallurgy	11,013	Hotels and tourism	14,596
Food and drink production	5,508	Administration	8,524
Clothing	4,047	Legal and commercial services	3,621
Chemicals	2,004	Public utilities	3,535
Timber and furniture	1,792	Other services	29,953
Textiles	715		
Other manufacturing industries	3,295	Total employed population	268,898

Source: *Statistisches Jahrbuch der Stadt Zürich 1977*. Statistisches Amt der Stadt Zürich 1978.

The map extract provides only a very limited amount of information about industry in the city. There is no indication of the type of production carried out in even the largest factory premises, which are shown by solid black shading on the map as at Oerlikon (832518) and along the Limmat valley towards Schlieren. However, the map extract may again be supplemented by the population data and figure 33 which shows the distribution of working population. It must be emphasised that with a working population of approximately 300,000 Zürich is the largest single centre of industry in Switzerland and, as the table above indicates, is important for both its manufacturing industry and its commercial and financial activities.

Exercises

1. Examine the figures in the table on p. 113 which show the percentage population changes by districts between 1960 and 1975. Map these figures and comment on the pattern of change.

Photograph 29. The Oerlikon Engineering Company. Founded in 1876, the company now employs c. 6,000 workers in the production of hydro-electric and turbo-generators, transformers, electric locomotives and switchboard gear.

The Oerlikon Engineering Co. Ltd., Zürich

2. Explain why such a large proportion of Zürich's working population is employed in service industries.
3. To what extent does the distribution of working population in Zürich (figure 33) reflect the pattern of residential population (figure 32)?
4. How has Switzerland become an industrial country in spite of geographical disadvantages? (O. and C.)

Further reading

CAROL, H. 'The Hierarchy of Central Functions within the City', *Annals of the Association of American Geographers*, **50**, 1960.
DICKINSON, R. E. *'The City Region in Western Europe'*, chapter 5, section 5, 'Zürich: An Example of the Regional Relations of the City', Routledge & Kegan Paul, 1967.
DIEM, A. 'Planning in the Zürich Region', *Canadian Geographer*, **13**, 1969.
ELVIN, R. 'Zürich; Portrait of a City', *Geographical Magazine*, August, 1952.
MURPHY, R. E. and VANCE, J. E. 'Delimiting the CBD; A Comparative Study of Nine Central Business Districts' and 'Internal Structure of the CBD', *Economic Geography*, **30** 1954, and **31**, 1955.
MURPHY, R. E. *The Central Business District. A Study in Urban Geography*, Longman, 1972.
SCHÄRER, W. W. 'Die Suburbane Zone von Zürich', *Geographica Helvetica*, **11**, 1956.
ZWINGLI, U. 'Zürichs Stadtquartiere', *Zürcher Statistische Nachrichten*, no. 3, 1954.
ZWINGLI, U. 'Criteria for the Delimitation of Urban Zones, particularly the Town Centre, and their application to the City of Zürich', *Urban Core and Inner City Symposium*, Amsterdam, 1966.

LA CHAUX DE FONDS NEUCHÂTEL SWITZERLAND

A Jura landscape

Relief

The frontier zone south-east of Basle between France and Switzerland forms part of the range of uplands known as the Jura. Rolling hills, wide vales and occasional deeply incised river valleys succeed one another in a belt over 80 km in width. Although the hills cannot compete with the Alps in their height or grandeur, nevertheless the Jura region has always been a barrier to movement and has preserved its own geographical individuality distinct from the rest of both France and Switzerland. Map 26 shows a small part of the Jura north of Neuchâtel in the vicinity of Le Locle and La Chaux de Fonds.

The greatest altitudes are found in the south-east where heights of over 1,400 metres are recorded on the narrow ridge by Tête de Ran (5511). The ridges on either side of the depression between Le Locle and La Chaux de Fonds are lower (c. 1,200 metres) while north-west of the Doubs Valley, heights of only 1,000 metres mark the crests. Valleys show considerable variation both in height and width. One may contrast the tortuous and deeply incised valley of the River Doubs with the higher, wider and less steep-sided depression between Le Locle and La Chaux de Fonds, or with the steep-sided but wide and flat-floored valley of La Sagne. The pattern of valleys is worth detailed examination. The major axes of drainage are clearly on lines running north-east and south-west parallel to the ridges, but the direction of flow varies from place to place. The most southerly valley, that of La Sagne, falls in a south-westerly direction; the central depression drains north-east and south-west from a watershed near Le Crêt du Locle; the River Doubs follows its deep valley to the north-east. Where valleys cut across ridges there is a marked steepening of the sides and a gorge often results. This is noticeable in the course of the stream which rises south-east of Le Locle (4910) and flows to a confluence with the River Doubs south-west of Les Brenets.

There are several points which may be made from the map and the photograph concerning rock type. Parts of the central ridge have areas of marsh close to the crest while on the same ridge there are several dry valleys (compare 4916 and 4614). The valley of La Sagne in the south is without streams while the valley of Le Locle appears to have intermittent surface drainage. On the aerial photograph a white rock shows in the quarry at 459113. On the map, north-west of the Doubs Valley and west of Le Barboux (4418) lie several depressions reminiscent of limestone country. Finally, the word *combe*, occurring in 4612 and 4811, is frequently used in France for a steep-sided valley carved out of limestone. It is difficult to be certain from map and photograph evidence alone, but most of the evidence suggests that limestone is the most widespread surface rock.

This Jura landscape derives its form from the Alpine mountain building period and subsequent erosion. Although the basement rocks are crystalline these never outcrop at the surface. They were folded in the Hercynian orogeny, eroded to a peneplain and covered with sediments of Permian, Triassic, Jurassic and later ages. Generally, today's surface rocks are limestones of Jurassic age although pockets of Cretaceous and Tertiary rocks still remain in certain down-folded sections. The valley of La Chaux de Fonds and Les Eplatures (5115) contains such a Tertiary remnant. Folding was accomplished in Tertiary times and affected all rocks younger than the Bunter division of the Trias. In the north-east of the Jura, pressure was concentrated against the Hercynian block of the Black Forest and folding is intense. In the central Jura, however, the Hercynian horsts had less controlling effect and folding is less strongly developed. The present relief corresponds directly with the various folds: anticlines form the ridges while synclines form the valleys. The ridges either side of Roche aux Crocs (5513) and Tête de Ran owe their steepness to structure: here the dip of the beds is very great and a 'hog's back' landform is the result. For an explanation of the many gorges which cut through the ridges of the Jura one must invoke an antecedent drainage system. That is to say, the drainage pattern existed before the ridges were uplifted and downcutting by the rivers kept pace with the uplift. Thus the wide open *val* sections contrast with the gorge-like *cluses* in many rivers' courses.

Land use

Land use in the Jura is marked by an emphasis upon wood and pasture land. Reference to the map and the photograph confirms this view. Woodland is abundant wherever slopes are steep: note particularly the slopes of the Doubs Valley in the north-west and those of the valley of La Sagne in the south-east. In other areas gradient seems to have less influence: the ridge north-west of La Chaux de Fonds shows many large woods on gently sloping land. Perhaps soil conditions or the history of settlement and land use are the important influences here. Farming is dominated by pastoral interests. The appearance of the fields in the photograph, and the figures opposite bring out this point very clearly.

In every one of the Swiss communes shown the proportion of agricultural land devoted to pasture is above 90%, and in only one, La Sagne, does it fall below 95%. Pastureland is of various types, by far the greatest proportion being natural pasture though there are small but important areas of improved pasture in the valleys of La Chaux de Fonds and La Sagne. Arable land

Land use 1975

Commune (Parish)	Total area in hectares	Agricultural land as % of total area	Pastureland as % of agricultural land
La Chaux de Fonds	5,586	65	97·8
Les Planchettes	1,174	40	98·0
La Sagne	2,566	57	91·2
Les Brenets	1,153	50	98·8
Le Locle	2,312	58	98·7

Source: Service Cantonal de Statistique, Neuchatel, 1977.

plays a very small part in farm economies and is usually given over to cereals. Surprisingly little land is devoted to root crops.

The reasons behind this pattern of land use are readily understood. Winters are quite cold and summers only moderately warm, while during the spring period the rise in temperature is very slow. Precipitation is heavy and a considerable amount falls as snow. The following statistics refer to La Chaux de Fonds (990 metres a.s.l.).

Mean temperature:
January −2·8°C
July 15°C

Precipitation: 1,300 millimetres

Throughout the Jura the short and cool growing season restricts plant growth and few crops are capable of showing profit in such conditions. Even the limit of tree growth lies at between 1,372 and 1,585 metres compared with an average of 2,134 metres in the Alps.

Occupations

Percentages of total working population

Commune	Agriculture	Forestry	Industry	Building	Trade
La Chaux de Fonds	2	0·4	61	5	11
Les Planchettes	53	3·0	8	0	6
La Sagne	34	0·2	44	3	7
Les Brenets	9	0·8	63	1	4
Le Locle	7	0·4	67	6	5
Average for all communes	4	0·4	63	5	9

Source: Bureau Fédéral de Statistique, Berne.

The employment figures shown above cover the five Swiss communes shown on the map. They reveal aspects of the economic geography of the region which are not discernible either from the topographical map or from the photographs. In spite of the large area of woodland only a minute percentage of the working population is employed in forestry. Even agriculture only employs 4% of the total working population, though in La Sagne and Les Planchettes the figure is much larger. The Swiss Jura is shown to be an industrial rather than an agricultural region with a very high proportion of its people engaged in manufacturing industry. The following figures illustrate the nature of industry in La Chaux de Fonds:

Employment in La Chaux de Fonds 1976

	Number of enterprises	Number of workers
Primary (agriculture)	170	404
Secondary	639	10,022
of which:		
Watchmaking	343	7,131
Building	176	1,267
Chemicals	6	25
Machinery	70	926
Electronics	20	204
Printing	23	400
Tertiary (inc.	1,357	9,348

Administration, Retail, Commerce, Transport, Hotels, Professions)

Source: Rapport du Conseil Communal au Conseil Général, La Chaux de Fonds, 1977.

The dominant industry in this part of the Swiss Jura is that of watchmaking. Unlike many manufacturing industries today, that of watches and clocks is not concentrated in a few large factories. The assembly of watches is carried on in three different types of establishment. Firstly there are a few large factories which both manufacture parts and assemble the final product. In La Chaux de Fonds there are four such establishments employing about 600 workers, while in Le Locle there are two, the well-known Tissot and Zenith works, but these are of larger size employing 1,400 people. The second type of factory buys most of the parts from specialised manufacturers and assembles the watch. There are 70 of these *entreprises d'établissage* in La Chaux de Fonds, while in Le Locle there are ten factories of this type. Both the first and second type of factory work under licence and their products carry their own names. The third form of assembly is through *ateliers de terminage*. These are sub-contractors and work for the licensed firms assembling parts provided by these firms. Two hundred workers are employed in 35 *ateliers de terminage* in Le Locle and La Chaux de Fonds. The manufacture of parts is mostly the work of specialised firms, though a few large organisations manufacture their own. In particular the production of the casings which house the movement of the watch has been dominated by state-organised factories, though these are mainly outside the region of the map extract. These came into being as a direct consequence of the depression of the 1930s which hit this part of the industry particularly hard. As with the assembly stage there is a large amount of work put out to independent men working in their own workshops. Certain branches of this specialised manufacture of parts are highly concentrated in this part of Switzerland. Thus 70% of the Swiss workers producing gold watch cases work in La Chaux de Fonds while for the manufacture of dials, glasses and hands the corresponding figure is 40%. Altogether there are 245 workshops

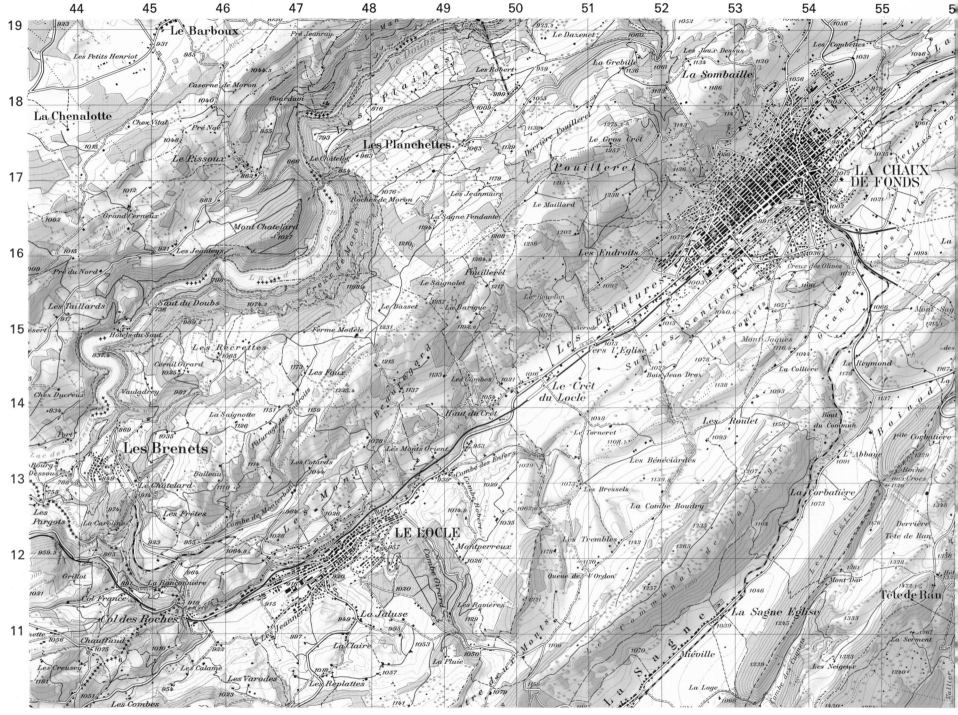

LA CHAUX DE FONDS
NEUCHÂTEL
SWITZERLAND

Extracts from Sheets 231
(Le Locle) and 232
(Vallon de St. Imier).
Swiss 1:50,000 Series.

Sheet 231 Published 1959.
Sheet 232 Published 1953.
Revised 1960.
Vertical Interval of
Contours 20 metres.
Intermediate Contours at
10 metres on gentle slopes.

*Extract from the Swiss National
Map 1:50,000, reproduced with
permission of the Topographical
Survey of Switzerland of 18th
September, 1968.*

Map 26

Photograph 30. Jura landscape near Le Locle and La Chaux de Fonds. Note the parallel arrangement of ridges and valleys, the combination of dispersed farmsteads and nucleated towns, and the predominance of natural pasture and the plentiful woodland.

Swissair-Photo AG, Zürich

Photograph 31. La Chaux de Fonds. Note the relationship between the plan of the town and the relief of the area, the type of houses and their alignment.

Aerofilms Ltd

factory to collect work and return to their home with a supply of watch cases or bracelets for engraving and finishing work. This is a craftsman's job and the skill involved is passed from one generation to the next.

The reasons for the growth and pattern of organisation of this industry in the Swiss Jura are connected very closely with the geography of the region. The Jura forms a difficult environment by reason of its height and the limited productivity of its farms and forests. In part this is due to relief and soil conditions; in part it is a result of a climate with a harsh and long winter. The development of craft industries in such circumstances is not uncommon and one may cite the woodwork industries of the Alps or Black Forest as comparable examples. The working of small deposits of iron was common in early times in the Jura and from this there sprang an interest in metal working, especially in armour and nails. The early development of clock manufacture came at the end of the seventeenth and beginning of the eighteenth centuries. By 1741 there were several hundred clock makers in the valleys of La Chaux de Fonds and Le Locle. In great part the development of the industry owed its inspiration to one man, Daniel Jean Richard, who was the first to organise it as an assembly industry. Possibly comparisons could be made with the figure of Josiah Wedgwood in his influence on the English pottery industry. The nineteenth century saw a tremendous growth in the population of La Chaux de Fonds as a result of the success of the watch industry. From 2,266 in 1760 the figure reached 16,915 in 1860 and 40,640 in 1917. In the main the success of the industry has been a result of the expansion of the export trade with the development of communications linking these isolated parts of Switzerland to the outside world. Furthermore, the high value of the product in comparison with its bulk makes the costliness of transport of little consequence.

The manufacture of watches is certainly an example of an industry in which the labour factor dominates location. The raw materials are not expensive and the finished product is many times more valuable. The training of skilled craftsmen is very strongly localised in this area. Originally a father taught his craft to his son; today the technical schools of Le Locle and La Chaux de Fonds fulfil the same function, supplying the labour needs of the future. The fact that many branches of the industry, both in manufacture and assembly, can never lend themselves to any large economies of scale (as with an integrated steel works) allows the family business to persist. The watch industry is in part an assembly industry. Thus, as with the automobile industry, there is a strong tendency towards keeping the manufacture of parts within the vicinity.

Apart from watchmaking, the most important industrial activity in La

employing over 8,100 workers in La Chaux de Fonds and Le Locle concerned with the manufacture of parts of watches. The two centres of La Chaux de Fonds and Le Locle today produce over 30% of the total export of watches from Switzerland. The contrasts between the two towns stem largely from the scale of operations. There is a tendency in Le Locle towards the large firm while in La Chaux de Fonds there are many small enterprises. This seems to be largely explained by the retention of the family business in La Chaux de Fonds to an extent far greater than in Le Locle.

As an employer the watch industry spreads its influence far beyond the two towns. Farming in this region of the Jura is neither a very profitable business nor does it provide full employment throughout the year. Especially during the winter it is still common for a farming family to come to the

Chaux de Fonds is the manufacture of machinery, instruments, metal goods and scientific apparatus. It must be emphasised that this is mainly precision work and is frequently linked closely to the watch industry. These developments appear to be a natural step from existing watchmaking interests, since similar raw materials and a similar type of skill are required. In the past few years the watchmaking industry has itself faced intense competition in overseas markets from Japanese and other manufacturers whose products have been developed through advances in electronics technology. The digital watch achieves a high level of reliability together with accuracy and represents a major threat to the traditional watch, especially in the middle and lower price ranges of the market. Evidence of decline is shown in the numbers employed in watchmaking in La Chaux de Fonds. These have fallen from 11,108 in 1967 to 7,131 in 1976. It would seem to be sensible to encourage a broader range of industrial production in the Jura area if major problems of unemployment are to be avoided.

Power

Some evidence is offered by the map extract to suggest the source of the power used in industry. The River Doubs is dammed to form a lake which stretches upstream to the waterfall known as Saut du Doubs. The lake has an area of 0·911 square kilometres and contains about 16 million cubic metres of water. The barrage at Le Châtelot has a height of 97 metres. From the dam a pecked blue line indicates an underground gallery which leads to the H.E.P. station at Le Torret (495192) which lies at a height of about 620 metres, compared with the lake surface at 713 metres. Electricity production, begun in 1953, reached a total of 117 million kilowatt hours in 1965–6, of which part was fed into the French system while the remainder was taken by the electricity authority for the Canton of Neuchâtel. Consumption within La Chaux de Fonds and Le Locle reaches 54 and 24 million kilowatt hours per annum respectively.

Settlement

The pattern of settlement is one of a series of dispersed farms together with strong nucleation in La Chaux de Fonds, Le Locle and Les Brenets. Perhaps the most striking feature of La Chaux de Fonds (and to a lesser extent of Le Locle) is the regular gridiron layout of streets and houses (see photograph 31). The town is a creation of the nineteenth century, since the old settlement was largely destroyed by fire in 1790. Although the architect of the time conceived a town similar to Karlsruhe or Versailles, his successor thought differently and designed a settlement on a grid pattern reminiscent of American cities. The main axis, Avenue Leopold-Robert, lies at the bottom of the valley, while further streets were constructed parallel to this axis along the slopes. Though lacking in variety, the town nevertheless bears a logical relationship to the topography of its surroundings. There are in addition certain advantages in respect of climate. Winds tend to blow along the valley either from north-east or south-west. Houses are also aligned in this direction. Thus the drifting of the considerable snowfalls of winter will be less of a hindrance to entrances of houses than if these lay athwart the main wind direction.

La Chaux de Fonds is a good example of the way in which a landscape, unpromising in its endowment of natural resources, has nevertheless been induced to support a moderately dense population at a high standard of living. The resources of soil, timber and power have of course been important, but the decisive factor has certainly been the ingenuity and capacity for work of the people of the region.

Exercises

1. Discuss the relationships between communications and relief in the area of the map.
2. Discuss the nature and possible origin of the features called Col des Roches (4511).
3. 'The human factor is a resource sometimes neglected when discussing the location of industry.' Discuss.
4. Draw a profile of the country between Le Barboux (4519) and the hotel at Tête de Ran (5511), using a vertical scale of 1 centimetre to 100 metres.
Below your profile, plot separately the distribution of woodland, settlements and routeways along your section. Comment on the relationships which are revealed.
5. Daniel Jean Richard is quoted as playing a vital rôle in the establishment of the watch and clock industry at La Chaux de Fonds. In Study 15 Dom Perignon is mentioned as being important in the growth of the wine industry of Champagne. Assess the importance of individual enterprise of this type as a location factor in economic activity.

Further reading

FRÜH, J. *Geographie der Schweiz*, Volume 3, Zollikoser, St. Gallen, 1938.
MUTTON, A. F. A. *Central Europe*, 2nd edn, Longmans, 1968.
SHACKLETON, M. R. *Europe*, 7th edn, Longmans, 1965.

Study 22
THE GORNER GLACIER
VALAIS
SWITZERLAND

Extract from Sheet 284.
Mischabel.
Swiss 1:50,000 Series.

Map published 1941.
Revised 1965.
Vertical interval of contours 20 metres. (Form lines with 10 metre vertical interval are marked on parts of the glacier.)

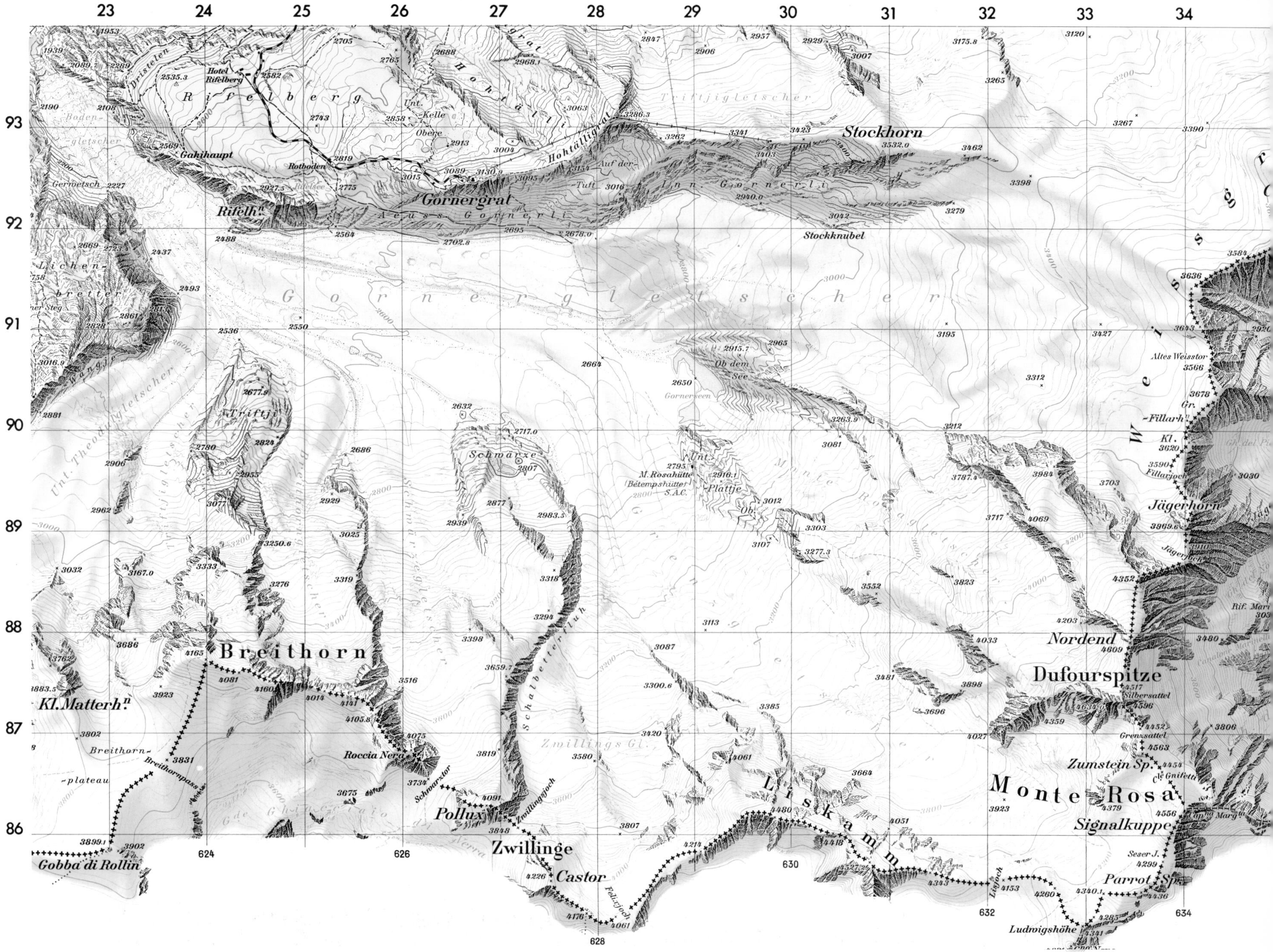

Map 27

Map labels (selection):

Gornergletscher · Gornergrat · Stockhorn · Stockknubel · Triftjigletscher · Hohtälligrat · Hohtälligletscher · Aeuss. Gornerli · Inn. Gornerli · Hotel Riffelberg · Riffelberg · Rotboden · Gagihaupt · Gerroetsch · Lichen-bretter · Unt. Theodulgletscher · Unt. Kelle · Obere · Auf der Tuft · Riffelh. · Triftji · Schwärze · Ob dem See · Gornerseen · Unt. Plattje · M. Rosahütte (Betempshütte) S.A.C. · Monte Rosagletscher · Breithorn · Kl. Matterh. · Roccia Nera · Schwarztor · Breithornpass · Breithorn-plateau · Gde. di Gr. · Gobba di Rollin · Pollux · Zwillinge · Castor · Zwillingsjoch · Zwillings Gl. · Schaltbetter Luh · Felikjoch · Liskamm · Monte Rosa · Signalkuppe · Ludwigshöhe · Parrot Sp. · Zumstein Sp. · Dufourspitze · Nordend · Silbersattel · Grenzsattel · Jägerhorn · Altes Weisstor · Gr. Fillarh. · Fillarjoch · Kl. · Grenssattel · Lisjoch · Seser J. · Weiss

Photograph 32. Tributaries of
the Gorner Glacier and corries
on the flank of the Breithorn.

Swiss National Tourist Office, London.

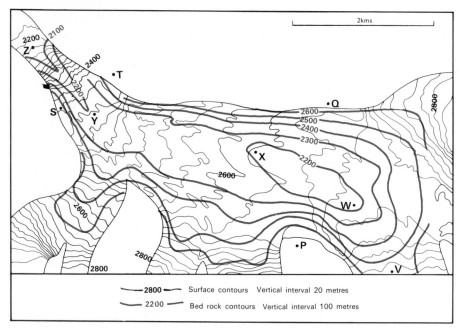

Figure 34. Surface and bed rock contours of the Gorner Glacier.
Based on Geologischer Atlas der Schweiz, 1:25,000, Blatt 535.

——2800——	Surface contours	Vertical interval 20 metres
—— 2200 ——	Bed rock contours	Vertical interval 100 metres

Certain of the highland regions of North-West Europe still contain active glaciers. The region shown on the map extract is part of the Pennine Alps of southern Switzerland. To the north, the Gorner Glacier drains to the valley of the Mattervispa which is tributary to the Rhône, while to the south of the watershed lies the Valle d'Aosta drained by the Dora Baltea, which is tributary to the River Po. The highlands of the area culminate in the Monte Rosa massif (4634 metres) in the south-eastern corner of the map. These are formed mainly of crystalline and metamorphic rocks. (A useful general account of the structure of the Alps can be found in A. F. A. Mutton's *Central Europe* or M. R. Shackleton's *Europe*.) Comparison of maps and photographs will suggest certain features of glacier movement, erosion and deposition. Perhaps the most characteristic feature of mountain glaciation is the corrie. Photograph 32 shows details of the corrie at the head of the Breithorn Glacier. The precipitous back and side walls are covered at their lower levels with the steep-surfaced corrie glacier (gradient of 1 in 1, or 45°). After a more gentle slope in the base of the corrie the glacier steepens once again in an impressive ice fall where a maze of crevasses runs transversely across the ice. Crevassing is shown on the map by discontinuous blue lines, and careful examination of the map shows a tendency for these to occur wherever the slope of the glacier steepens. Because of

great pressure, ice may flow in a pseudo-plastic manner in its lowest layers, but, in its upper layers, it behaves as a crystalline mass, and irregularities of the valley floor which cause a steepening of its surface may encourage cracks which lie transversely to its course. Crevasses may also be found at the margins of glaciers as a result of tensions produced by the differing rates of movement of the centre and sides of the glacier. Because of the higher velocity towards the centre, tensions are produced which crack the ice along lines at 45° up-glacier, though these are soon rotated and deformed by differential flow. Longitudinal crevasses are often formed where the valley widens. Reference to squares 2392, 2489, 2589, 2888 and 3189 will illustrate the various types mentioned. In places the glacier surface has a number of convexities which relate to confluent tributaries. Unlike rivers, the contributions of tributaries do not mix with the main stream. The main ice mass is the Grenzgletscher, and this ice reaches the snout. That of the tributary on the northern side of Ob dem See (2990) does not reach the snout but only as far as the Rifelhorn (2492).

The map and photographs show abundant evidence of melt-water flow during the summer. By far the greater part finds its way beneath the surface ice (note the disappearance of surface streams down moulins to issue beyond the rocky terminal moraine as a wide and rushing torrent near Zermatt, which lies 3 km to the north of the map). At 2890 and 2990 and on photograph 33, lakes are to be found where the Monte Rosagletscher joins the main ice stream. Examination of the contours will show that the surface of the Grenzgletscher is over 20 metres above the surface of the lakes and in fact blocks the path of melt-water from Monte Rosagletscher, so forming these two lakes. Numerous surface depressions may be noted on the surface of the lower section of the glacier. Many of these relate to hollows formed and abandoned by meandering melt-water streams which have found outlets below the ice further upstream. In the summer these hollows are occupied by melt-water which, warmed by insolation, tends to enlarge them.

On photograph 32, below the ice fall of the Breithorngletscher, a marked light and dark arc-shaped banding is evident. These bands are *ogives* and their origin is a matter of some controversy. The foot of an ice fall is a zone of intense compression while the ice fall itself is an area of tension. It is thought that ice passing over the fall in summer is partially melted and recrystallisation with compression at the foot of the ice fall produces a dark band. In winter however there is no melting and compression produces a different form of ice which shows up as a white arc.

The frost-shattered slopes above the ice are the source of debris which accumulates as lateral moraine along the sides of glaciers. The convergence

of two such lateral moraines produces a medial moraine as on the north side of Schmärze (spot height 2632 metres in 2690). Towards the snout of the glacier (2392, 2292 and 2293) the ice is almost completely covered with rocky debris, so that it is difficult to tell where the glacier ends and the terminal moraine begins.

The map gives no indication of the retreat of this glacier. Figures provided by measurement over a period of years show that the lower part of the glacier is wasting away rapidly. Near the snout a lowering of the surface at a rate of over 3 metres per year has occurred since 1930. Further upstream the rate declines until between Ob dem See and Schmärze the loss has been about 1·4 metres. This wastage affects the position of the snout, which is now at least $\frac{1}{2}$ km to the south-east of the position shown on the map.

Exercises

1. Find the widths, in metres of the various glaciers shown on photograph 33. What is the distance in kilometres from the small peak in the left foreground to the peak (Dufourspitze) in the background?
2. Determine the point from which photograph 32 was taken.
3. Draw a longitudinal profile down the centre of the Grenzgletscher and Gornergletscher between the following spot heights: 4436 (Parrot Sp.—3385), 3923, 3113, 2664, and 1939. (Use mm/cm graph paper and a vertical scale of 1 cm : 200 metres).
(a) Comment on the profile so obtained; *(b)* Calculate the vertical exaggeration of your section; *(c)* Calculate the actual surface gradients of
(i) The steepest section of the glacier. (ii) The least steep part of the glacier.
4. With reference to fig. 34, construct the following three sections: *(a)* Down the centre of the Grenzgletscher to the 2200 metre contour through points V, W, X, Y, Z; *(b)* across the glacier between points P and Q; *(c)* across the glacier between points S and T.

On each section show (i) the surface of the glacier (ii) the bedrock. Comment on and try to account for the features revealed by your sections.
5. On a sheet of tracing paper mark *(a)* the landscape which is not covered with ice; *(b)* the pattern of moraines. Attempt to classify these moraines. Comment on the sources of material and position of these features.
6. Compare and contrast the corries on the eastern and western sides of the ridge from Signalkuppe (3486) to spot height 3636 (3491).
7. 'The modification of mountain landscapes by ice action can take many and varied forms.' Discuss.
8. Why do glaciers retreat?

Further reading

HOLMES, A. E. *Principles of Physical Geology*, 3rd edn, Nelson, 1978.
MUTTON, A. F. A. *Central Europe*, Longmans, 1968, chapter 4.
SHACKLETON, M. R. *Europe*, 7th edn, Longmans, 1965, chapter 23.
SHARP, R. P. 'Glaciers', *Condon Lectures, Eugene, Oregon*, 1960. University of Oregon Press.
SPARKS, B. W. *Geomorphology*, 2nd edn, Longman, 1972

Photograph 33. The Gorner Glacier and Monte Rosa.

Swissair - Photo AG Zurich.

Key Symbols

Only those symbols necessary for interpretation of the map extracts have been listed. These are not comprehensive lists of symbols.

Belgian 1 : 50 000 Map Series

COMMUNICATIONS

- 1st class road, more than 9 m
- 2nd class road, from 6–9 m.
- 3rd class road, less than 6 m
- 3rd class road, narrow or neglected
- Earth road
- Railway (steam) with multiple tracks
- Railway (steam) single track
- Electric railway with multiple tracks
- Electric railway, single track
- Tramway and depot
- Underpass and overpass
- Level crossing, tunnel
- Foot and vehicular ford, ferry and footbridge

VEGETATION

- Woods and forests
- Orchards, willows, poplars

BOUNDARIES

- Province
- Parish
- 60 Population number in hundreds

HUMAN FEATURES

- Completely built-up area
- Trig. point (church – trig. point)
- Church (no trig. point)
- In built-up areas no blue accentuation circle
- Chapel, cross

- Cemetery
- Houses
- Shed or warehouse, garage
- Factory, gas tank
- Water-mill
- Tower or chimney
- Radio mast
- Ordinary pylon
- High tension cable
- Water tower
- Lock

LAND AND WATER FEATURES

- Contour lines
- Slag heap
- Slope
- Embankment } at least 1:50 m.
- Cutting
- River, small river, canal over 50 m. wide
- from 31–50 m.
- from 16–30 m.
- } Navigable part
- Ditch
- Spring, fountain, well

ABBREVIATIONS

- **Anc.**   Old
- **Charb.**   Coalmine
- **Ch^{au}** Castle
- **Gend^{ie}** Police station

French 1 : 50 000 Map Series

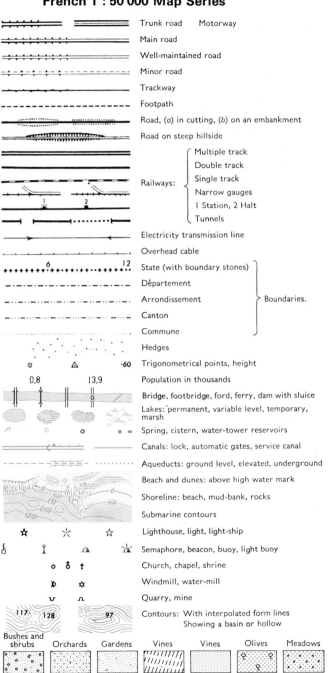

- Trunk road   Motorway
- Main road
- Well-maintained road
- Minor road
- Trackway
- Footpath
- Road, (a) in cutting, (b) on an embankment
- Road on steep hillside
- Railways: Multiple track / Double track / Single track / Narrow gauges / 1 Station, 2 Halt / Tunnels
- Electricity transmission line
- Overhead cable
- State (with boundary stones)
- Département
- Arrondissement
- Canton
- Commune } Boundaries.
- Hedges
- Trigonometrical points, height
- Population in thousands
- Bridge, footbridge, ford, ferry, dam with sluice
- Lakes: permanent, variable level, temporary, marsh
- Spring, cistern, water-tower reservoirs
- Canals: lock, automatic gates, service canal
- Aqueducts: ground level, elevated, underground
- Beach and dunes: above high water mark
- Shoreline: beach, mud-bank, rocks
- Submarine contours
- Lighthouse, light, light-ship
- Semaphore, beacon, buoy, light buoy
- Church, chapel, shrine
- Windmill, water-mill
- Quarry, mine
- Contours: With interpolated form lines / Showing a basin or hollow

Woods | Bushes and shrubs | Orchards | Gardens | Vines | Vines | Olives | Meadows

Symbols vary slightly from sheet to sheet in this series according to edition.

French 1 : 25 000 Map Series

- N.P.7 ou N.31
- N.P.19 ou N.228
- N.696
- D.P.5 ou D.12
- D.47
- D.38

- Motorway
- Trunk or National roads { 1st class / 2nd class / 3rd class
- Département Roads { 1st class / 2nd class / 3rd class
- Cobbled Surface { 1st class / 2nd class
- Works road
- Track way
- Footpath
- Roads on embankments
- Roads in cuttings
- Walled road
- Multiple track railway
- Single track railway
- Narrow gauge railway
- Railway sidings
- State boundary
- Département, arrondissement boundaries
- Canton, commune boundaries
- Electricity transmission lines
- Bridges; stone, wood, iron, suspension, footbridge
- Dam with sluice, ford, ferry
- Stream, dried-up stream
- Canals, with lock, dock
- „ not navigable
- „ diversion, dried up
- Aqueducts, on the ground, on a viaduct
- Spring, fountain, well, cistern, water tower
- Reservoirs
- Lakes, permanent, temporary
- Shingle, gravel; marsh; peat bog

- Trigonometrical points
- Churches, bell tower, chapel, small chapel
- 'Mairie', police station, monument, chimney
- Barracks, hospital, convent
- Important buildings, factory with chimney
- Camp, kiosk, market or warehouse
- Water-mill, windmill
- Gasometer, blast furnace, mineshaft, cave
- Walls, walls in ruins, ruins
- Cemeteries; Christian, Jewish
- Rocks, scree
- Quarry, sandpit
- Form lines
- Basin or hollow
- Hedge, hedge with trees
- Aerodrome
- Woods
- Coniferous woods
- Tall bushes or brushwood
- Low bushes or brushwood
- Gardens
- Orchards
- Nursery
- Poplars
- Osiers

ABBREVIATIONS

Briq^{ie}	— Briqueterie	Brickfield
Ch^{au}	— Château	Castle, Manor
Ch^{nee}	— Cheminée	Chimney
Cim^{ie}	— Cimenterie	Cement work
Cim^{re}	— Cimetière	Cemetery
H^{ts} F^{neaux}	— Hauts Furneaux	Blast furnaces
R^{au}	— Ruisseau	Stream
R^{voir}	— Réservoir	Reservoir

West German 1 : 50 000 Map Series

⊢⊢⊢⊢⊢⊢⊢	'Länder' boundary
— — — —	'Regierungsbezirk' boundary
— — — —	'Kreis' boundary
Bahnhof	Railway, standard gauge multi-track with station
Haltepunkt	Railway, standard gauge single track with halt
	Narrow gauge railway
	Rack railway
	Tramway or industrial railway
im Bau 10	Autobahn – under construction
	Main road
	A class with bordering trees
	A class with kilometre stone
	All weather road, light surface
	Fair weather road, loose surface
	Track
	Footpath with stiles

₀	Church with two spires
₀	Church with one spire
+	Chapel
†	Shrine
	Cemetery
⊥	Monument
⌁	Tower
○	Chimney
	Tower or Chimney on a building
	Ruins
	Water-mill
	Forester's house
	Mine, in use
	Mine, disused
∩	Cave
○	Sports ground
	Windmill
	Windpump
○ ₂	Isolated trees
	Bank

▲	Camping place
·149	Spot height
△307	Trigonometrical point
δ δ ○	Trig point on church, tower, chimney
⇌	Iron bridge
	Wooden bridge
W.F.	Ferry; railway, vehicle, pedestrian
	Steep edge (usually artificial)
	Embankment, with track
	Embankment, without track
	Stone quarry, pit
○ ○	Tumulus
	Wall fence
	Hedge
	Low bank with hedge
	High tension cable

	Deciduous forest
Schneise	Coniferous forest
	Tree nursery
	Mixed forest
	Trees and shrubs
	Regularly spaced trees
	Orchard, with or without meadow
	Heath with scattered trees and shrubs
	Pasture with marsh, trees and bushes
	Vineyard
	Hop garden
	Garden
	Park

ABBREVIATIONS

A.T.	Observation tower
Bf.	Railway station
Br.	Well
El.Wk.	Power station
Fbr.	Factory
H.Hs.	Hut, house
Hbf	Main railway station
Hp.	Halt
Jg.Hb.	Youth hostel
K.D.	Monument of cultural interest
K.O.	Lime works
Kp.	Chapel
Krkhs.	Hospital
M.	Mill
N.D.	Outstanding natural feature, eg, large rock

N.S.G.	Nature reserve
P.Wk.	Pumping station
R.	Ruin
Sch.	Barn
Schl.	Castle
St.	Stable
S.Wk.	Sawmill
T.	Tower
U.Wk.	Transformer station
W.T.	Water tank
W.F.	Car ferry
Whs.	Inn
Wbh.	Water tower
Zgl.	Brick yard
Molk.	Dairy
Sp.Pl.	Sports ground
U.	Transformer

Contours

	100 metres
	10 metres
	5 metres
	2.5 metres

Swiss 1 : 50 000 Map Series

	Important railway station
	Railway station
	Railway: standard gauge double track with halt
	Railway: standard gauge, single track with halt
	Railway: narrow gauge with halt
	Railway: narrow gauge alongside road with halt
	Works railway
	Téléferique for passengers
	Téléferique for goods transport
	Railway tunnel
	1st class road over 5 m. wide
	2nd class road 3-5 m. wide
	3rd class road 2 2-3 m. wide
	Minor road
	Unsurfaced road
	Footpath
	Covered bridge
	Vehicle bridge; footbridge, aqueduct
	Road tunnels
	Level crossings
	Road over railway
	Road under railway
	National boundary with numbered boundary stones
	Canton boundary with numbered boundary stones
	District boundary with numbered boundary stones
	Commune boundary with numbered boundary stones
△2042.6	
·1966.6 ·1165.0	Triangulation points
·1482 ·2364	Spot heights
	House, country house, guest house
δ	Church, chapel
	Gasometer, tower or high chimney, observation tower
	Walls, dry walls
△ †	Monument, cross
∩ ○	Cave, erratic boulder
	Rock and scree
	Cemetery
	Radio station, transformer station (above ground)
	Electricity transmission line

Over rocks	Over ice	Contours
		200 m interval
		20 m interval
		10 m interval

	Hollow, Hill
	Quarry, sand or gravel pit; clay pit
	Lake, Depth in metres in black; Mean surface level in blue, 1 Jetty, 2 Harbour, 3 Bathing place, 4 Marshy shore
	Lake of variable level; Pool, swimming pool
	Reservoir, fountain, storage tank
	River, old bed, embankment
	River: vehicle ferry, passenger ferry
	Streams; 1 Embankment, 2 Waterfall, 3 Spring, 4 Intermittent flow, 5 Ravine
	Marsh
	1 Forest, 2 Open woodland, 3 Bushes
	Park; tree-lined avenue; isolated tree
	Hedge; chestnut trees

BERN	Town of more than 50000 inhabitants
AARAU	Commune or settlement with 5000–50000 inhabitants
Hochdorf	Commune 1000–5000 inhabitants
Seen	Settlement with 1000–5000 inhabitants
Kerns	Commune or settlement less than 1000 inhabitants
Wasen	District with 100–1000 inhabitants
Huben	Hamlet with 50–100 inhabitants
Eichmatt	Small Group of houses

Grand Combin Jungfrau *Birghorn Doldenstock*	Mountains
Val de Nendaz Val Champex *Suldtal Sefinental*	Valleys
Col du G.d St Bernard Pas de Chevoille *Simplonpass Ramilpass Gamchilücke*	Cols.
Champagne Forêt des Râmes *Brunauerboden Bannwald*	Regions
RHÔNE Rhône Sarine Eau Noire	Rivers
LE LÉMAN *Walensee Silsersee*	Lakes

Linear Scales

1:100,000
Kilometres (1 cm: 1 km)
1000m 0 1 2 3 4 5 6 7 8 9 10 11 12 13 14 15 16 17 18 19 20 21 22 23
Miles (0·6336 ins: 1 mile)
8 4 0 1 2 3 4 5 6 7 8 9 10 11 12 13
Furlongs

1:50,000
Kilometres (2 cm: 1 km)
1000m 0 1 2 3 4 5 6 7 8 9 10 11
Miles (1·2672 ins: 1 mile)
8 4 0 1 2 3 4 5 6
Furlongs

1:25,000
Kilometres (4 cm: 1 km)
1000m 500m 0 1 2 3 4 5
Miles (2·5344 ins: 1 mile)
8 7 6 5 4 3 2 1 0 1 2
Furlongs

1:20,000
Kilometres (5 cm: 1 km)
1000m 500 0 1 2 3
Miles (3·1675 ins: 1 mile)
8 7 6 5 4 3 2 1 0 1
Furlongs

1:10,000
Kilometres (10 cm: 1 km)
1000m 500 0 1
Miles (6·335 ins: 1 mile)
8 7 6 5 4 3 2 1 0
Furlongs

Tables for Conversion from Metric Measurements

Hectares to Acres

Hectares	Acres
1	2·47
2	4·94
3	7·41
4	9·88
5	12·36
6	14·83
7	17·30
8	19·77
9	22·24
10	24·71
25	61·78
50	123·56
100	247·12

Kilometres to Miles

Kilometres	Miles or Kilometres	Miles
1·609	1	0·621
3·218	2	1·242
4·827	3	1·864
6·437	4	2·485
8·046	5	3·107
9·655	6	3·728
11·265	7	4·350
12·874	8	4·971
14·483	9	5·592
16·093	10	6·214
40·232	25	15·535
80·465	50	31·070
160·930	100	62·140
402·320	250	155·350
804·650	500	310·700
1609·300	1000	621·400

Metres to Feet

Metres	Feet or Metres	Feet
0·305	1	3·281
0·610	2	6·562
0·914	3	9·842
1·219	4	13·123
1·524	5	16·404
1·829	6	19·685
2·134	7	22·966
2·438	8	26·247
2·743	9	29·528
3·048	10	32·808
7·620	25	82·022
15·242	50	164·043
30·480	100	328·086
76·200	250	820·220
152·420	500	1640·430
304·800	1000	3280·860

Millimetres to Inches

Millimetres	Millimetres or Inches	Inches
25·400	1	0·039
50·800	2	0·079
76·200	3	0·118
101·600	4	0·157
127·000	5	0·197
152·400	6	0·236
177·800	7	0·276
203·200	8	0·315
228·600	9	0·354
254·000	10	0·394
635·000	25	0·984
1,270·000	50	1·969
2,540·000	100	3·937
6,350·000	250	9·843
12,700·000	500	19·685
25,400·000	1000	39·370

°Centigrade to °Fahrenheit

°Centigrade	°Fahrenheit
+25	+77
+20	+68
+15	+59
+10	+50
+ 5	+41
0	+32
− 5	+23
−10	+14
−15	+ 5
−20	− 4
−25	−13
−30	−22
−35	−31
−40	−40

To convert °C to °F
$$x°C = \frac{9}{5}x + 32 \quad (°F)$$